RHODES BESIEGED

RHODES BESIEGED

A New History

Robert Douglas Smith & Kelly DeVries

First published in 2011

The History Press
The Mill, Brimscombe Port
Stroud, Gloucestershire, GL5 2QG
www.thehistorypress.co.uk

© Robert Douglas Smith & Kelly DeVries, 2011

The right of Robert Douglas Smith & Kelly DeVries to be identified as
the Authors of this work has been asserted in accordance with the
Copyrights, Designs and Patents Act 1988.

All rights reserved. No part of this book may be reprinted
or reproduced or utilised in any form or by any electronic,
mechanical or other means, now known or hereafter invented,
including photocopying and recording, or in any information
storage or retrieval system, without the permission in writing
from the Publishers.

British Library Cataloguing in Publication Data.
A catalogue record for this book is available from the British Library.

ISBN 978 0 7524 6178 6

Typesetting and origination by The History Press
Printed and bound by TJ International Ltd, Padstow, Cornwall

Contents

Acknowledgements   7

Introduction   9

Part One

The Knights, the Ottoman Turks and Rhodes before 1480   13

The Siege of 1480   43

The Uneasy Calm, 1480–1522   63

The Siege of 1522   95

Part Two

A Story of Stone, Cannon and Men   123

Appendix 1: The Artillery   133

Appendix 2: The Walls   169

Appendix 3: The Grand Masters' Coats of Arms   193

Bibliography   195

Index   203

Acknowledgements

The role of serendipity is seldom acknowledged in the study of the past, but the meeting of an academic, a medieval military historian and an expert on the study of artillery working in an arms and armour museum has proved a fruitful relationship for many years. Bringing together the skills of the historian and the museum professional has enabled us to develop a much broader and fuller approach to the study of medieval warfare, resulting initially in the study of the late fourteenth- and fifteenth-century artillery of the dukes of Burgundy. It was the successful completion of this project that led us to speculate whether this approach, using as wide a range of sources as possible, could be used elsewhere – preferably somewhere warmer and with a better exchange rate than Switzerland.

We both owe a large debt to Ruth Rhynas Brown, not just for suggesting that we study the two sieges of Rhodes as our next project, but for sharing her knowledge, expertise and research skills with us. She also accompanied us on our various expeditions: to Rhodes, to study the walls, and on our artillery safaris to Nuremberg, Paris and Istanbul. She has been the inspiration behind much of what we have written and without her this work would have been considerably the poorer.

We gratefully acknowledge a generous grant from the British Academy to facilitate travel to Robert Smith, and the financial and moral support of Loyola College in Maryland (which during the completion of this book went through a name change to Loyola University Maryland), especially the Center for the Humanities, Dean of Arts and Sciences, and Department of History, to Kelly DeVries. Dean James Buckley has provided especially valuable support for this research and should be singled out, especially as he is on the verge of his retirement and will be missed. Thanks should also be given to the Midgley family of Menston, Yorkshire, and the members of the Wharfdale Branch; to the Royal Armouries Library, Leeds, and Robert Woosnam-Savage for friendship, lodging, encouragement and aid in research. On our various research trips we were helped and assisted by many friends and colleagues; Sylvie Leluc and Antoine Leduc, of the Musée de l'Armée in Paris were very generous with their time and expertise; Johan Willers, formerly at the Germanisches Nationalmuseum in Nuremberg; the staff at the St John's Museum in Clerkenwell, London; Dr Jonathon

Rhodes Besieged

Riley, Director General and Master of the Armouries, and Captain Koçer, Military Attaché at the Turkish Embassy in Istanbul, were instrumental in obtaining permission for us to study at the Military Museum in Istanbul; Gulsen Arslanboga, Curator of Artillery at the Military Museum in Istanbul; Stephen Spiteri for permission to use some of his wonderful drawings of the fortifications; Anna-Maria Kasdagli and Katerina Manoussou-Della at the Department of Medieval Town and Archaeological Site, Municipality of Rhodes; and James Millar and Dominic Aston, formerly of Granada Television and Producer/Director and Assistant Producer of the National Geographic series, *Ground War*. (All researchers should have a National Geographic film crew with them – the doors that are opened ...)

A number of friends and colleagues helped in many ways: Vicky Avery shared her knowledge of Venetian artillery and accompanied us on our visit to Istanbul; Steven Walton and Guy Wilson gave us their support; Renato Ridella and Carlo Beltrame supplied us with images of cannon from the collection at the Askeri Muze in Istanbul; and, especially, Heather Lane who wielded her formidable pen to improve our, too often idiosyncratic, text.

Finally, our thanks go to the jolly Greek owner of the bar in Rhodes, where we stopped each afternoon under a large shady tree for a beer or a glass of wine, who greeted us like long-lost friends with grapes and smiles.

All photographs © Robert D. Smith except p. 172 top right; p. 178 top left and top left lower; p. 187 lower left; p. 190 upper centre; © Stephen Spiteri. All colour images courtesy Epernay.

Introduction

When armies meet, on the battlefield or in a siege, the course of events and the final outcome are never predictable. Overwhelming superiority in numbers or technology does not always guarantee success. The quality of leadership, morale, the element of surprise, even the weather and luck, all play their part to a greater or lesser degree, and politics, intrigue and treachery, food and water supplies, and disease, among other things, can be important factors.

If attempting to predict the outcome of a conflict is difficult, understanding the course of events of past battles and sieges is rarely, if ever, easy. Even when we have good contemporary sources and reliable eyewitness accounts it is often difficult to see just why a certain turn of events occurred or be sure of the underlying motives that drove a particular action. Why, for example, did Balian of Ibelin, the commander of Jerusalem, negotiate surrender with Saladin in 1187 when he had vowed to God that he would never give up the city without waiting for a relief army from Europe or fighting to the last man?[1] Or why did the Turks leave Malta in the late summer of 1565 after a gruelling four-month siege? They were on the verge of success – just one more assault would probably have resulted in victory.[2] Of course, hindsight is, as has been famously noted, as good as it gets – essentially 20-20 vision.

Throughout the fourteenth and fifteenth century the power and influence of the Ottomans was in the ascendancy – victories, such as at Adrianople in 1361, Nicopolis in 1396, Varna in 1444 and the second battle of Kosovo in 1448, established them as truly formidable, seemingly invincible enemies. And, of course, the taking of Constantinople in 1453 established them as the dominating power of the Eastern Mediterranean. Their presence was a looming threat to the established order of Western Europe.

But, though their mastery in the Eastern Mediterranean was, by the later decades of the century, almost complete, the tiny island of Rhodes, just some two dozen or so kilometres from the south-western coast of Turkey, was a particular thorn in their side. The island was governed and ruled by 'warrior monks', the Knights Hospitaller, an Order which continued the Crusade against the adherents of Islam wherever they were to be found, finding expression, especially after the beginning of the fifteenth century, in a constant running fight with the Ottoman Empire. Vice versa, the Turks ravaged Hospitaller possessions and shipping whenever they had a chance, even making a couple of half-hearted attempts to take the island.

By 1480 the Turks decided to make a more determined effort to conquer the island of Rhodes. The Sultan, Mehmed II, launched a full-scale attack to finally rid himself of those troublesome Christians. Yet, despite having a superbly efficient war machine and superior numbers, and seemingly with everything in his favour, the siege lasted just two months, ending with the withdrawal of the Turks – the outcome neither a decisive victory for the Hospitallers nor a decisive defeat for the Turks. Within that short time the Turks threw everything they could at the city, both in terms of artillery and men, and they were well led and well supplied. Why did they not succeed? How did the Knights manage to hang on and prevent the Turks storming the city? What shaped the course of events and led to the final outcome?

Though the Turks finally packed up and left, the Hospitallers knew that they would return; they were growing stronger, more powerful, decade by decade, and eventually they would be back, probably sooner rather than later. There was not a moment to lose. The defences had to be rebuilt, reshaped in the newest and latest fashion to counter the newest and latest threats. New artillery also needed to be bought. The city had to be put into, and maintained in, a state of preparedness.

However, a series of events in the Ottoman world meant that the impetus of the 1480 siege was lost and the Empire turned its attention away from Rhodes. But in 1522 a new Sultan, Suleyman, later to be known in the West as 'the Magnificent', decided that it was time to remove the Hospitallers from their island stronghold. The siege he personally led in the summer, autumn and winter of 1522 finally succeeded. Again the outcome was not decisive, at least as far as destroying the Knights Hospitaller – a negotiated settlement allowed them to march out of the city and sail away with almost all their possessions. After some years without a secure base, they eventually found a home on the Central Mediterranean island of Malta, which they successfully defended against the Turks in 1565.

Much happened in the western world between 1480 and 1522 – the world seemed to 'turn on its axis'. The Catholic Church's Christian supremacy was being questioned and sea routes to the Far East and America were being opened up, resulting in Europeans beginning to look beyond their narrow physical and mental confines. Warfare, too, began to change as the truly awesome power of gunpowder was making a real impact. By 1480 gunpowder had been around for some 150 years, but it was the last decades of the fifteenth century and the first of the sixteenth century that saw the developments in artillery and gunpowder which could only be countered by very significant changes in fortifications. The walls that the Turks tried to breach in 1480 were thin and could accommodate mainly small- and medium-sized artillery. Those that Suleyman encountered in 1522 were thicker, stronger and augmented with larger, many-tiered outer works. More importantly, large artillery could be mounted on top of and within these fortifications, enabling the Knights to project their fire more effectively into the Turkish camp.

Introduction

But nothing is ever simple: resources, finances, manpower and time were not then, nor are they ever, limitless, and changes and developments always take place within the framework that they dictate. The Turks left Rhodes in July 1480, and though the Hospitallers knew that they would return, they did not know when. The coffers of the Order were not bottomless. New defences were very costly to build, money had to be raised and work managed effectively to get the most from every ducat.

In addition, the Hospitallers had to find new ways to counter the increased effectiveness of the new artillery that was developing at the same time. In 1480 Turkish bombards fired stone balls of immense size and weight. In 1522, though they were still using some large stone-throwing guns, they added long cannon firing cast-iron shot at greater velocity and greater range.

But people are so often the key to any military situation. Leadership, charisma, strength of character, personal charm, among many character traits, are all crucial as are the morale, outlook and attitude of the soldiers. Grand masters, knights and sergeants, mercenaries, city militia and even the townspeople were integral to the defence of Rhodes. An understanding of their roles in the sieges of 1480 and 1522 is of equal importance to those of the stones and cannon.

This is a story of cannon, stone and men. It unapologetically follows a chronological narrative – from the lead-up to the siege of 1480 through to the immediate aftermath of that in 1522. Appendices cover in detail both the walls and the surviving artillery. Using a unique combination of available evidence – narrative eyewitness accounts, contemporary illustrations, surviving artillery and the very walls of Rhodes themselves – this book is an attempt to look at the changing faces of siege warfare in the period when it went through perhaps the fastest and most enduring changes before the age of Vauban in the later seventeenth century.

Notes
1. Marshall Baldwin, 'The Decline and Fall of Jerusalem, 1174–1189', in *A History of the Crusades. Vol. I: The First Hundred Years*, ed. M.W. Baldwin (Madison: University of Wisconsin Press, 1969), pp. 590–621.
2. Ernle Bradford, *The Great Siege: Malta, 1565* (London: The Reprint Society, 1961)

Part One

The Knights, the Ottoman Turks and Rhodes before 1480

On 18 May 1291, after a century in Christian hands, the city of Acre fell to the Mamluks. It took a relatively short siege of just six weeks. For all intents and purposes this ended the Western European Crusades in the Holy Land, for although Sidon, Haifa, Beirut, Tartus and Atlit were still in Christian hands, all fell to the Mamluks before the middle of August. Indeed, Acre had been the last real hope for a Crusader presence in the Middle East. It was strongly fortified, with sufficient supplies and provisions inside the city to last its garrison and population for many years, long enough to survive until a relief army could arrive from Europe. It was a symbolic city. Taken in 1191 by the Third Crusaders, under the command of kings Richard I the Lionheart of England and Philip II Augustus of France, Acre was the last major conquest of a Crusader army in the Holy Land – although one might suggest a poor substitute for the original goal of the Third Crusade, the recapture of Jerusalem, which had fallen to Saladin four years previously.

Retaining Acre was so important that each of the popes from 1276 to 1291 – Gregory X, Innocent V, Adrian V, John XXI, Nicholas III, Martin IV, Honorius IV and Nicholas IV – had called for soldiers from all over Europe to defend it. Only the Knights Templar, the Teutonic Knights and the Knights Hospitaller, the three monastic military orders which had their origins in the years following the First Crusade, responded in any numbers, but these did not prove sufficient for the task of defending such a large city. Although eyewitnesses record numerous feats of military skill and bravery from the Templars and Hospitallers, they were ultimately unable to keep the Mamluks from overwhelming the fortifications and entering the city. The Teutonic Knights, the Hospitallers and the townspeople capitulated, and, on 28 May, after a desperate ten-day stand at their fortified headquarters, so too did the Templars.[1]

Over the following decades most European leaders, including the popes, blamed the failure at Acre on the military orders. Indeed, the Templars were unable to recover from this shame and infamously met their demise with the dissolution of their Order in 1307–12. Many veterans of Acre were among those burned at the stake for heresy.[2] The activities of the Teutonic Knights in north-east Europe soon eclipsed their failures in the Holy Land. Of the three Orders defending Acre, only the Hospitallers remained involved in crusading activities in the Eastern Mediterranean, first on the island of Cyprus and then on Rhodes. Though at first their fight was against the Mamluks, throughout the fourteenth and fifteenth centuries they increasingly turned their attention to the Ottoman Turks.

While the early history of the monastic military orders is disputed for lack of original source material, it is generally accepted that the earliest was the Knights of the Order of the Hospital of St John. It was certainly founded before 1113, the date of its confirmation as an Order by Pope Paschal II. It appears that originally it was not a military order. It was established by the Blessed Gerard, their recognised founder, to provide lodging and care for pilgrims, possibly around 1070, even before the launching of the First Crusade. Still, soldiers were needed to protect pilgrims travelling to, through and from the Holy Land in those dangerous years following the success of the First Crusade. Though the Crusaders took a number of places in the Middle East, including Antioch, Edessa, Bethlehem and Jerusalem, as well as several large coastal cities, these could not guarantee safe movement through those territories nor freedom from attack by enemies or brigands. It is possible that the Hospitallers were transformed into a military order for this purpose, probably by the middle of the twelfth century.[3]

That the Crusades produced monastic military orders is not surprising when one considers the difficulty in recruiting for a campaign so far away from Western Europe. Voyages to the Holy Land, either overland or by sea, were long and expensive; such a trip amounted often to a lifetime of military commitment. Numbers going on the First Crusade had been significant, with estimates of between 60,000 and 100,000, as it had the benefit of papal endorsement and publicity, something which would not always be given for later Crusades. Recruitment was never sufficient to protect all the lands that had been acquired by the First Crusaders, let alone provide troops for further expansion. Medieval monastic orders, principally the Hospitallers and Templars (which received papal recognition around the same time as the Hospitallers), became the basis of a standing Crusader army.[4]

For the next two centuries, between its founding and the final siege of Acre, the Hospitallers played an active role in all Crusader activities.[5] They retained their principal responsibilities as providers of short- and long-term hospital care, both at their castles and their urban convents, and as performers of religious rites and ceremonies.[6] But, more conspicuously, they also took part in all aspects of military and political life throughout the Crusader principalities.

These became especially noticeable in the middle of the twelfth century following the disastrous Second Crusade. Although the Grand Master of the Hospitallers

The Knights, the Ottoman Turks and Rhodes before 1480

at that time, Raymond du Puy, attended the council in June 1148 which foolishly decided to attack Damascus, there is no record of Hospitallers participating in the doomed campaign which followed. Hospitaller knights did fight at the successful siege of Ascalon in 1153, on the unsuccessful campaign into Egypt in 1168 and with the Count of Tripoli in his largely unsuccessful campaigns in the north. They also fought against Saladin at the battles of the Spring of the Cresson, on 1 May 1187, and Hattin, on 4 July 1187, where almost all were killed in the fighting or, if captured, were massacred. The garrison of the Hospitaller castle of Belvoir was also massacred when it was captured by Saladin on 5 January 1189 after a siege lasting almost a year and a half.

They were more effective in the Third Crusade: providing trebuchets for the siege of Acre in 1189–91; campaigning with Richard the Lionheart from Acre to Jaffa in 1191; fighting at the Battle of Arsuf on 7 September 1191; and intercepting a Muslim supply caravan at Bait Nūbā in June 1192. They were also active in the warfare of the Fifth Crusade, especially at the siege of Damietta in 1218, where they provided ships and siege engines, as well as soldiers. Although this siege of Damietta was a failure, the attack undertaken by the French King Louis IX (Saint Louis) in 1249–50, also with the Hospitallers' participation, was successful – even though the rest of the Crusade was not.[7]

The Hospitallers also became deeply involved in Crusader Kingdom politics. Early on, this primarily focused on the Kingdom of Jerusalem, where the grand masters were especially influential in advising the King on military matters, including pushing King Alamric I to invade Egypt in 1168. But by the middle of the twelfth century their influence had spread throughout the principalities and they frequently found themselves at odds with the Templars, especially in succession claims. In 1201 the Hospitallers supported Raymond-Rupen as Prince of Antioch over the Templar-supported Bohemond of Tripoli. Although Raymond-Rupen was young his inheritance claim was more direct and, besides the support of the Hospitallers, he had that of the Papacy and of Leon, King of Cicilian Armenia, uncle to Raymond-Rupen's mother, Alice. Ultimately his claim was recognised and for the rest of his reign, and that of his uncle in Armenia, the Hospitallers were favoured with patronage, lands and gifts in the northern Holy Land. For a generation in the thirteenth century this shifted the Hospitallers' political focus to that region. It returned to the Kingdom of Jerusalem in 1225 when they opposed, this time in concert with the Templars, the kingship of the Holy Roman Emperor Frederick II. He was currently under his second of three excommunication bans and as such was not to be given support by any temporal or ecclesiastical lords. In 1242 they also became embroiled in the succession crisis of the Kingdom of Jerusalem, this time on the side of Frederick II's son, Conrad IV, who was not affected by his father's ecclesiastical problems. Finally, in 1256–58, the Hospitallers became involved in resolving the political disputation known as the 'War' of St Sabas, 'fought' between Genoa, supported by the Hospitallers, and Venice, supported by the Templars, over ownership of property previously held by the Monastery of St Sabas in Acre. On this occasion the Genoese, and their Hospitaller supporters, lost out to the Venetians.

From 1191, when the city was taken by the Crusaders, to 1291, when it fell to the Mamluks, the Hospitallers had their headquarters at the convent in Acre.[8] The loss of the city meant that they had to establish a new headquarters elsewhere. Although by this date their holdings had diversified throughout Europe, Hospitaller veterans wished to remain in the Eastern Mediterranean to enable them to take part in any new Crusade. Initially Cyprus was chosen, and Pope Nicholas IV agreed to the establishment of a hospital in Limassol in 1292, though not it seems as a permanent headquarters.[9] Alternative sites were suggested, such as Cilician Armenia or Provence, but they were rejected.[10] Some Hospitallers wanted to return to Acre and attack the Mamluks, either alone or with the Templars, but these aspirations went no further than a few limited naval engagements between Hospitaller and Mamluk ships and coastal raids on Syria and Egypt.[11]

When Rhodes was first mentioned as a site for the Hospitaller headquarters is not known. The island was not in European or Catholic hands and, unlike many other Eastern Mediterranean islands, had rarely been part of any Crusader activities, even during the time of the Latin Kingdom of Constantinople (1204–61). The Rhodians were Byzantine Greeks who followed Greek Orthodox Christianity and, when forced, were politically and economically loyal to the emperors in Constantinople. However, there were not many of them, with estimates of the population of Rhodes at less than 10,000.[12] Still, Rhodes would provide the Hospitallers with several important advantages. Its proximity to both Asia Minor and the Holy Land would keep the Hospitallers aware of any potential crusading action, allowing them to choose whether to participate or not. Its natural harbours, especially those of the city of Rhodes, would also serve the Hospitallers well, by giving them an influence in trade and piracy that would undoubtedly lead to increased economic prosperity. It would also give them an independence that they did not have on Cyprus. Finally, it was likely that the inhabitants would put up very little resistance against a Hospitaller invasion. It was also doubtful that the Byzantines would try to defend the island, especially as their focus had recently been diverted to military problems caused by the rise of a small group of Turks, the Ottomans.

By 1306 increasingly difficult relations between the Hospitallers and the rulers of Cyprus led them to attempt to capture Rhodes. Matters came to a head when Amalric de Lusignan tried to usurp the power of his brother, King Henry II of Cyprus. Although the Hospitallers had their difficulties with Henry they offered to mediate between the two brothers. Nevertheless, their position in Cyprus grew more difficult.[13]

The initial conquest of Rhodes did not go as smoothly as had been hoped. Counting on surprise, Grand Master Foulques de Villaret led a small armed fleet – two galleys and four other ships – containing thirty-five Hospitaller knights, six Turcopoles and 500 infantry, supplemented by two Genoese galleys hired for the campaign, on what Anthony Luttrell has described as 'essentially a piratical Latin assault on a Christian, if schismatic Greek island'. However, the Rhodians learned of the Hospitallers' plans and retreated behind the walls of the island's fortifications which, while not in the best condition, still provided enough protection to prevent a speedy occupation. Sufficient land was captured, though, that Villaret was able to establish a camp on the island and, once reinforcements had arrived in early 1307, campaigning began anew. Some time later in 1307 Lindos, the largest city in the southern part of the island, was captured, but the city of Rhodes with its Byzantine walls held out, despite being continually attacked by Hospitaller catapults and other siege engines. Only on 15 August 1309 did the city surrender to save the lives and property of the citizens, although parts of the island were not entirely subjugated until 1310.[14] The Byzantine Emperor tried twice to relieve Rhodes, in 1307 and 1308, but on both occasions his force failed to break the determination of the Hospitallers. By 1310 he, too, had abandoned the island.[15]

The condition of Rhodes following its conquest by the Hospitallers is not known. The city of Rhodes seems to have been reasonably prosperous, largely as a result of trade, smuggling and piracy, but little had been spent on public works. Water and sewage still ran through the conduits built by the ancient Greeks, whose city greatly dwarfed that of the early fourteenth century, and their roads stretched from it throughout the island. In the rural regions agriculture provided more than the island's population could consume, and the surplus was traded abroad, as were timber, iron and the slaves taken in the course of piracy.

The churches seem to have been well maintained but elsewhere significant repairs had to be made.[16] The harbours were far too small for the Hospitallers' needs, if only to house their own fleet of galleys, warships and trading vessels, and the walls needed to be repaired and enlarged. The Byzantine walls, the remains of which can still be followed today, only protected about a quarter of the city. The Hospitallers proceeded to build their administrative, religious and military complex within these walls. Castles throughout the island, some built many centuries earlier, had to be restored or reconstructed, and new fortifications added where needed.[17]

Of course, uppermost in the minds of the Hospitallers was the construction of their headquarters convent. Pope Clement V recognised the Hospitallers' right to Rhodes on 5 September 1307,[18] even before the conquest had been completed, with the implied permission to relocate their headquarters there. Sufficient funds had also been collected, gathered in part when Grand Master Villaret toured Europe from 1307 to 1310,[19] and also, no doubt, in part from the Hospitallers' acquisition of a large number of the Templar properties after the Order's dissolution in 1312. However, by 1317 accusations of financial extravagance, including expenses associated with the conquest of Rhodes, brought about the removal of Foulques de Villaret as Grand Master. His replacement was Maurice de Pagnac, but, after a personal meeting with Pope John XII in Avignon two years later to discuss the Hospitallers' finances, he too was replaced – by Hélion de Villeneuve.[20]

Rhodes Besieged

The headquarters on Rhodes had to be large enough to house all of the brother knights, the brother sergeants, non-military brothers, their servants (and slaves), the Order's administrators, and visitors and guests. It also had to provide space for churches and a hospital. How quickly these were erected, and in which order, is unclear, but there does not appear to have been much of a delay between the capture of the city of Rhodes and the beginning of construction. Before the end of 1309 the Hospitallers had begun to move some of the Greek inhabitants away from the northern part of the older, walled Byzantine city – known as the *collachium* – where they planned to build their convent, to the rest of the city – known as the *borgo* – although there is evidence that a complete expulsion of the citizens was not attempted.[21] It is assumed that building commenced shortly afterwards, and eventually two hospitals, a Catholic cathedral, arsenal, treasury, mint, admiralty, various 'auberge' dormitory buildings and the Grand Master's Palace were constructed. The walls around the *collachium* were also strengthened, allowing the Hospitallers to control access into and out of this part of the city. When all of this was completed cannot be determined; however, it is known from visitors' travelogues that by 1420 one hospital and the arsenal had been finished and by 1437 the *collachium* could be closed off.[22] Archaeological evidence indicates that by 1480 the two hospitals, the auberge of Spain, the Grand Master's Palace and the house which today carries the arms of Grand Master Hélion de Villeneuve had been completed.[23] The illuminations in Guillaume Caoursin's manuscript, *Obsidionis Rhodiae urbis descriptio*, the painting of Rhodes found in the Epernay City Hall – both of which date to the five years following the siege – and the illustration of the city in Grünemberg's manuscript – which dates to 1486 – all show an entirely finished Hospitaller convent complex.[24]

Unfortunately the Grand Master's Palace in Rhodes today does not bear any likeness to that of the fourteenth and fifteenth centuries, other than the fact that it is built on the same foundations. The original was destroyed in 1856 by an explosion of ammunition stored in the crypt of the Church of St John of the Collachium.[25] Archaeological excavations on the remains of the palace, carried out between its destruction and the rebuilding in 1937–40, revealed that the foundations actually pre-date the Hospitaller construction. The Grand Master's Palace appears to have been built on a Byzantine structure, probably the citadel, or *akropolis*, which had existed there since the end of the seventh century. It also reused a large Byzantine tower in its original construction.[26]

Studies of the Grand Master's Palace carried out before its destruction in the nineteenth century show that the original was a large building on the northern side of a square courtyard around which were stables, kitchens, storehouses and other structures. On the main floor of the palace was a large hall in which council meetings and legal proceedings were held – lavishly decorated according to the illuminations in Caoursin's manuscript – and on the first floor, reached by stairs from the courtyard, were the Grand Master's spacious and vaulted personal apartments. Other rooms included a large private dining hall decorated with tapestries and with a minstrels' gallery for the Grand Master, also shown in the Caoursin manuscript,[27] a dining hall for the brothers, vaulted with two marble pillars, located in an upper storey, and a wine cellar in the basement.[28] In the courtyard a gateway flanked by two small rounded towers and walls enclosed the courthouse. On the gateway were the arms of Hélion de Villeneuve, Grand Master from 1319 to 1346, and the Papacy, although there is some evidence that the gateway itself was not built until after Villeneuve's death.[29] Documents from Cyprus put the Grand Master's staff at thirty-two – including squires, chaplains, stablemen, scribes, sergeants, a smith, a barber, a cook, a seneschal, a butler, a standard-bearer and other valets and servants – although it is not known how many lived in the Grand Master's Palace.[30]

The Grand Master had his own small chapel dedicated to St Catherine and possibly St Mary Magdalene, although its exact location in the palace is not known.[31] The Conventual church, St John's of the Collachium, was located just outside the gate to the palace and was probably built at the same time, as the Hospitaller brothers had certainly begun meeting in it by 1318.[32] It, too, was destroyed by the explosion of 1856, but appears to have been a traditional Christian basilica-style Gothic-vaulted church with a nave, two aisles and a square apse that was neither particularly long nor wide (50 x 30m) or tall. Contemporaries actually considered it 'small',[33] no doubt because of the number of tombs of grand masters and other brothers placed inside. Yet, it seems to have been large enough for all of the Hospitallers to meet there for general chapter assemblies, religious ceremonies and the election of the Grand Master.

There were three other Catholic churches in Rhodes before 1480, all the remaining churches being Greek Orthodox. The cathedral, located at the south-east corner of the *collachium*, had served the townspeople of Rhodes since at least the eleventh century when the current building was constructed. It was reconsecrated as a Catholic cathedral quite early in the Hospitallers' occupation of the city, probably in 1309. Initially, religious functions and rites were performed in the cathedral by Hospitaller chaplains, but in 1322 they were replaced by archbishops appointed by the Pope. It is probable that under their direction the Byzantine religious decoration – of which traces can still be seen today – were replaced by Latin artworks, more of which are extant. Eventually the windows and roof were also changed, the latter from a dome to ribbed vaults. After 1322 Santa Maria del Castello (Our Lady of the Castle), as the cathedral came to be known, seems to have served the townspeople rather than the Hospitallers.[34]

Another Catholic church dedicated to Santa Maria was located outside the *collachium* in the *burgo* and consequently gained the name Santa Maria del Borgo (Our Lady of the Town). It is thought that this church may have been built on the site of a Latin Christian church that had previously served those Catholics who lived in or traded with the Byzantine town. The new, large Gothic church, the ruins of which still exist, including three large rounded apses, was probably built between 1309 and 1346.[35] Finally, a Catholic church dedicated to St Anthony was built outside the walls of the city to the north by the sea. It was completed before Grand Master Villeneuve's death in 1346, and its cemetery served as the principal burial site for the Hospitallers. During the 1480 siege it was where the Ottomans set up their bombards to fire on the Fort St Nicholas and was destroyed.[36]

There is evidence that the first Hospitallers' hospital in Rhodes was established within existing buildings close to the eastern wall of the *collachium*. Plans for a more permanent hospital were quickly made, however – in 1314 – and by 1345 it had been completed (although parts of the building were already being used in 1338). A second, larger hospital was constructed around 1440, south of the first hospital inside the *collachium*.[37]

Numerous other Hospitaller buildings were constructed over the following two centuries. Some of these were built to house the knights and their servants, divided into various language or national groups, called *langues* or tongues. Although *langues* probably existed among the Hospitallers prior to the move to Rhodes, it is only there that living arrangements were divided in this way. This probably dates from 1347 when German Hospitallers purchased a residence for their *langue*. It was followed in 1348 by the establishment of the *langues* of Italy and Auvergne, and later by those of Provence, Spain, France and England. All still exist today, although with much reconstruction.[38] An arsenal, mint and treasury were also constructed in the *collachium* by the Hospitallers before the middle of the fourteenth century.[39]

Although their focus was on construction within the *collachium* during most of the fourteenth century, the Hospitallers were also responsible for some administrative, legal and charitable buildings in the *borgo*, including the hospice of St Catherine, built in 1391,[40] as well as markets, warehouses and stores to supply the Hospitallers and townspeople.[41]

Anthony Luttrell has suggested that, while a large amount of construction was going on in the city in the early decades following the Hospitallers' conquest of Rhodes, little was done to the walls beyond the shoring up of old Byzantine fortifications around the *collachium*.[42] The reason for this was simple: at the beginning of the fourteenth century there was no real threat to their security or that of the city, despite the walls not entirely encircling it. The Byzantines were weak and busy with internecine squabbles with a small but determined new force in Anatolia, the Ottomans, while the Mamluks were too distant and had concentrated their efforts on defending their Middle Eastern lands from the Ilkhanid Mongols. This remained the situation until well into the fifteenth century. The city of Rhodes, which had grown since the Hospitallers had occupied it, remained largely unprotected by fortifications.

The loss of the Holy Land to the Mamluks remained uppermost in the minds of the Hospitallers long after their move to Cyprus and then Rhodes. But a new enemy soon replaced the Mamluks: the Ottoman Turks.

By the time of the Hospitaller conquest of Rhodes in 1306–10 the Ottomans were beginning to cause military problems for the Byzantines in Anatolia. The meteoric rise of the Ottoman Turks at the very end of the thirteenth and early fourteenth centuries is one of the more interesting stories of medieval history, but is so shrouded in myth that what actually happened will probably never be known. The Ottoman Turks rose to power under the leadership of Ghāzī 'Osmān, from whom they also took their name. 'Osmān, head of a small Turkish clan, defeated a far larger Byzantine army at the Battle of Baphaeus in 1301.[43] Even then the Byzantines thought that they were only dealing with a simple rebellion by a Muslim minority, more of an irritant keeping Constantinople from facing more 'fearsome' enemies. This opinion began to change when 'Osmān nearly captured Philadelphia in 1304, especially as his siege was raised only when the Latin Grand Company from Greece intervened. It was to change completely when 'Osmān's son and successor, Orkhān I, defeated a Byzantine army led by Emperor Andronicus III Palaeologus at the Battle of Pelekanon in 1327, captured Nicaea after a siege of nearly three years in 1331 and conquered Nicomedia after a siege of nearly four years in 1337.[44]

By this time the Hospitallers on Rhodes had already encountered the Ottoman Turks but, at least initially, seem not to have had major dealings with them. Although the Venetian traveller-diarist Marino Sanudo Torsello believed that the Hospitallers were effectively 'sow[ing] discord among the Turks and their neighbours',[45] it was not until 1312 that they had their first military encounter with them. That year a Hospitaller fleet attacked twenty-three Ottoman ships near Amorgos, burned them and massacred their crews, some 800 Turks. But they suffered their own casualties, 57 Hospitallers and 300 others according to a possibly exaggerated account by Francesco Amadi. (This had increased further to the killing of 1500 Turks with a loss of a total of only eighty-five Christians by the time it was reported to the Papacy at Avignon later that year.)[46] Other naval engagements followed in 1318, 1319 and 1320, each time with the Hospitallers victorious, destroying large numbers of ships, killing large numbers of men (also women and children on occasion) and capturing large amounts of booty and slaves. A small Turkish invasion of Rhodes was also thwarted in 1320.[47]

As the Ottomans became stronger during the reigns of Orkhān I, Murād I and Bāyezīd I, the Hospitallers became less successful in their encounters with the Turks. Triumphs such as those in May 1344, when Hospitaller ships participated in a victory near Smyrna and fifty-two Turkish ships were sunk, or in June 1347, when Hospitaller and other Western European ships captured 118 Ottoman vessels near Imbros, were matched by losses, such as at Lampsakos in 1359, when an undermanned (and 'undershipped') attack of a Turkish fortification was counter-attacked with great force, and in 1394 when the Hospitaller-controlled island of Astypalia was so comprehensively destroyed by Ottoman attacks that no one would live there.[48] The Knights were forced to spend more of their funds on fortifying the coastlines of Rhodes and other Eastern Mediterranean holdings against an ever increasing number of Turkish raids during the fourteenth and fifteenth centuries.[49] Yet, at other times, the Hospitallers and Ottoman Turks allied with each other, at least in purpose if not in a formal pact, for example against the Byzantines in late 1333/early 1334 when they succeeded together in conquering the Byzantine island of Lesbos.[50]

Apart from these encounters, though, there was very little conflict between the Hospitallers and the Ottoman Turks before the beginning of the fifteenth century. In large part this was due to the Ottomans' focus on enlarging their territory in Anatolia and in the Balkans rather than in the Greek islands of the Eastern Mediterranean. They acquired Seres and Demotika in 1361, Macedonia in 1371, Armenia in 1375, Sofia in 1385, Nis in 1386, Bulgaria in 1393, Salonika and Rūm in 1394, and Dobrudja in 1395. In two major battles, at Kosovo in 1389 and Nicopolis in 1396, Ottoman armies crushed western opponents: a Serbian army at Kosovo, and at Nicopolis, a crusading force drawn from England, Burgundy, France, Germany, Hungary, Wallachia, Transylvania and the Teutonic Knights. Only twice during this period did the Ottoman Turks lose significant military engagements: at Rovine in 1395 when a Hungarian and Wallachian army defeated them in battle, but were unable to halt their Balkan campaign; and at Ankara in 1402 when Tamerlane and his Mongols trounced the Ottoman army, capturing Sultan Bāyezīd I and sacking the former Turkish capital of Bursa.[51] During this time, with their military efforts directed elsewhere, Rhodes was largely ignored. When recognised, such as in 1393 when Bāyezīd approached the Hospitallers with a peace proposal, diplomacy was pursued instead of military action; the Knights refused this treaty, however, as it contained provisions for free trade and the requirement to return any Turkish slaves who escaped to Rhodes or other Hospitaller holdings.[52]

Certainly the Hospitallers were very concerned about the growth of Ottoman power and territory during this period. Especially frightening was the prospect of the fall of Constantinople, which was besieged in 1394. While the Byzantines had been enemies of the Hospitallers since their conquest of Rhodes, their control of parts of the Eastern Mediterranean was greatly preferred to that of the Ottoman Turks. Beginning in the last decade of the fourteenth century, the Hospitallers participated more frequently in campaigns against the Ottomans. For example, Hospitallers, led by Grand Master-elect Philibert de Naillac, fought at the Battle of Nicopolis in 1396, although they wisely did not participate in the ill-considered attacks that led to the Crusaders' humiliating defeat and were able to escape the massacre which followed.[53] The Order subsequently raised money to help ransom those who had been captured at Nicopolis.[54] In 1403 they provided the base for, and participated in, French Marshal Boucicault's raids on the Anatolian and Syrian coasts. Boucicault considered these to be revenge for his imprisonment after Nicopolis, but they did no real damage and brought no great benefit to him or the Hospitallers.[55] Licences for privateering Ottoman vessels, like those awarded to Hospitaller brothers Jean de Pietris and Richard de Pontailler on 14 April 1413, were also regularly awarded during this time.[56]

By the turn of the fifteenth century the Hospitallers had built up a reputation for military strength that made the Ottomans fear their influence and possible interference, especially after the dreadful loss to the Timurid Mongols in 1402 had destabilised the Ottoman government and army.[57] By defeating the Ottomans at Ankara, Tamerlane did Christianity in the Eastern Mediterranean a great favour. For more than a decade following the battle, the Ottoman Turks were embroiled in a succession crisis as Bāyezīd I's sons, Suleyman, Isa and Mehmed, all fought one another over who was to follow their father on to the Sultan's throne. Even after Mehmed I triumphed in 1413 he was unable to do much more than reconquer some Balkan and Armenian lands before his death at the age of 32 in 1421.[58]

But Murad II, Mehmed's son, who ruled from 1421 to 1451, returned to the Ottoman policy of expansionism, especially in south-eastern Europe and in what remained of the Byzantine Empire. In the Balkans his capture of Smyrna in 1424, Salonika in 1430, Albania in 1432, and his defeat of the Hungarians at the Battle of Golubac in 1428 prompted Pope Eugenius IV to call for a crusade against the Ottoman Turks in 1440. In response, in 1441, Vladislav, King of Poland and Hungary, raised the siege of Belgrade; in 1442 the Hungarian János Hunyadi defeated the Ottomans invading Transylvania; in 1443 the Albanians revolted and regained their independence; and in 1444 Hunyadi won the battle on Mount Kunovica. However, even this was not sufficient to discourage the Ottomans. Following Murad II's defeat of a crusading army at the Battle of Varna in 1444 and Hunyadi at the Second Battle of Kosovo in 1448, he recovered control of the Balkans, except for Albania and Belgrade, putting an end to any hopes of stopping the Turks from further conquest in south-eastern Europe.[59]

None of these campaigns directly affected the Hospitallers. Although the Knights participated in some of the campaigns and engagements, most notably at Smyrna, Rhodes and their other Eastern Mediterranean lands and fortifications were untouched by conflict. Still, neither the Hospitallers nor anyone else in Christian Europe could ignore the unrelenting Ottoman conquests of Murad's reign, and it is against this backdrop that they began to think more actively about their defences, especially those of the city of Rhodes.

The Turks may have been the most worrisome of the Hospitallers' enemies in the mid-fifteenth century, but it was the Egyptian Mamluks who tried first to remove them from Rhodes. Why Rhodes was their target is not known – the main account of the siege is from a Catalan eyewitness, Francesc Ferrer, who wrote *Romanç de l'armada del soldà contra Rodes* (Romance of the Sultan's Armada against Rhodes)[60] – although it may be that the Mamluk ruler, Az-Zahir Sayf ad-Din Jaqmaq, saw this both as a means of ridding the Eastern Mediterranean of the Hospitallers and gaining an island from which they could launch attacks against the Ottoman Turks.

On 10 August 1444 a Mamluk fleet of seventy-five ships arrived at Rhodes and laid siege to the city. Attacks were concentrated on St Anthony's Gate and the Tower of St Nicholas, with a major assault made on 10 September. But the fortifications held, and three days later, after a fleet made up mostly of Burgundian, Catalan and Hospitaller vessels began to pester the Mamluk ships lying at anchor, they raised the siege and left the island. On the whole the city seems to have suffered relatively little

Rhodes Besieged

damage, although Anna-Maria Kasdagli and Katerina Manoussou-Della have conjectured that it did raise awareness among the Knights that more work was needed on the walls, leading to the construction projects of Grand Master Jean de Lastic.[61]

Written and archaeological evidence suggests that the defences of Rhodes changed very little from the time the Knights captured the city in 1309 to the end of the fourteenth and the beginning of the fifteenth centuries.[62] The old Byzantine wall that surrounded the *collachium* was rebuilt and strengthened, but little more seems to have been done to enclose the, by then, much larger city or protect the harbour. Grand Master Juan Fernandez de Heredia (1376–96) carried out work on the north side of the city as his arms can still be seen on the square towers to the west of St Paul's Gate. It was his successor, Philibert de Naillac (1396–1421), who was responsible for a completely new tower, the Tower of Naillac, which stood on the promontory on the west side of the commercial harbour. Unfortunately demolished by an earthquake in April 1863, it was a striking construction with four corner turrets and emphasised, perhaps, that at this period it was attack on Rhodes from the sea that was seen as the greatest threat by the Hospitallers.[63]

This changed in the fifteenth century, although by whom and when the major walls of the city were built is not entirely clear. The arms of the grand masters set into many places in the walls are of great value to date them, but this is not without problems. The arms of Grand Master Antonio Fluvian de Riviere (1421–37) and Grand Master Jean de Lastic (1437–54) are very similar – both consist of a horizontal bar across the shield. The difference between the two is that in those of Fluvian the bar is red set in a golden shield, while in those of Lastic the bar is white set in a red shield. The problem is that when carved from a single piece of stone which has since lost its painted colouring these can look identical – essentially a white shield with a recessed horizontal bar also in white. And while there are a few which can be positively identified as those of Lastic and made from contrasting coloured stone – red and white – most are, as noted above, all white. Only in one place can it be certain that a shield is that of Fluvian as it occurs together with the arms of Pope Martin V, who was pope between 1417 and 1431. Without further evidence it would appear that the majority of the walls that can be seen today were originally built by grand masters Fluvian and Lastic. Certainly their arms appear at fairly regular intervals on most of the walls still remaining today.[64]

The arms of succeeding grand masters, Jacques de Milly (1454–61), Piero Raimondo Zacosta (1461–67) and Giovanni Battista Orsini (1467–76), also appear on the walls, albeit in far fewer numbers, and strongly suggest that they continued the work begun by Fluvian and Lastic. Orsini in particular seems to have carried out extensive work on the harbour walls, where his arms appear no fewer than six times. The seaward defences were further strengthened by the construction of the Tower of the Mills on the end of Windmill Mole, which juts out to form the north-east side of the merchant's harbour, some time around 1440–54. Built to protect the mole as well as help to defend Rhodes from the sea, this tower also housed one end of a chain stretched across the harbour to Naillac's Tower. This great iron boom protected the inner, commercial harbour. As first built, the Tower of the Mills consisted, like the Tower of St Nicholas, of a cylindrical tower with a separate, detached staircase tower. Around its base was a low wall pierced with simple gun loops.

Although Grand Master Zacosta may have done little to the main walls of the city, he was responsible for one of the most important features of the 1480 siege, for it was during his mastership that the Tower of St Nicholas was built, in 1464–67. Its construction was partly paid for by a generous donation of 12,000 gold *soldi* by Philip the Good, Duke of Burgundy, whose arms can still be seen on the tower to this day.[65] Constructed as a fortification on the end of the mole leading north from the city, it greatly strengthened the defences of the harbour. Originally built as a circular drum, with a detached staircase tower, it was encircled by a lower polygonal apron with gun loops on two levels. The Tower of St Nicholas commanded the sea to the north and east, as well as access to the military harbour to the west. It was a major focus for the Ottoman forces in 1480, and the fact that it was not captured by the Turks contributed to the failure of the siege.

It is clear, then, that the walls that confronted the Turks in 1480 were essentially created in a period of just over thirty years – from 1421 to 1454. It should be understood, however, that those walls differed from those that can be seen today and, in order to better understand what the Turks faced, an attempt must be made to recreate them. First, it is clear that the walls of 1480 were thinner – their width was greatly increased by Grand Master Fabrizio de Carretto largely between 1513 and 1517. Substantial stretches, for example the section between the Tower of Spain and the Tower of the Virgin, were also lower in height. Along the top of this main wall ran a parapet behind which was a relatively narrow fighting platform. Parallel to the main wall, at some 3–4m in front of it, was another lower one, called a *faussebraye*. Like the main wall it had a parapet and a platform from which bows, crossbows and handguns could be fired. At intervals along the *faussebraye* were a series of square towers. These were not then, as they are today, attached to the main city wall but stood away from it, connected by wooden bridges which could be easily demolished if necessary. Finally, the moat was considerably narrower.

This form of city wall was essentially the same all over Europe at the time. Defenders relied on a series of obstacles to prevent direct attack in force. The first was usually a moat to keep attackers at a distance, as well as making it difficult for them to storm the main wall. Though many moats were filled with water, making them even harder to cross, dry moats, like that at Rhodes, were also common. Having a *faussebraye* was unusual but not uncommon, providing the defender with a first line of attack when the enemy stormed the moat. Detached interval towers were also common, allowing the defender a commanding position over the enemy. In the event that the towers were taken they could easily be cut off from the wall, the main defence of the city. High walls, of course, were difficult to scale.

Rhodes Besieged

Medieval fortifications were built to withstand attacks from men, individually or en masse, while also protecting their inhabitants from machines built to break through them, from the traction and counterweight trebuchets of the High Middle Ages to the gunpowder weapons of the Later Middle Ages. The trebuchet was the major siege weapon from the twelfth to the middle of the fourteenth century, although it remained in limited use into the first part of the fifteenth century. Capable of accurate and consistent fire, the trebuchet had by this time reached the extent of its capabilities and was countered successfully by engineers who recognised its limitations and were fully capable of making their defences more resistant to its attack. Gunpowder weapons were first used in Europe in the second quarter of the fourteenth century, but their full potential was not attained until the later fifteenth century. Before then gunpowder and barrel-making technologies were still in their infancy, and the enormous power that gunpowder artillery would achieve was not yet evident. Similarly the changes needed to counter this power were not realised and the builders of fortification and city walls could only respond to current threats.

As noted above, the main walls of the city of Rhodes were essentially built in a single period, from 1421 to 1454, and it is safe to assume that they were built in response to the latest gunpowder weapons and could be taken as an example of the most up-to-date fortifications of the time. However, this period was one of significant changes in artillery and there is sufficient evidence to suggest that there was a dramatic increase in the size of artillery barrels. Though large-calibre pieces had previously been made, the years between 1430 and 1460 saw a large increase in size – bombards with bores in excess of 50cm in diameter.[66] The development of the very large-calibre bombard in the middle of the century meant that the Turks were able to do more damage to the walls than earlier in the century; however, it is likely that the fortifications were resistant to much of the artillery of the period.

Still, the outcome of a siege in the middle of the fifteenth century was never certain. Using a large number of gunpowder weapons and with the time and patience to wage a determined siege, a fortified city could be captured. This was well demonstrated when, on 5 April 1453, Sultan Mehmed II laid siege to the Byzantine capital, Constantinople, and showed Europe just what he and his armies were capable of.[67] His army was huge, estimates putting it at 200,000 strong, although it is more likely that only 80,000–100,000 soldiers were present. Among these were a large force of Janissaries, some of the most skilled and determined warriors in the world at the time. His siege train was also huge, consisting of all sizes and shapes of gunpowder weapons. According to contemporary sources, many of these had been made especially for this siege and some were operated by mercenary gunners recruited from Germany and Hungary.[68] Constantinople was also blockaded from the sea, with some of Mehmed's ships being dragged overland to bypass the great chain which stretched across the mouth of the Golden Horn and cut off the city's harbour.

Facing him was a paltry force, no more than 7,000, including more than 2,000 European adventurers and Ottoman exiles, but they were all behind the city's walls.

Built between 408 and 413 by Emperor Theodosius II, the walls extended across 2.8km of land between the Golden Horn and the Sea of Marmara, and had been maintained and added to over the next millennium. By 1453 they had been increased in height and width, with ninety-six towers, a *faussebraye*, a wide, deep moat, eight fortified gates and a wall surrounding the city along the sea.[69] Only defeated by the Fourth Crusaders in 1203–04,[70] the walls of Constantinople had held up for centuries against enemies as diverse as the Huns, Arabs, Bulgars, Slavs, Russians, Seljuk Turks, Mongols and even early attempts by Ottomans. At times enemies simply avoided Constantinople in their campaigns, defeating the peoples around the city but not bothering to invest what would certainly be a large amount of time and money to besiege the city. In the last decade of the fourteenth and first of the fifteenth centuries the Ilkhanid Khan, Tamerlane, avoided the city during his invasion and occupation of Byzantine lands in central and eastern Anatolia. Similarly, in their territorial expansion the Ottoman Turks, who by 1453 occupied all the lands surrounding Constantinople, only attempted a siege of the city in 1422 into which they put little effort and from which they decided to withdraw after barely more than two months.[71]

By 1453 there was almost nothing left of the Byzantine Empire except Constantinople. Attacking it became a matter of strategy and not just honour. Mehmed becoming the first Ottoman Sultan to defeat Constantinople is mentioned frequently in the Turkish sources as a motivating factor in his siege of the city.[72] Learning from the failures of the past, Mehmed took with him a very large army and a large artillery train. He had built the latter virtually from scratch, recognising the need for some means to penetrate the strong city walls. In 1453 the construction of such an artillery train was still relatively novel for the Eastern Mediterranean region. The Ottoman Turks had guns, but not of the size or number that Mehmed felt were necessary to take down the walls of Constantinople. It was necessary to build these. Kritovoulos, a Greek writer hired by Mehmed as his biographer, was quite impressed by the guns the Sultan had built:

> He devised machines of all sorts ... among others various stone throwers and especially the newest kind, a strange sort, unbelievable when told of but, as experience demonstrated, able to accomplish everything.[73]

Apparently limited in native manufacturers and operators of these weapons, Mehmed hired Germans and at least one Hungarian to make and fire his guns.[74] The story of the Hungarian, Urban or Orban by name, has become legendary:

> There came from Constantinople [where he had previously offered his services to the Byzantine Emperor but been turned down] a craftsman who had great skill in the casting of cannon, a Hungarian ... Mehmed asked him if he was able to cast a cannon large enough to fire a shot which would make an impression on the walls of the city, in spite of their strength and thickness. He replied, 'if you wish, I can cast cannon as large as the

shot which is being shown to me now. I know what the walls of the city are like. The shot from my cannon could reduce them, and even the walls of Babylon itself.' ... The operation of casting was completed within three months, and the result was a monstrosity of the most fearful and extraordinary kind ... In January [the Sultan] ... decided to test the cannon which the Hungarian had made. It was carefully set in position before the main gateway leading into the palace [at Adrianople] which he had built that year, the ball was fitted into it, and its ration of powder weighed out. It was planned to fire it the next morning, and public announcement throughout Adrianople, to advise everyone of the loud and thunderous noise which it would make so that no one would be struck dumb by hearing the noise unexpectedly or any pregnant woman miscarry. In the morning the gunpowder was lit, there was a great rush of hot air, and the shot was driven forth, leaving the cannon with a loud explosion which filled the air with clouds of smoke. The sound was heard a hundred stadia away (18.5 km), and the shot travelled a thousand paces from the point of firing, making a hole six feet deep at the point where it landed.[75]

Mehmed placed his larger cannon against 'the most vulnerable and weakest parts of the wall', according to Kritovoulos.[76] For fifty-five days they fired continually against them. Giacomo Tedaldi calculates the number of shots and how much gunpowder was used by Mehmed's forces:

Each day the cannon were fired between a hundred and a hundred and twenty times, and the siege lasted for fifty-five days. It has been calculated that they used a thousand pounds weight of powder each day, so that in fifty-five days they used fifty-five thousand pounds weight of powder.[77]

Initially the Byzantines tried to fight back with their own gunpowder artillery,[78] but they ultimately proved to be insufficient to defeat Mehmed's guns and determination.[79]

Before too long the destruction of the walls had become significant. Kritovoulos describes the impact of each gunshot:

And the stone, borne with tremendous force and velocity, hit the wall, which it immediately shook and knocked down, and was itself broken into many fragments and scattered, hurling the pieces everywhere and killing those who happened to be near by. Sometimes it demolished a whole section, and sometimes a half-section, and sometimes a larger or smaller section of a tower or turret or battlement. And there was no part of the wall strong enough or resistant enough or thick enough to be able to withstand it, or to wholly resist such force and such a blow of the stone cannon-ball.[80]

The Turks had also been active in moving the siege forward elsewhere. Mehmed's ships, including those dragged overland past the harbour chain, had fought against and destroyed Byzantine and allied vessels in the seas around the city, while they and artillery from the shore kept relief ships away from the harbour.[81]

On 28 May Mehmed began his final assault of Constantinople. First he ordered his gunners to fire against the weakened and wrecked parts of the walls, making breaches in several places.[82] Mehmed then sent his non-professional, irregular troops forward first into these breaches. There were many casualties on both sides.[83] Finally, Mehmed ordered his most powerful military force, his Janissaries, into the attack. 'They were to keep up so heavy a fire that those defenders would be unable to fight, or to expose themselves because of the clouds of arrows and other projectiles falling like snowflakes,' Kritovoulos writes.[84] The city was soon taken.

News of the fall of Constantinople resonated throughout Western Europe with the inevitable fear-mongering and was highlighted by stories, no doubt apocryphal, of depredations committed by the Turks in their conquest. To Cardinal Bessarion, a Byzantine cardinal of the Catholic Church educated in Constantinople, these included the desecration of the symbols of Christianity:

> As for the venerable image of the Blessed Virgin Mary, which the entire population of Constantinople used to worship before all else with the greatest devotion, those impious butchers detached its gold, silver and precious stones, cut up their meat on it for a long time, before finally trampling it beneath their feet, breaking it up with an axe, and burning it. The representations of our Saviour in the vaults of the church, which were too high up to reach by hand and pollute with excrement, they shot arrows at shamelessly hurling abuse: 'Let's see if the God of the Christians knows how to escape from our hands.'[85]

Despicable acts were also said to have been committed against innocent people. Michael Ducas, an eyewitness to the fall of Constantinople, writes:

> Who can recount the calamity of that time and place? ... The commonest Turk sought the most tender maiden. The lovely nun, who heretofore belonged only to the one God, was now seized and bound by another master. The rapine caused the tugging and pulling of braids of hair, the exposure of bosoms and breasts, and outstretched arms.[86]

Beliefs that the Ottoman Turks would soon attack Central and Western Europe were widespread. Calls for crusade were made by both ecclesiastical and secular leaders. Philip the Good, the powerful and wealthy Duke of Burgundy, immediately started planning a crusade against Mehmed II and the Ottoman Turks. Announcing his plans at the famous Feast of the Pheasant, held at Lille on 17 February 1454, Philip called for others to join him. He vowed:

> with the help of our blessed creator ... to undertake and carry out [a crusade against the conquerors of Constantinople] by recruiting as many troops as he can find, both from

> those who have made a vow for the aid and defence of our said Christian faith, and from among those who are resolved to go. And . . . to set out next Spring in person on this journey.[87]

Elaborate plans were drawn up and funds allocated. Spring 1455 proved to be too ambitious and the date that the Crusader army was to set out for the Eastern Mediterranean was delayed for another year. It was hoped that this would be the start of a massive movement that would gather numbers and strength as the Burgundians marched across Europe. Pope Callixtus III lent his support, urging those throughout the West to join the Crusade.[88]

But this crusade never happened. Philip the Good was forced to delay his start in 1456 because of an uprising in Utrecht over his choice to be Prince-Bishop of the city and the unsuccessful siege of Deventer that followed. Delays continued, and in the end the Duke of Burgundy never marched east,[89] nor did any of the others who had taken the cross in the aftermath of the fall of Constantinople and the defeat of the Byzantine Empire.

Unfortunately, in not responding to the fall of Constantinople and the threat of Ottoman expansion in south-eastern Europe, the Western European powers missed the opportunity to defeat the Turks. Had their troops been with those of János Hunyadi and the 71-year-old Franciscan friar, Giovanni Capistrano, at Belgrade on 22 July 1456, they might have inflicted a more decisive defeat on Mehmed II's forces. They were only pushed back from their unsuccessful siege of the city and were not dealt a more substantial blow.[90]

Aeneas Silvius Piccolomini, who as a cardinal had tried with considerable effort to encourage Western European leaders to avenge the fall of Constantinople, attempted to do the same as Pope Pius II at the conference of Mantua – described by Jocelyne G. Russell more as 'a series of bilateral meetings of the Pope and individual "national" embassies or groups of embassies' – held in 1459.[91] Pius, in trying to rationalise the reason why none of the European kings or princes had answered the Catholic Church's calls to crusade in the six years since the fall of Constantinople, concluded that there were two probable reasons: first, the Western European Christian powers had been too busy fighting other Christians, either in international or civil war; and second, Western European realms were too frightened by the Turks to fight against them.[92]

Even before the end of the siege of Constantinople the Hospitallers had become alarmed by the Turkish threat to their headquarters on Rhodes. On 6–7 July 1453 Grand Master Jean de Lastic ordered the mobilisation of the priories of France and St Gilles,[93] and until his death he made further decrees for Hospitaller mobilisation and the delivery of funds and goods to Rhodes.[94] Lastic also made general calls for assistance to 'all the faithful'.[95] He even went so far, in a letter to French Prior Nicole de Giresme, as to predict an attack on the island in April 1454 by Turkish galleys.[96]

In another 1454 letter, Jean de Lastic mentions that the Turks had demanded a 2,000-ducat tribute from the Knights, apparently at the time of demanding the same from Venice. On 18 April 1454, in order to preserve Crete, Cyprus and their other Eastern Mediterranean and Black Sea lands, Venice chose to pay what was requested, as well as granting other concessions to the Turks. The Hospitallers refused – perhaps providing the reason behind Lastic's prediction of an attack in April of that year.[97]

No doubt the Knights Hospitaller had reason to feel that they would be the Ottoman Turks' next target. With most of Anatolia under their control it was only natural that the Knights would believe that Mehmed II would want to clear the nearby islands of enemies. The attack on Belgrade in 1456 and Trebizond, in northern Anatolia, in 1461 proved that Ottoman military interests lay elsewhere. The raiding of Hospitaller lands – in particular Syme, Nisyros, Cos, Chios as well as Rhodes – and vessels by the Turks continued, but so too did the raids on Turkish lands and ships by Hospitallers.[98]

Fear of the Turks and anticipation of an attack on the city of Rhodes continued into Jacques de Milly's term as Grand Master. Elevated to the position after the death of Lastic in 1454, Milly continued to warn the Knights of the Ottoman threat, but he also attempted to make peace with the Turks. In 1455 he sent legates to Mehmed II at Edirne, bearing gifts and the proposal of a peace treaty, one based largely on trade between the Hospitallers and the Turks. The feeling here was simple: positive economic connections make warfare between two powers unprofitable. The treaty was to allow the Hospitallers freedom to trade in Anatolia, principally along the coasts of Caria and Lycia, while the Ottomans would be able to trade freely on Rhodes. The Turks appear to have been interested in signing such a treaty, but they would not do so until an annual tribute from the Hospitallers was agreed first, and Milly refused to even consider this – paying tribute to the Turks had been officially banned by Pope Nicholas V. Mehmed II even threatened war with the Hospitallers should they not agree to a tribute, but Milly still refused.[99]

The Ottoman failure to take Belgrade the next year meant that they could not immediately carry out their threats against the Hospitallers. Belgrade cost the Turks a large number of soldiers, vehicles and vessels, gunpowder weapons and, most importantly, morale and confidence. It bought what the threatened south-eastern European and Eastern Mediterranean states needed most: time to recuperate and rebuild.[100] While the Ottomans were recovering from the defeat, the Hospitallers continued to build their walls and to gather their own stores, guns and money.[101] The Turkish defeat also boosted their confidence: if the Belgradians, with a few Hungarians and some motley Crusaders who followed John of Capistrano, could defeat the same soldiers who had conquered Constantinople, then there was certainly hope that the Knights Hospitaller could do the same.[102] This hope, together with the anticipation of and preparations for an Ottoman attack, would continue through the rule of grand masters Jacques de Milly, Piero Raimondo Zacosta and Giovanni Battista Orsini.

During this time the Knights continued their role as opponents of Islamic expansion wherever they could. This included: providing money and supplies to the papal fleet operating in the Eastern Mediterranean in 1457;[103] protecting the islands of Lemnos and Thasos in 1458–59 when asked to do so by Pope Callixtus III;[104] assisting in the defence of Cyprus when it was attacked by Mamluks in 1460;[105] promising to provide three galleys for Pope Pius II's Crusade in 1463;[106] providing a haven for a Venetian fleet attempting to capture Lesbos and other recently conquered islands in 1464; aiding Venice in the attempted reconquest of Negroponte in 1470;[107] and joining the Christian League initiated by popes Pius II and Sixtus IV – with Venice, Naples and Aragon – which sacked Smyrna, Adalia, Seleucia and Corycus in 1472.[108] But it also included attacks in 1460, 1464 and 1465 on Venetian ships conducting trade with Islamic lands in violation of papal directives. Venice answered these incidents, the first by attacking some villages on Rhodes, the second with a naval demonstration in view of the city, and the third by landing on the island of Rhodes, until the Hospitallers returned booty and Muslim prisoners from the vessels.[109]

However, the Knights also sent delegations to the Ottoman court. For example in March 1462 they sought peace and trade agreements, although they continued to refuse to pay tribute to the Sultan.[110] At times, trade agreements and treaties were put into effect, but they never held for long before one side or the other violated a part of the agreement, such as the Sultan's request for tribute again in 1464 and 1466, which the Hospitallers continually refused.[111]

The Hospitallers and the Ottoman Turks, both ardent adherents of their religions, co-existed, but only barely. Kenneth Setton has astutely summed up relations between the Hospitallers and Turks during the period: '... for decades life in the Aegean was disrupted by almost continuous warfare, punctuated by piracy, between the Ottoman government and the Hospitallers at Rhodes.'[112]

Western Europe knew of the situation in Rhodes and there was widespread concern that the Knights Hospitaller would not survive the inevitable Turkish onslaught. Some, like Pope Paul II writing in response to a letter from Grand Master Orsini written 20 January 1471, promised both psychological and physical help:

> We have received your letter ... and gathered clearly enough that you are doubtful and apprehensive about the city of Rhodes because of the power and increasing impetus of the terrible Turks. Certainly we must fear, but not so as to cease the search for aid and remedies. Not at all. We shall have to move with greater care and speed. Do not fail yourselves, but take heed. We are managing, along with the Italian and other Christian powers, to take such steps ... as will help that city, which we love as our own, to the fullest extent of our ability. But since we understand that the towers of [Fort] St Nicholas, of the Harbour, and of the Mole are not being so well and diligently guarded as they should be, and that, furthermore, the city has not been well fortified along the moats, we have wanted to warn you to take every precaution against negligence and too little concern in this matter ... and there must be no delay here, but haste![113]

Ultimately, though, it was to be the Hospitallers alone who would face the Ottoman Turkish attack, and it was to be one man, Grand Master Pierre d'Aubusson, who would lead them through it to victory.[114]

Giovanni Batista de Orsini, Grand Master of the Knights Hospitaller, whose entire rule had been spent preparing for an attack by the Ottoman Turks, never saw it take place; he died on 8 June 1476. His successor, d'Aubusson, was chosen nine days later. There really was no other candidate. The fifth and youngest son of Jean d'Aubusson of Le Monteil, whose other brothers rose to prominence in French royal and ecclesiastical service, probably had little choice in determining his occupation. With no land, title or inheritances, the only occupational avenues open to Pierre d'Aubusson were a regular or monastic order or a military monastic order. He chose the latter, although the precise date of his initiation has not survived. The most prestigious military monastic order in the mid-fifteenth century was the Hospitallers – the Teutonic Knights having suffered severe military and organisational setbacks since their ignominious defeat at the Battle of Tannenburg. By 1468, at the latest, he had risen to lead the priory of Auvergne, from where he was summoned by Orsini in November of that year to Rhodes to lead the fortification efforts of the Knights.[115] By August 1474 he had become Captain General, in charge of all Hospitaller military functions,[116] and on 17 June 1476 he was elected Grand Master.[117]

Initially d'Aubusson simply followed the lead of his predecessor in anticipating an Ottoman attack and doing whatever he could to strengthen Hospitaller numbers, supplies, gunpowder weapons and walls. Almost immediately after his election he wrote a barrage of letters to Knights Hospitaller abroad to send money and men. On 11 October 1476 he summoned all Hospitallers to come to Rhodes for the anticipated Turkish invasion.[118] The following July d'Aubusson called a general chapter meeting for all Knights to discuss the preparations for a Turkish attack on Rhodes and other Hospitaller holdings.[119] And on 19 May 1480 d'Aubusson hired a German bombardier, Johannis Berger de Nordlingen, to provide expertise to the Hospitallers at Rhodes.[120] He was certainly not the only mercenary hired for these and other tasks.

Money and supplies were also needed. On 1 March 1479/80 the Grand Master wrote to the preceptor of St Gilles to send the priory's *dimidicum* (subsidy) and annual pensions 'for the defence of the convent'.[121] On 28 June 1477 he wrote to the bailiff of Majorca, Fra John de Cardonna, to prepare ships for the transport of grain, victuals and munitions to Rhodes.[122] On 11 October 1478 he ordered Fra Raymond Ricardi to take his ship to Sicily for food and grain.[123] And on 4 November 1478 he gave a licence to Manoli Calodi Rhodius to trade wood and pitch from Egypt and Syria for grain and victuals.[124]

Money was also received and had to be allocated. On 24 December 1476 d'Aubusson decided to use funds sent by King Louis XI of France to strengthen the island's fortifications.[125] On 4 Sept 1477 6,800 ducats were received from the priories of St Gilles, France and Auvergne 'for the defence of Rhodes'.[126] On 24 June 1479 the 8,000 gold pieces received from Louis XI and Pope Sixtus IV were also to be used for the fortifications of Rhodes.[127]

Rhodes Besieged

Only once in these letters does d'Aubusson get angry with the recipient, on 22 February 1480, when he threatened the priory of France that if it failed to pay all its dues, its members would be deemed rebels and removed from the Order.[128]

To all these letters and appeals was appended the urgent reason for the request: the Turks were due to attack soon. In one letter, written on 13 September 1479, the Grand Master said that he expected them to attack Rhodes during the following year, 1480, a prediction which was to come true. This expectation was gained from the intelligence d'Aubusson gathered from travellers and merchants visiting the city. On 4 November 1478, for example, in granting permission for Manoli Calodi Rhodius to trade his wood and pitch from Egypt and Syria for grain and victuals, he instructed the merchant to 'report back on munitions in those places'.[129] On another occasion, on 19 June 1478, Pope Sixtus IV gave a similar licence to trade goods with Egypt and Syria to a merchant of Rhodes named Anthony, so long as he would report to the Hospitallers the munitions and provisions he saw there.[130] Of course, the Ottomans were also seeking information and on 3 August 1478 Sixtus IV issued a licence to trade to another merchant, Nicholas, so long as he promised 'not to reveal any information about Rhodes'.[131] And, as the attack by the Turks was sure to come, on 10 June 1478, Grand Master d'Aubusson showed an impatient side; as if trying to push Mehmed II into a war he granted Petro Jerachi permission to attack Turkish ships near to Rhodes which held Christian prisoners on them.[132]

The walls of Rhodes were a special priority for the Grand Master, whose coat of arms appears frequently around the circuit as it stands today. Although it is impossible to tell whether most of these were erected before or after the 1480 siege, on the Marine Gate, the entry from the harbour into the city, d'Aubusson's coat of arms is set above an inscription: 'D F PETRUS DAUBUSSO RHODI MAGR HAS TURRES EREXIT MCCCCLVIII' (Brother Petrus d'Aubusson, Master of Rhodes, built these towers, 1478). This is confirmed by the illumination (f. 9v) that accompanies Guillaume Caoursin's *Obsidionis Rhodiae urbis descriptio*, which shows d'Aubusson directing work on the walls facing the harbour, and by statements made by Caoursin and others that in the last few years leading up to the siege the Hospitallers worked diligently on building and repairing the city's fortifications.[133] D'Aubusson was determined to have Rhodes ready for the Turks.

On 28 May 1480 Grand Master Pierre d'Aubusson announced to all Knights Hospitaller outside Rhodes that the Ottomans had begun besieging the city the week before. He was about to become one of the great generals of the Middle Ages.

Notes

1. Despite its importance surprisingly little has been written on the siege of Acre in 1291, although the recent book by David Nicolle, *Acre, 1291: Bloody Sunset of the Crusader States* (London: Osprey, 2005) is worth a look.
2. Trying to pick the scholarly wheat from the popular chaff on the Templars is a difficult task, but one can always rely on Malcolm Barber's works for their strong scholarly quality, for example, *The New Knighthood: A History of the Order of the Temple* (Cambridge: Cambridge University Press,

1994) and *The Trial of the Templars* (Cambridge: Cambridge University Press, 1978).
3   Helen Nicholson, *The Knights Hospitaller* (Woodbridge: The Boydell Press, 2001), pp. 1–17; David Nicolle, *Knights of Jerusalem: The Crusading Order of Hospitallers, 1100–1565* (Oxford: Osprey, 2008), pp. 14–8; Anthony Luttrell, 'The Earliest Hospitallers', in Montjoie: *Studies in Crusade History in Honour of Hans Eberhard Meyer*, ed. Benjamin Z. Kedar, Jonathan Riley-Smith and Rudolf Hiestand (Aldershot: Ashgate, 1997), pp. 37–54; Jonathan Riley-Smith, *Hospitallers: The History of the Order of St John* (London: The Hambledon Press, 1999), pp. 3–54; and Alan Forey, 'The Militarisation of the Hospital of St John', *Studia monastica* 26 (1984), pp. 75–89.
4   There are several very good histories of the monastic military orders during the times of the Crusades, including Alan Forey, *The Military Orders: From the Twelfth to the Early Fourteenth Centuries* (Toronto: University of Toronto Press, 1992); Desmond Seward, *The Monks of War: The Military Religious Orders* (London: Eyre Methuen, 1972); and Helen Nicholson, *Templars, Hospitallers and Teutonic Knights: Images of the Military Orders, 1128–1291* (Leicester: Leicester University Press, 1995).
5   For a general history of the Hospitallers during the Crusades see J. Delaville le Roulx, *Les Hospitaliers en Terre Sainte et Chypre, (1100–1310)* (Paris: Ernest Leroux, 1904) and Nicholson, *Knights Hospitaller*, pp. 18–42. On their and the Templars' fighting capabilities in the Crusades see Alan Demurger, 'Templiers et Hospitaliers dans les combats de Terre Sainte', in *Le combattant au moyen âge*, 2nd ed. (Paris: Publications de la Sorbonne, 1995), pp. 77–92. An interesting recent perspective on the Hospitallers during the Crusades is Judith Bronstein, *The Hospitallers and the Holy Land: Financing the Latin East, 1187–1274* (Woodbridge: Boydell and Brewer, 2005).
6   On these Hospitaller duties see Riley-Smith, pp. 18–30.
7   Contemporary chronicler, Matthew Paris, claims, however, that both the military orders, Hospitallers and Templars, advised against the ill-fated Battle of Mansurah, although when their dedication to 'God's work' was challenged they did participate, with tragic results. See Nicholson, *Knights Hospitaller*, pp. 28–9.
8   Riley-Smith, pp. 41–4.
9   Nicolle, *Knights of Jerusalem*, pp. 24–5, suggests that the instability of the island's political and military system made it unsuitable for the establishment of the Order's headquarters.
10 Armenia was seen as too weak and vulnerable, and Provence, which was favored by Grand Master Guillaume de Villaret, was seen as too distant.
11 Nicolle, *Knights of Jerusalem*, pp. 26–7.
12 Anthony Luttrell, *The Town of Rhodes, 1306–1356* (Rhodes: City of Rhodes Office of the Medieval Town, 2003), p. 63.
13 Anthony Luttrell, 'The Hospitallers at Rhodes, 1306–1421', in *A History of the Crusades, vol. III: The Fourteenth and Fifteenth Centuries*, ed. Harry W. Hazard (Madison: University of Wisconsin Press, 1975), p. 281.
14 Luttrell, 'The Hospitallers at Rhodes, 1306–1421', pp. 283–6; Luttrell, *The Town of Rhodes*, pp. 76–81; Delaville de Roulx, pp. 272–83; and Nicholson, *The Knights Hospitaller*, pp. 46–7.
15 Nicholson, *The Knights Hospitaller*, pp. 46–7.
16 Luttrell, *The Town of Rhodes*, p. 63.
17 Luttrell, *The Town of Rhodes*, p. 67.
18 Luttrell, 'The Hospitallers at Rhodes, 1306–1421', p. 285.
19 Luttrell, 'The Hospitallers at Rhodes, 1306–1421', pp. 285–6.
20 Luttrell, *The Town of Rhodes*, p. 78, and J. Delaville le Roulx, *Les Hospitaliers à Rhodes jusqu'à la mort de Philibert de Naillac, 1310–1421* (Paris: E. Leroux, 1913), pp. 11–27.
21 Luttrell, *The Town of Rhodes*, pp. 81–3.
22 Luttrell, *The Town of Rhodes*, pp. 81–5.
23 Elias Kollias, *The Knights of Rhodes: The Palace and the City* (Athens: Ekdotike Athenon S.A., 1991), pp. 91, 143–64.
24 Although Kollias (pp. 93–7) claims that most of the Hospitaller buildings seen today date to between the two sieges, 1480–1522, many are clearly depicted in these artistic sources.

Rhodes Besieged

25   Kollias, p. 143.
26   Kollias, pp. 143–4, and Luttrell, *The Town of Rhodes*, pp. 90–1.
27   Kollias, pp. 153–5.
28   This can be found in the account of the 1480 siege by Mary Dupuis, when he describes a Turkish courtau ball smashing into the dining hall of the Hospitallers which 'destroyed the vault and broke two large marble pillars holding up the vault in the middle of the room. These two pillars were so large that two men could not reach around them' (p. 94). Dupuis goes on to write that 'the stone went through everything and fell into a cellar underneath onto a tonne of wine which was broken into pieces and the wine lost'. See Mary Dupuis, in *The History of the Knights of Malta*, ed. Abbé Vertot (London, 1728), I:94.
29   Luttrell, *The Town of Rhodes*, pp. 91–4. Albert Gabriel, *La cité de Rhodes* (Paris: E. de Boccard, 1921–23), II:5–12, pl. 2–7, contains the best reconstruction of the medieval palace based on the illuminations in Caoursin and pre-1856 illustrations and photographs. See also Kollias, pp. 143–64, endplans II–IV, for a description that includes archaeological work done subsequent to Gabriel.
30   Luttrell, *The Town of Rhodes*, pp. 93–4. This is based on a document from 1302: *Cartulaire general de l'Ordre des Hospitaliers de St Jean de Jerusalem, 1100–1310*, ed. J. Delaville le Roulx, 4 vols (Paris: Ernest Leroux, 1894–1906), no. 4574.
31   Kollias, pp. 159–60.
32   Luttrell, *The Town of Rhodes*, pp. 94–9; Gabriel, II:167–72; and Kollias, pp. 100–1. A fragmentary tomb slab from St John's also dates to 1318 (Luttrell, *The Town of Rhodes*, p. 43).
33   This comment was made by a visitor, Niccolò da Martoni, in 1394. See Luttrell, *The Town of Rhodes*, p. 99 (Martoni's visit is described on pp. 279–81).
34   Luttrell, *The Town of Rhodes*, pp. 100–9; Gabriel, II:170–4, figs 113–8; and Kollias, pp. 102–3.
35   Luttrell, *The Town of Rhodes*, pp. 141–4; Gabriel, II:179–80; and Kollias, pp. 101–2.
36   Luttrell, *The Town of Rhodes*, pp. 112–3; Gabriel, II:14–5; and Kollias, p. 106. Although the original St Anthony's Church was rebuilt after the 1480 siege, this church was destroyed following the 1522 siege and replaced by the mosque of Murad Reis, which still stands.
37   Luttrell, *The Town of Rhodes*, pp. 99–100, 267–78, and Gabriel, II:9–10.
38   Luttrell, *The Town of Rhodes*, pp. 113–8.
39   Luttrell, *The Town of Rhodes*, pp. 119–20.
40   Luttrell, *The Town of Rhodes*, pp. 121–2.
41   Luttrell, *The Town of Rhodes*, pp. 122–3.
42   Luttrell, *The Town of Rhodes*, p. 81.
43   The best books covering the rise of the Ottomans are Halil Inalcik, *The Ottoman Empire: The Classical Age, 1300–1600*, trans. Norman Itzkowitz and Colin Imber (New York: Praeger Publishers, 1973) and Colin Imber, *The Ottoman Empire, 1300–1650* (Houndmills: Palgrave Macmillan, 2002).
44   For these early Byzantine-Ottoman wars see Mark C. Bartusis, *The Late Byzantine Army: Arms and Society, 1204–1453* (Philadelphia: University of Pennsylvania Press, 1992), pp. 76–94.
45   Quoted in Anthony Luttrell, 'The Hospitallers of Rhodes Confront the Turks: 1306–1421', in *Christians, Jews and Other Worlds: Patterns of Conflict and Accommodation*, ed. P.F. Gallagher (Lanham: University of America Press, 1988), reprinted in Anthony Luttrell, *Hospitallers of Rhodes and their Mediterranean World* (Aldershot: Ashgate, 1992), p. 84.
46   Francesco Amadi, in *Chroniques de Chypre d'Amadi et de Strambaldi*, ed. R. de Mas Latrie (Paris, 1891–93), I:393, and Luttrell, 'The Hospitallers of Rhodes Confront the Turks', p. 86.
47   Luttrell, 'The Hospitallers of Rhodes Confront the Turks', pp. 86–7.
48   Luttrell, 'The Hospitallers of Rhodes Confront the Turks', pp. 91–7.
49   Luttrell, 'The Hospitallers of Rhodes Confront the Turks', pp. 88, 91–2.
50   For the Byzantines see Luttrell, 'The Hospitallers of Rhodes Confront the Turks', pp. 88–9, and for the Genoese see Luttrell, 'The Hospitallers of Rhodes Confront the Turks', pp. 83–4.
51   Inalcik, pp. 10–17 and Imber, pp. 11–17. For a more detailed account of these conquests see Kenneth Setton, *The Papacy and the Levant (1204–1571). I: The Thirteenth and Fourteenth Centuries* (Philadelphia: The American Philosophical Society, 1976).

52 Luttrell, 'The Hospitallers of Rhodes Confront the Turks', pp. 96–7.
53 On the Battle of Nicopolis the best work is still Aziz Suryal Atiya, *The Crusade of Nicopolis* (London: Methuen and Co. Ltd, 1934), but it can now be supplemented and updated by David Nicolle, *Nicopolis, 1396: The Last Crusade* (London: Osprey, 1999) and the articles in Jacques Paviot and M. Chauney-Bouillot, ed., 'Nicopolis, 1396–1996: Actes du Colloque international', *Annales de Bourgogne* 68 (1996).
54 Luttrell, 'The Hospitallers of Rhodes Confront the Turks', p. 98.
55 Luttrell, 'The Hospitallers of Rhodes Confront the Turks', p. 101, and Setton, *The Papacy and the Levant*, I:384–8.
56 National Library of Malta, Section 5, Libri Bullarum, f. 179v.
57 Luttrell, 'The Hospitallers of Rhodes Confront the Turks', pp. 98–9. Despite its incredible importance the Battle of Ankara has not received adequate study by military historians. For the upheaval this defeat caused to the Ottomans see Imber, pp. 17–19 and Inalcik, pp. 17–19.
58 Imber, pp. 18–19 and Inalcik, pp. 18–19.
59 On these campaigns see Joseph Held, *Hunyadi: Legend and Reality* (Boulder: East European Monographs, 1985); Pál Engel, 'János Hunyadi: The Decisive Years of his Career, 1440–1444', in *War and Society in Eastern Central Europe, vol. III: From Hunyadi to Rákóczi: War and Society in Late Medieval and Early Modern Hungary*, ed. J.M. Bak and B.K. Király (New York: Brooklyn College Press, 1982), pp. 103–23; and F. Szakály, 'Phases of Turco-Hungarian Warfare before the Battle of Mohács', *Acta orientalia academia scientia Hungarensis* 33 (1979), pp. 65–111. On the campaign and Battle of Varna see Oscar Halecki, *The Crusade of Varna* (New York: Polish Institute of Arts and Sciences in America, 1943); Kenneth M. Setton, *The Papacy and the Levant (1204–1571), vol. II: The Fifteenth Century* (Philadelphia: American Philosophical Society, 1978), pp. 82–107; and Colin Imber's collection of original sources, *The Crusade of Varna, 1443–45* (Ashgate: Aldershot, 2006).
60 Francesc Ferrer, *Romanç de l'armada del soldà contra Rodes*, in L. Nicolau d'Olwer, 'Un témoinage catalan du siege de Rhodes en 1444', *Estudis universitaris catalans* 12 (1927), pp. 376–87; Setton, II:88 n. 2; and Nicolson, *The Knights Hospitaller*, p. 58.
61 Anna-Maria Kasdagli and Katerina Manoussou-Della, 'The Defences of Rhodes and the Tower of St John', *Fort* 24 (1996), 19.
62 Here, as elsewhere, the best reference to the defences of Rhodes is Gabriel, although we have frequently added our own observations.
63 Setton, II:351–2, note especially footnote 19 in which Setton extensively reviews the literature on what the Naillac Tower was before its destruction.
64 Kasdagli and Manoussou-Della suggest that the unsuccessful siege of Rhodes by the Mamluks in 1444 provided Grand Master Lastic 'with additional incentive for the reinforcement of the fortifications', p. 19.
65 National Library of Malta, Valletta, Section 5, Libri Bullarum, f. 160r; J. Maria van Winter, *Sources concerning the Hospitallers of St John in the Netherlands* (Leiden: Brill, 1998), p. 59 no. 69; and Nicolas Vatin, *Rhodes et l'Ordre de Saint-Jean-de-Jérusalem*, (Paris, 2000), p. 79.
66 This can be clearly seen in extant European bombards, including Mons Meg in Edinburgh Castle, made in 1449, and Dulle Griet on the Kanonplein in Ghent, made at the same time, as well as several bronze Turkish bombards (see below, Appendix 2). Written records confirm the increased size of bombards dating from the 1430s to 1450s. See Robert Douglas Smith and Kelly DeVries, *The Artillery of the Dukes of Burgundy, 1363–1477* (Woodbridge: The Boydell Press, 2005), pp. 204–11.
67 The best account of the siege of Constantinople is still Steven Runciman, *The Fall of Constantinople, 1453* (Cambridge: Cambridge University Press, 1965), but see also Roger Crowley, *Constantinople: The Last Great Siege, 1453* (London: Faber and Faber, 2005) and David Nicolle, *Constantinople 1453: The End of Byzantium* (London: Osprey, 2000).
68 Kelly DeVries, 'Gunpowder Weaponry at the Siege of Constantinople, 1453', in *War, Army and Society in the Eastern Mediterranean, 7th–16th Centuries*, ed. Yaacov Lev (Leiden: E.J. Brill, 1996), pp. 355–6.

69 An excellent recent study of the walls of Constantinople is Stephen Turnbull, *The Walls of Constantinople, AD 324–1453* (London: Osprey, 2004).
70 The best study on the Fourth Crusade is Donald E. Queller and Thomas F. Madden, *The Fourth Crusade: The Conquest of Constantinople, 1201–1204*, 2nd ed. (Philadelphia: University of Pennsylvania Press, 1997), but see also Jonathan Phillips, *The Fourth Crusade and the Sack of Constantinople* (New York: Viking, 2004).
71 Djurdica Petrovic, 'Fire-arms in the Balkans on the Eve of and after the Ottoman Conquests of the Fourteenth and Fifteenth Centuries', in *War, Technology and Society in the Middle East*, ed. V.J. Parry and M.E. Yapp (London: Oxford University Press, 1975), p. 190; Mark C. Bartusis, *The Late Byzantine Army: Arms and Society, 1204–1453* (Philadelphia: University of Pennsylvania Press, 1992), p. 117; and John W. Barker, *Manuel II Palaeologus (1391–1425): A Study in Late Byzantine Statesmanship* (New Brunswick: Rutgers University Press, 1969), pp. 358–65.
72 See, for example, Kritovoulos, *History of Mehmed the Conqueror*, trans. Charles T. Riggs (Princeton: Princeton University Press, 1954).
73 Kritovoulos, p. 37. On gunpowder weapons at the siege of Constantinople, see DeVries, 'Gunpowder Weaponry at the Siege of Constantinople, 1453'.
74 Zorzi Dolfin, 'Cronaca', in *The Siege of Constantinople, 1453: Seven Contemporary Accounts*, trans. J.R.M. Jones (Amsterdam: Adolf M. Hakkert Publisher, 1972), p. 127.
75 Michael Ducas, 'Byzantine History', in *The Siege of Constantinople, 1453: Seven Contemporary Accounts*, trans. J.R.M. Jones (Amsterdam: Adolf M. Hakkert Publisher, 1972), pp. 70–2.
76 Kritovoulos, p. 46. Tursun Beg (p. 35) adds that these cannon were placed in specially dug trenches.
77 Giacomo Tedaldi, 'Letter to Alain de Coëtivy, the Cardinal of Avignon', in *The Siege of Constantinople, 1453: Seven Contemporary Accounts*, trans. J.R.M. Jones (Amsterdam: Adolf M. Hakkert Publisher, 1972), p. 3.
78 George Sphrantzes, *The Fall of the Byzantine Empire: A Chronicle of George Sphrantzes, 1401–1477*, trans. M. Philippides (Amherst: University of Massachusetts Press, 1980), p. 103. See also Kritovoulos, pp. 40, 48–9; Ducas, p. 83; and Laonicus Chalcocondylas, 'Turkish History', in *The Siege of Constantinople, 1453: Seven Contemporary Accounts*, trans. J.R.M. Jones (Amsterdam: Adolf M. Hakkert Publisher, 1972), pp. 16–7.
79 Sphrantzes, p. 115, and Leonard of Chios, 'Letter to Pope Nicholas V', in *The Siege of Constantinople, 1453: Seven Contemporary Accounts*, trans. J.R.M. Jones (Amsterdam: Adolf M. Hakkert Publisher, 1972), pp. 16, 27, 29.
80 Kritovoulos, p. 45. See also Kritovoulos, pp. 43–6; Ducas, p. 87; Tursun Beg, p. 38; and Nicolo Barbaro, *Eidemerides de Constantinopoli anno 1453 obsessa atque expugnata*, in *Patrologia Graeca*, 158, ed. J.P. Migne (Paris: Vrayet, 1866), p. 1075.
81 Kritovoulos, pp. 20–2, 50–3, 58, 64; Ducas, pp. 70, 90; Leonard of Chios, pp. 21–2; Tedaldi, p. 5; Sphrantzes, p. 113; Chalcocondylas, p. 46; and Barbaro, p. 1074.
82 Kritovoulos, p. 65. See also Tursun Beg, p. 36.
83 Kritovoulos, p. 67, and Sphrantzes, pp. 125–6.
84 Kritovoulos, p. 69.
85 L. Mohler, ed., 'Bessarions Instruktion für die Kreuzzugspredigt in Venedig (1463)', *Römische Quartalschrift* 35 (1927), pp. 337–49. A translation is found in Norman Housley, *Documents on the Later Crusades, 1274–1580* (New York: St Martin's Press, 1996), pp. 147–54. This quote is on p. 148.
86 Ducas, p. 227.
87 This is from a report written by Charles the Bold, Philip's son, to the sovereign-bailiff of Namur on 20 December 1454. It can be found in Richard Vaughan, *Philip the Good: The Apogee of Burgundy* (London: Longman, 1970), pp. 359–60. A list of the numerous works devoted to Philip's plans for a crusade can be found in Kelly DeVries, 'The Failure of Philip the Good to Fulfill His Crusade Promise of 1454', in *The Medieval Crusade*, ed. Susan Ridyard (Woodbridge: The Boydell Press, 2004), n. 13. On the Feast of the Pheasant see Agathe Lafortune-Martel, *Fête noble en Bourgogne au XVe siècle. Le banquet du Faisan (1454): Aspects politiques, sociaux et culturels* (Montreal: Bellarim, 1984); Marie-Thérèse Caron, '17 février 1454: le Banquet du Voeu du Faisan,

fête de cour et stratégies de pouvoir', *Revue du nord* 78 (1996), pp. 269–88; and the numerous articles in Marie-Thérèse Caron and Denis Clauzel, ed., *Le Banquet du Faisan* (Arras: Artois Presses Université, 1997).

88 Franz Babinger, *Mehmed the Conqueror and His Time*, trans. Ralph Manheim, ed. William C. Hickman (Princeton: Princeton University Press, 1978), p. 145.

89 DeVries, 'The Failure of Philip the Good', pp. 157–70.

90 Setton, II: 171–80; R.N. Bain, 'The Siege of Belgrade by Muhammed II, July 1–23, 1456', *English Historical Review* 7 (1892), pp. 235–45; and Kelly DeVries, 'Conquering the Conqeror at Belgrade (1456) and Rhodes (1480): Irregular Soldiers for an Uncommon Defense', *Revista de história das ideias 30* (2009), pp. 219–32.

91 Jocelyne G. Russell, 'The Humanists Converge: The Congress of Mantua (1459)', in *Diplomats at Work: Three Renaissance Studies* (Stroud: Sutton, 1992), pp. 51–93. Pius II's account of the Congress can be found in Pius II, *The Commentaries of Pius II*, trans. F.A. Gragg (Northampton: Smith College, Department of History, 1937, 1940, 1947, 1951, 1957), pp. 191–217. The Hospitallers had sent a delegate to Mantua to ask for assistance against the Turks. See Setton, II: 208.

92 Pius II, pp. 213–6. See also Kelly DeVries, 'The Lack of a Western European Military Response to the Ottoman Invasions of Eastern Europe from Nicopolis (1396) to Mohács (1526)', *Journal of Military History 63* (1999), pp. 539–59.

93 National Library of Malta, Valletta, Section 5, Libri Bullarum, f. 5b, also published in R. Valentini, 'L'Egeo dopo la caduta di Costantinopoli nelle relazioni dei Gran Maestri di Rodi', *Bullettino dell'Istituto storico italiano per il medio evo e Archivio Muratoriano* 51 (1936), pp. 159–61.

94 National Library of Malta, Libri Bullarum, ff. 5 v, 8r, 9v–b, 37v, 38v, 116r–v, also published in Valentini, pp. 159–62.

95 National Library of Malta, Libri Bullarum, ff. 196v, 200b, also published in Valentini, pp. 163–4.

96 National Library of Malta, Libri Bullarum, f. 5v, also in Valentini, pp. 159–61.

97 Halil Inalcik, 'The Ottoman Turks and the Crusades, 1451–1522', in *A History of the Crusades, vol. VI: The Impact of the Crusades on Europe*, ed. Norman P. Zacour and Harry W. Hazard (Madison: University of Wisconsin Press, 1989), p. 317, and Anthony Luttrell, 'The Hospitallers at Rhodes, 1421–1523', in *A History of the Crusades, vol. III: The Fourteenth and Fifteenth Centuries*, ed. Harry W. Hazard (Madison: University of Wisconsin Press, 1975), pp. 314–60.

98 Setton, II:144–5; Babinger, pp. 130–2; and Luttrell, 'The Hospitallers at Rhodes, 1421-1523', p. 321.

99 Babinger, pp. 129–30. The proposed treaty can be found in National Library of Malta, Libri Bullarum, f. 176. On Nicholas V's prohibition, which Venice had already violated, see Inalcik, 'The Ottoman Turks and the Crusade', p. 317.

100 Inalcik, *The Ottoman Turks and the Crusades, 1451–1522*, pp. 324–5.

101 National Library of Malta, Libri Bullarum, ff. ccxiiii a-b [246r–v] (authorisation of money for wall repair and construction, 4 May 1459); ff. ccxv a–b [247r–v] (papal authorisation to use money intended for other religious works for the construction of walls and mole, 8 May 1459); f. clii a (regulation of sale of grain in order to build up stores, 2 October 1460); f. v b–vi a (request for chancellor and procurator of the Hospitallers' Roman curia to Avignon to gain subventions, 6 November 1460); and f. ccxi (order to repair castle and walls of Bodrum), 18 April 1460/61.

102 See, for example, Milly's congratulations to the Knights on the island of Simi for surviving a Turkish attack, dated 21 November 1460, National Library of Malta, Libri Bullarum, ff. 217v–218r. National Library of Malta, Libri Bullarum, ff. 164r–v (Zacosta's order to raise 50,000 gold florins, 12 October 1461); ff. 164v–165r (order by Zacosta's lieutenant to Knights at the preceptory of Verona and priory of Venice to purchase saltpetre and other supplies in Venice, 17 November 1461); f. 214r (pension awarded for assistance in building the walls of the castle of St Peter, 18 August 1462); f. 193v (order to procurators giving full power to raise money for the Hospitallers in Rhodes, 4 November 1462); f. 193r (defence of money spent in preparing defensive works of Rhodes and other Aegean holdings, 4 November 1462); ff. 193v–200 (Zacosta's report of recent military actions [1451–62] to justify expense in building defences, 4 November

Rhodes Besieged

1462); ff. 206r–v (tax on people of Rhodes to pay for the construction of a moat around city, 1 March 1464/65); ff. 144, 145(159)r–146(160)r (division of Rhodes wall to eight 'tongues' for city's defence, 3 February 1465); f. 160r (Zacosta's confirmation of 10,000 gold *soldi* received from Philip the Good, Duke of Burgundy, to build a tower, 20 June 1465); f. 174v (compensation for houses demolished to repair walls); f. 1r–3r (summoning of Order members to discuss defence of Rhodes, 6 April 1465); f. 108r (order all Hospitallers on Cyprus to Rhodes to defend city, 23 April 1465); ff. 108r–v, 109v–110r (orders to purchase grain from France and Sicily for eastern holdings, 24 July 1465); f. 110v (order to collect money to pay for debts incurred because Rhodes was in danger of attack, 4 February 1465/66); f. 117v (compensation for stones used in repairing castle of Villanova, 12 August 1466); ff. 236r–237v (bull concerning repairs of Rhodes fortifications, 17 August 1471); f. 179r (request of 10,000 florins from merchants of Rhodes to pay for construction and repair of walls, 27 August 1471); f. 170r (providing of ammunition to Rhodes from Capua, 26 September 1466); f. 206r (discussion of appearance and decoration of tower of St Nicholas, 22 December 1466); ff. 60r–v (summoning of Pierre d'Aubusson to Rhodes to lead fortification construction and repair, likely November 1468); ff. 2r–5v (warning of Turkish preparation of a war fleet, 17 August 1469); f. 212v (on repair of fortifications of Langonis, 23 November 1471); ff. 3r–4r , 57v–58r (concerning collection of money from 'tongues' for moat, 26 November 1471); ff. 197v–198v (appointment of preceptor of Langonis to oversee repairs to fortifications, 23 December 1471); f. 71v (assessment of 3,000 *soldi* for construction of moat, 26 November 1471); f. 128r (German knights to pay for moat, 12 March 1471/72); ff. 90r–v (assessment of priory of Portugal for moat costs, 12 May 1472); ff. 195v–198v (allocation of money to expanding and stabilising Rhodes' walls and fortifications, 12 June 1472); ff. 115r–v (necessity of providing funds for moat, 28 July 1472); f. 202r (reallocation of funds from new infirmary to building walls of port, 17 September 1472); ff. 102v–103v (demand that preceptor of Auziza produce doctor's assurance he is ill and cannot come to Rhodes, 4 January 1472/73); f. 116v (complaining that annates not sent for sustenance of Rhodes, 24 January 1472/73); f. 207r (assent for expenditures because of imminent Turkish war, 7 March 1473/74);); f. 80v (procession to safeguard Christians from Turks, 20 April 1475); ff. 229v–230 (safe-conduct given to ship with Islamic prisoners to Rhodes, 9 December 1474); f. 198r (announcement of a three-year repair and reconstruction program for Salakos Castle, 16 January 1474/75); f. 198v (expectation of Ottoman fleet requires wood for fortifications, 6 April 1475); f.201v (tower in front of mole of the windmills to replace mill there, 3 November 1475); ff. 204v–205r (salary for captain of Naillac Tower, 3 February 1475/76); National Library of Malta, Valletta, Section 2, Libri Conciliorum, f. 13 (arming of two galleys, 25 March 1470); f. 16v (concerning land and sea preparations against Turks); f. 14 (repair of castle of St Peter, Bodrum, 14 April 1470); f. 27 (concerning safety of Rhodians, 28 June 1470); f. 19v–20v (on repairing Rhodes, 23 July 1470); f. 36 (on Turkish captives taken at sea, 8 August 1470); f. 37 (concerning the Order's artillery, 8 August 1470); f. 47v (the sending of 100 men and 2 gunners to Lango, 27 October 1470); f. 48 (prior of Capua writes to Pope and King Ferdinand of Aragon for assistance against the Turks, 31 October 1470); f. 52 (responding to King of Cyprus concerning war with Ottomans, 16 November 1470); f. 55 (about fortifications in Jewish Quarter of Rhodes, 21 January 1471); f. 59 (on fortifications of Rhodes, 21 February 1471); f. 96 (concerning moat from Tower of Spain to St Anthony's Gate, 29 September 1471); f. 139v (disarming of Rhodian galley, 24 August 1472); f. 157 (repair of Rhodes fortifications, 4 January 1473); f. 157 (report on the fortifications of Rhodes, 17 February 1473; ff. 62(70)r–63(71)r (measures of defence of Rhodians against Ottomans, 3 March 1475); f. 11v (garrisoning city of Rhodes and seas, 7 April 1473); f. 12 (inhabitants of castle of Sienna ask to be assigned elsewhere because of Turkish attacks, 9 April 1473); f. 18v (arming of galleys, 24 July 1473); f. 19 (concerning Admiral of Rhodes, 14 July 1473); f. 20v (arming of galleys, 30 July 1473); f. 49 (on the provisioning of island of Rhodes, 26 June 1474); f. 49v (repair of island fortifications, 6 July 1474); f. 52 (news of Turkish ships being armed, 19 August 1474); f. 52 (providing for garrisons, 19 August 1474); f. 56 (concerning the castle of Sienna, 20 September 1474); f. 58 (gathering of provisions, 18 October 1474; ff. 72v–74 (deliberations on defence of Rhodes, 30 March 1475); f. 75v (naming of captain of Tower of St Nicholas, 3 April 1475); f. 75 (offering of prior

of Toulouse to guard the Tower of the Mills, 4 April 1475); f. 75v (naming of captain of Tower of St Nicholas, 3 April 1475); f. 77–78v (provisions for war, 10 April 1475); f. 81v (concerning repair of moats, 2 June 1475); f. 87 (defence of island of Rhodes, 11 August 1475); f. 97 (prohibitions of items sold to Muslims, 13 October 1475); f. 107v (concerning the walls and news of Turkish ships, 27 March 1476); ff. 147r–148r (warning of Hospitaller penury with war imminent); f. 112 (concerning the wall from the Tower of St Peter to the Tower of the Plagnes, 22 April 1476); f. 112 (demolition of the ancient wall, 28 April 1476); and ff. 114v–115v (on repair of the island, 7 May 1476). See also Setton, II:238–9.
103 Setton, II:188.
104 Inalcik, 'The Ottoman Turks and the Crusades, 1451–1522', p. 320. However, this did not keep Mehmed II from conquering them in 1459–60.
105 Luttrell, 'The Hospitallers at Rhodes, 1421–1523', pp. 321–2.
106 Setton, II:261–3.
107 Luttrell, 'The Hospitallers at Rhodes, 1421–1523,' p. 322.
108 Luttrell, 'The Hospitallers at Rhodes, 1421–1523', pp. 322–3, and Setton, II:316–7.
109 Luttrell, 'The Hospitallers at Rhodes, 1421–1523', p. 322, and Setton, II:276–7.
110 National Library of Malta, Libri Bullarum, f 214; Babinger, pp. 129–30; Inalcik, 'The Ottoman Turks and the Crusades, 1451–1522', p. 317; and Luttrell, 'The Hospitallers at Rhodes, 1421–1523', p. 322. Luttrell claims that the Knights were willing to pay a 'gift' but not a 'tribute'.
111 Luttrell, 'The Hospitallers at Rhodes, 1421–1523', p. 322.
112 Setton, II:189.
113 As quoted in Setton, II:309–10.
114 Gilles Rossignol's *Pierre d'Aubusson: 'le bouclier de la chrétienté' Les Hospitaliers à Rhodes* (Besançon: Editions la Manufacture, 1991) is the only modern biography of d'Aubusson that exists, and it has clearly drawn from fanciful later tradition where gaps in the more credible sources occur.
115 National Library of Malta, Libri Bullarum, ff. 60r–v.
116 National Library of Malta, Libri Conciliorum, f. 52.
117 National Library of Malta, Libri Conciliorum, ff. 122v–125.
118 National Library of Malta, Libri Bullarum, ff. 44v–45r.
119 But there seem to have been some of the Order, although not specifically Knights, who remained elsewhere, no doubt maintaining the Hospital priories in Europe, and in July, September and November 1479, when the Ottoman attack became more imminent, they too were asked to come to Rhodes. National Library of Malta, Libri Bullarum, f. 1r.
120 National Library of Malta, Libri Bullarum, f. 164r.
121 National Library of Malta, Libri Bullarum, f. 35v.
122 National Library of Malta, Libri Bullarum, ff. 137v–138v.
123 National Library of Malta, Libri Bullarum, ff 223v–224r.
124 National Library of Malta, Libri Bullarum, ff. 192v–193r.
125 National Library of Malta, Libri Bullarum, ff. 7v–8r.
126 National Library of Malta, Libri Bullarum, ff. 139v–140r.
127 National Library of Malta, Libri Bullarum, f. 152r.
128 National Library of Malta, Libri Bullarum, ff. 13r–14r.
129 National Library of Malta, Libri Bullarum, ff. 170–171.
130 National Library of Malta, Libri Bullarum, f. 190v.
131 National Library of Malta, Libri Bullarum, ff. 189r–v.
132 National Library of Malta, Libri Bullarum, ff. 222r–v.
133 See, for example, National Library of Malta, Libri Bullarum, f. 190r and ff. 191r–192r.

The Siege of 1480

Attending to this counsel were very skilled engineers (*machinarum viri periti*), among their number was George, a man of vast and subtle intelligence who had defected from Chios to the Turks a little while before. Living in Constantinople he provided for his wife and children and he was loved by the Turks and given many rewards. He had been at Rhodes for a time and was able to make plans of the city. It was not as well walled then as now for it had been twenty years since he had seen the city. Some said that the Turks needed to order more large engines for the siege of Rhodes. But George surpassed them. With great reason he concluded that a siege of the city could be successful if done with great strength as there were no walls thick enough that the power of their existing siege engines could not bring them down, for the Turks had such great power as had brought down two empires, twelve kingdoms and a large number of provinces and cities.[1]

How Guillaume Caoursin heard about this account of Master George of Constantinople, 'a man of vast and subtle intelligence', is not known. Did he really know Rhodes so well that he could make plans of the city accurate enough to convince Mehmed II that a siege of the city should be pursued with their existing siege engines?

As Master George is to have a role in the story of the siege of Rhodes in 1480 it would be nice to know the veracity of what Caoursin writes about his skills. Master George was not a military commander. As far as we can tell he had no military experience at all. In fact, it is likely that had Master George been born a hundred years earlier his skills would not have been noticed or even have concerned a military ruler such as Sultan Mehmed II. But war had changed so much in that time that men with George's abilities had become very valuable. They were needed to build, transport, position and fire the new technology that was now so necessary for anyone conducting a military operation, whether a siege, such as the one of Rhodes in 1480, or a battle.[2] Master George, writes Mary Dupuis, was very adept at this and 'an excellent gunfounder' (*fort excellent homme en fait dartillerie*).[3]

Mehmed knew this well. His own reputation had been built on the conquest of Constantinople in 1453, where he had used gunpowder weapons in the taking of the heavily fortified city. Although he had briefly ruled the Ottoman Empire while still a child from 1444 to 1446, Mehmed had regained the throne only two years prior to undertaking the siege of the capital of Byzantium.[4] In that period he had built his gunpowder artillery train virtually from scratch, recognising the need for some means to penetrate walls that had stood for almost a millennium. They had only fallen once, in 1204, to a determined Fourth Crusade army, whose siege machines had eventually overcome the fortifications, but only after ten months.[5] Since then, they had again been strengthened.[6]

Besieging a well-fortified city with gunpowder weapons in the fifteenth century required a considerable amount of planning. Building an arsenal of gunpowder artillery was not something that could be done quickly. In 1453 the construction of such a force was still relatively novel for the Eastern Mediterranean region.

By 1480 gunpowder weapons were more common, to the point that their use in Ottoman military engagements had become less frequently commented on, at least with the awe Kritovoulos had for them before the siege of Constantinople in 1453. Urban/Orban was no longer with the gunpowder train, as far as is known, but clearly, as shown by the story of George, skilled craftsmen-operators were still needed. In 1453 Mehmed needed outsiders to make his gunpowder artillery; in 1480 he seems to have had people to make guns, '*machinarum viri periti*' in the words of Caoursin, but George knew Rhodes as well. To Mehmed, in 1453, there still seems to have been some uncertainty as to whether his gunpowder weapons could breach the walls and allow his troops access to the city. In 1480 George could assert that 'there were no walls thick enough that the power of their existing siege engines could not bring them down'. Mehmed's guns would make short work of Rhodes' walls.

Grand Master Pierre d'Aubusson was less certain of the decisiveness of the Ottoman cannon. In a letter dated 28 May 1480 'to all the members of the Order' announcing that the Ottomans had begun the siege of Rhodes, d'Aubusson writes: 'Moreover, the city of Rhodes – not without heavy cost – has walls, ramparts, moats and towers and we do not fear the enemy's power'.[7] D'Aubusson knew that the Turkish guns the Hospitallers faced were formidable, but he had faith in the walls of their city, in the power of their defensive ordnance, in the amount of their stores, and in the bravery and martial ability of their men.

In winter 1479 Ottoman galleys were seen making a reconnaissance of the island. This included landing parties who raided the Rhodian countryside, terrorising and assaulting the peasants, and stealing what they could. However, as spies reported to d'Aubusson, the real purpose of these attacks was to reconnoitre the Hospitaller defences in preparation for the siege.[8]

During the winter and spring of 1480 Mehmed had been gathering the men, guns, munitions, equipment, victuals and tools necessary to besiege Rhodes. When the weather improved, probably in March or April, the army began to march overland from several places in the Ottoman Empire, and the navy and supply ships began to sail. They met up across the straits from Rhodes, at a place Caoursin calls Phisco,

22 'miles' from Rhodes.[9] Just where Phisco was is difficult to ascertain as no record of this place name in the region survives. However, the closest harbour is Marmaris, some 30 miles (50km) away.[10]

Mehmed tried to keep these movements secret. He stopped all transit on the mainland and also spread rumours of his own death. Caoursin reports: 'The Turks, to keep this secret, closed ports and guarded passes and prohibited any news to go forth.'[11] However, the Knights were not fooled. D'Aubusson had, after all, been anticipating a siege since he was installed as Grand Master in 1478, and had been mobilising his forces and making plans since the previous autumn. In late spring he stepped up the preparations for war, fortifying the Hospitallers' outlying posts and moving the islanders into the city with their goods and livestock. He also ordered them to bring whatever foodstuffs they could, both for their own use as well as to deprive the Turks of it, 'that all the ripe and some of the unripe crops (for the harvest had not yet been gathered) be collected and the people to pick everything and take it into their homes so that there be nothing left around the town'.[12] Giacomo de Curti was clearly impressed with the amount gathered, reporting that Rhodes was filled with 'grain, wine, oil, cheese, salted meat and other food stuffs in great quantity'.[13] D'Aubusson also continued to plead for men and money from the Hospitaller priories all over Europe, even going so far on 22 February as to threaten the Knights of the priory of France that he considered them in rebellion and that they would lose their habits if they did not pay all their 'dues and responsions' into the common treasury so that he might draw from them for the 'anticipated Turkish siege'.[14] On 19 May he wrote to a German gunner, Johannis Berger de Nordlingen, in an attempt to employ him (for 80 Rhodian florens).[15]

On 23 May the Ottoman fleet was sighted. Curti notes that 'the sea was covered with sails as far as the eye could see'.[16] In his 28 May letter d'Aubusson numbers the Turkish fleet at 109 ships, claiming that they carried 70,000 soldiers as well as 'a great many cannon, bombards and wooden towers with other engines of war'.[17] Caoursin confirms the presence of a large number of gunpowder weapons and siege engines, which were sent directly to Rhodes from Constantinople.[18] Initially Caoursin does not tally the Turkish soldiers, although he does provide a later estimate of around 100,000, as reported by Master George after he had gone over to the Hospitallers, while Dupuis counts 170,000, which he also takes from George's testimony.[19] They were led by Mesīh Pascha from the Byzantine imperial house of Palaeologos, a somewhat odd choice so soon after the fall of Byzantium and the toppling of that same imperial family.[20] Not much is known about Mesīh Pascha Palaeologos before his command at the siege of Rhodes, although one can surmise that Mehmed had great faith in him to command in his stead while the Sultan was ailing in Constantinople.[21]

Of course, these numbers are probably exaggerated and it would be nice to have some confirmation from Ottoman sources. On the other hand, how large would a force need to be to effectively besiege a city the size of Rhodes? Rhodes has some 2.25km of walls facing the landward side, with about another kilometre of walls and

Rhodes Besieged

moles defending the seaward side which could not be besieged from land. With three-quarters of the land walls also protected by a moat, the Turkish army would need to stretch approximately 3km just to face the walls. That is without all the additional and necessary men – labourers, pioneers, medical personnel, carpenters (to build barricades and cannon mounts), masons (to carve stone cannonballs), smiths (to repair wrought-iron cannon and other weapons and to shoe horses), carters, horse wranglers, herdsmen, cooks, scullions, servants, etc., that would serve as support staff to the besieging soldiers. (And this does not include the number of sailors and marines on board the Ottoman ships trying to blockade the city.) The total numbers were quite clearly staggering, in the many tens of thousands, though probably not as high as the figures given by d'Aubusson and Caoursin. Nor should we doubt Mehmed's ability to recruit such a sizeable force. He could call on any male who lived in his vast lands – and could probably purchase the services of as many mercenaries as he might feel he needed to supplement their numbers. If he required a large army he could get it.

Facing these tens of thousands of Ottomans was a much smaller force, including Hospitaller knights and sergeants, mercenaries and whoever among the Rhodians was willing to defend their city, but just how many there were is difficult to determine. Eric Brockman, seemingly without supporting evidence, tallies the force as 'no more than 600 knights and servants-at-arms who were members of the Order, and perhaps as many as 1,500 mercenaries and local militia'.[22] Curti's numbers are larger for the overall force – 4,000 – but smaller for the numbers of Hospitaller knights – 500[23] – while Caoursin gives no figures.

The Turkish fleet, which Mary Dupuis identifies as consisting of 'galleys, *fusts*, *pallendrees, gappereries*, and other such ships',[24] arrived at Rhodes late in the day, the 'twentieth hour' according to Curti.[25] The soldiers disembarked first and began setting up their camp at the base of Mount St Stephen, which was less a mountain than simply the rising ground south of the city, although from its top the entire city could be seen, writes Dupuis.[26] Caoursin claims that the guns and other siege engines were unloaded behind 'where the mountain meets the sea which could not be seen from the town of Rhodes'.[27] This was no doubt done to keep them out of sight until needed.

Probably because of the lateness of the day or maybe, as Brockman asserts, because d'Aubusson 'could not afford the manpower',[28] there was no resistance put up against the Turkish arrival. No doubt encouraged by the lack of response, some Turks, both cavalry and infantry, note Dupuis and Caoursin, approached the walls, 'all the way to the moat', wearing large white feathers on their head and taunting those inside, 'saying that they wished to save the city'.[29] According to Dupuis, they were chased away by shots from those stationed on the walls and in the towers who felt that such 'pomposity' and 'arrogance' needed a response,[30] while Caoursin writes that they were driven away by a sortie from the town of 'certain confidently brave men' who 'put the enemy to flight, slaying several of them, some of whom were beheaded'.[31] Later, while the Knights dined, some Ottomans made another approach on the city. This too was answered by a sortie which chased them away, although one Hospitaller

The Siege of 1480

knight, who had 'incautiously split off from the group', according to Caoursin, was killed.[32] Dupuis, who seems to have known this brother knight, identifies him as a Catalan named Pierre (Pedro) de Bourges and is more detailed about his death, claiming that he fought 'strongly and valiantly' until hit on the head by a dart and knocked to the earth where he was beheaded.[33] His head was put on a lance and taken to the Turkish camp, while his body was recovered and taken into the town where it was buried with honours.

The siege began in earnest the following day when the Turks started to move their artillery into positions around the town. One battery was set up in the garden of the Church of St Anthony opposite the Fort of St Nicholas, which d'Aubusson later recalled consisted of 'three huge bronze bombards to batter down the town, whose size and power were incredible, and which fired balls of stone of nine palms'.[34] The Turks also set up other batteries around the town. D'Aubusson says that they 'surrounded the city with bombards and mortars, beating and destroying nine towers and a boulevard, and struck and demolished the palace of the grand master'.[35]

One of the most curious incidents in the siege happened at the very beginning. The day after the Ottoman Turks set up their bombards in the garden of St Anthony's church, Master George, the man who had been given credit by Caoursin for encouraging Mehmed II to undertake the siege of Rhodes, as quoted above, showed up on the edge of the moat facing the Grand Master's Palace and asked for refuge. His appearance was 'sudden' says Caoursin and Dupuis, who both give lengthy accounts of his entry into the town and interrogation before Grand Master d'Aubusson.[36] Caoursin, as vice-chancellor of the Order, would certainly have been present and Dupuis, as a Knight Hospitaller, may have been as well. Although some have suggested that Dupuis only copied Caoursin, the difference in details and the description of gunpowder weapons in particular, which is something that would have concerned Dupuis more than Caoursin, suggests that he was also at the interrogation or heard about it from another participant.

Word spread quickly of his arrival in the city. Master George was a 'tall man', writes Dupuis, 'well formed in his limbs and of good stature, well spoken and very entertaining', but he was also a 'very malicious man when one saw him or heard him speak'.[37] It is certainly possible that George's reputation had reached Rhodes, as both Dupuis and Caoursin call him an 'excellent gunfounder' – although that may have come from his own self-promotion – and it is surely possible that someone in the town might have remembered his previous visit. But it is more likely that it was George's willingness to defect so early in the siege and the potential information he brought with him that caused such a stir. D'Aubusson was certainly interested in meeting him and sent for him immediately. Dupuis, who has hindsight to benefit his scepticism, notes that before doing so 'a rope was tied around his neck', no doubt as a security measure.[38]

Any man coming from the Ottoman camp was bound to have some valuable intelligence, but as Master George was a man who knew all about the numbers and capability of the Turkish gunpowder weapons his knowledge was incredibly valuable

– if it could be trusted. Certainly his motivation for defecting to the Hospitallers at the very beginning of a siege that he had personally encouraged Mehmed to undertake – at least according to his own testimony – must be (and was) questioned. He claimed that the Turks had treated him and his family (who, by this defection, he was abandoning) very well. Mary Dupuis writes that George claimed a religious motivation, that as a devout Christian he could not stay with the Muslim Turks as they laid siege to the headquarters of a Christian military monastic order:

> The Lord Master interrogated him and asked him why he had come there, to which he responded that it was because of the great love and zeal he had for the Christian religion and also for the good and utility of the city and Christianity, and that he repented of the evil he had done or error he had made against Christianity.[39]

No doubt this satisfied some, as the sincerity of religious conversion was rarely questioned, but to others, including Dupuis it seems, there remained a distrust of the man. D'Aubusson may also have felt this but was desirous of gaining whatever information he could from him. He accepted George's explanation 'amiably' and asked about the numbers and placement of the troops besieging the city. There were around 170,000 men 'of all manners and conditions', he replied.[40] D'Aubusson then asked him about the gunpowder weapons the Turks had at the siege. George's answer was quite detailed:

> Of bombards among other pieces there are sixteen bombards which were twenty-two feet in length and one foot four inches in height, and they fire stone balls of nine to eleven palms in circumference, and six large mortars which fired stones as large as or larger than the bombards, and a large number of other smaller firearms.[41]

But was Master George's statement accurate? If so, then it was an incredible piece of intelligence, and most historians have accepted it as such.[42] There were certainly three large bombards then firing at the Tower of St Nicholas, although their size is not noted in d'Aubusson's, Dupuis' or Caoursin's accounts of the siege. And there were certainly several other gunpowder weapons in the Ottoman force. On the other hand, what could d'Aubusson have done with such information? It made very little difference to the defence of the city. The only possible result is that he might have considered the city would be defeated by such a force and have surrendered without further resistance. Could this be what Master George wanted?

There were diverse opinions concerning the trustworthiness of his testimony and the motives that drove him to surrender to the Hospitallers. Some said that he was a 'spy', while others believed that his repentance was sincere and that he wanted to help the Hospitallers and Rhodians. His situation was not helped by the fact that almost immediately after George's defection the Turks began shooting arrows into the town with letters attached to them saying: 'Beware of Master George' (*Gardez vous de Maistre*

George, in Dupuis' words).[43] But even if George could not be trusted he was still a valuable source of information, and so Grand Master d'Aubusson allowed him to go about the town accompanied by 'six men, [who were] commanded on pain of death to guard him night and day'.[44]

It is clear that the Ottomans' first objective was to destroy and take the fortification, the Tower of St Nicholas, on the end of the mole that extends north from the city and guards the mouth of the military harbour to the west (sometimes called the Mandraki) and the commercial harbour to the east. This seems somewhat strange – in hindsight it appears that the Turks wasted a great deal of time and energy on what appears to be an unnecessary tactic. However, the tower held a key position in the siege of the city. If the Hospitallers controlled it the whole of the seaward side of the city was open and reinforcements and supplies could reach the town relatively easily. The fortress also prevented any Turkish attack from the sea. Taking St Nicholas would have so weakened the Hospitallers' position that surrender would have been inevitable. Seen in this light, the importance of bombarding the tower is clear and, to a great extent, explains why such effort was expended.

An enormous effort was expended. Although some 250 yards (230m) separated the Church of St Anthony and the Tower of St Nicholas, shot from the bombards could and did reach the fortress, more than 300 in total according to d'Aubusson, a number confirmed by all the other sources.[45] Dupuis further claims that these fell only in the first fifteen days of bombardment, which means that each bombard fired six to seven times per day. While this does seem quite a slow rate of fire it must be considered that the loading and preparation for the firing of each bombard would have taken a considerable amount of time. The gunpowder needed to be placed into the powder chamber at the rear of the barrel, a wooden tompion securely and tightly rammed into place sealing the powder chamber, and the heavy stone ball craned into position, loaded into the barrel and secured in place.[46]

So what were the guns used by the two sides at the siege? Unfortunately this is not an easy question to answer. The biggest problem is that three of the four major sources for the siege of Rhodes in 1480 are in Latin. As Latin had no developed language, no vocabulary, for gunpowder weapons, the words that are almost always used are just '*machina*' or '*tormentum*' – both words had been adapted from other Latin usage and neither is actually the name of a specific type of weapon. The only other terms that the sources use are *bombard*, to mean a very large gun firing a large stone ball, and *mortar*, for a short barrel gun firing large stone balls in a very high trajectory. Otherwise there is no distinction made in the Latin sources between the types of guns that were used and those that certainly existed at the time – a fact that is proved beyond any doubt by other sources.[47] It is only in the single vernacular account of the siege, by the Hospitaller knight Mary Dupuis written in Old French, that gunpowder weapons are given a more distinct terminology: *bombards, mortars, courtaux, serpentines, canons, couleuvrines* and *batons de feu*.[48] This certainly helps, but there is still the problem of not always knowing to which weapons these names refer.

Rhodes Besieged

Of the two protagonists it is the Turkish cannon for which we have the most information. The battery that was set up in the grounds of St Anthony's Church was reported to consist of three bombards 'twenty two palms long . . . firing stones of nine or eleven palms around'.[49] Taking a palm to be 4in this equates to guns of 7ft 4in long (223cm) firing stones with a circumference of 36–44inches (91–110cm) – giving them a diameter of between 11.5 and 14in (29 and 35.5cm). These stone balls would have weighed between 140 and 255lb (63 and 116kg). Stones of these sizes can still be seen around the city of Rhodes today. But do we have a surviving Turkish cannon of the size described as firing them? In the collection of the Askeri Müze (Military Museum) in Istanbul is a bronze cannon with a length of 346cm, somewhat longer than the 223cm of the guns in the battery, and a bore of 37cm, very close in size to nine palms in circumference. Though there is no evidence linking this cannon to those besieging Rhodes in 1480, it is of the type and form that could have been used – it was probably made in the 1450s and is very likely an example of what the Ottomans were using at the siege.[50]

Though they are not referred to in any of the sources, there are some other existing Turkish cannon which also may also have been used in 1480. These are summarised below:

Place	Length - cm	Bore - cm	Approx weight of stone ball – kg
Military Museum, Istanbul	424	63	295
Rumeli Hisar 1	427	68	375
Rumeli Hisar 2	423	64	310
Artillery Museum, Turin	419	69	390

These are very large guns indeed and are of the same size as the largest surviving European bombards – Mons Meg and Dulle Griet:

Place	Length - cm	Bore - cm	Approx weight of stone ball – kg
Mons Meg, Edinburgh Castle	404	48	125
Dulle Griet, Ghent	501	64	310

The Siege of 1480

That these guns were able to do a great deal of damage is evident from the accounts of the siege in which the 300 shots from the battery by St Anthony's Church almost completely demolished the Tower of St Nicholas. The tower is described by Dupuis as: 'a very good and large round tower with a large and strong wall which from the base to the top was twenty feet high of good measure.'[51] Illustrations show that it was a simple cylindrical structure with an additional lower wall pierced with gunports surrounding it and a separate stair turret on the landward side. Although the tower was very badly damaged in the siege it was evidently rebuilt much as it had been and today the tower still has the coat of arms of Philip the Good on its very battered and much repaired southern face.[52] The destruction and defence of the Tower of St Nicholas well illustrates the counterpoint of attack and defence in the late medieval period and in fact provides us with a topos for both sieges – 1480 and 1522. It would appear that the Turkish guns were able to batter down, relatively easily, what were in effect quite thin and weak walls, which had only been built in the 1460s, when construction was evidently not greatly influenced by the growing power and force of artillery. However, the Tower of St Nicholas also had an outer encircling wall pierced with gunports from which the defenders could fire large guns, thus giving it an offensive purpose as well as being a strong, defensive position – the traditional role of the castle or fort. From the very beginning the relationship between cannon and walls had been a continually developing one in which changes in either were countered by developments in the other – leading eventually to the development of the bastion-type fortress and the powerful cast-iron firing cannon.

However, knocking down the walls of the city, castle or fortress is only the first part of a late medieval besieging strategy. The second, and as important but too frequently overlooked, was the storming of the breach, overwhelming the defenders and defeating them. That both are necessary is illustrated very well at the sieges of Rhodes. The Ottomans were able, time and again, to create breaches in the walls by their use of powerful and accurate cannon fire. Where they constantly failed was in the taking of the walls – the Hospitallers were able, by careful planning, courage and sometimes sheer good luck, to repair the breaches, construct counter-measures and hold the besiegers at bay. It is these skills which the Hospitallers were able to use in order to defeat the Turks in 1480. In the end it is not technology, gunpowder, cannon or masonry that always hold the key to military success, but leadership and the skills and courage of those fighting.

Against the Tower of St Nicholas it is clear that the Turkish bombards firing from St Anthony's church did a considerable amount of damage to the side facing the gunfire. D'Aubusson writes that 'a greater amount of the tower was destroyed, knocked down, and ruined; indeed, the enemy seeing this rejoiced in the destruction, filling the air with their shouts ...'[53] Dupuis is more detailed:

> ... about three hundred shots from the bombards battered the tower in such a way that the side facing the land where the bombards were firing seemed to be a large pile

of stones, all of the tower there battered and destroyed, and the stones fallen one onto another. But the other side of the tower, that which faced the sea, stood whole and entire in such a way that it seemed that it had never been hit by any bombard shot, so not only the top of the tower but also the crenellations were all clear and visible from the sea. And in fact that part of the tower which could be seen from the landward side where the bombards were firing seemed indefensible and that nobody dared to be inside it.[54]

This difference in damage can still be seen in the tower reconstructed after the siege of 1480, one side of which retains distinctive medieval machicolations and decoration absent from the other side.

But d'Aubusson, certainly realising the importance of the mole, was not going to give up simply because half the Tower of St Nicholas had been partly destroyed. He recounts his decision:

For we, being anxious for the safety of the tower, beholding its great and dreadful ruin, ordered that the remainder of the wall be propped up. But it seemed too little after so complete a downfall, we decided to build a fortification, to defend also the mole of St Nicholas. With vigilance, care and genius, a thousand labourers worked day and night, digging a deep ditch, and building a defence with timber on the top of the mole, around the tower, and in its foundations, and made the mole impregnable despite a great cost. There we placed a guard of our bravest warriors within the ruins of the mole, and placed stores and ammunition around them. In the foundations and foot, we placed other garrisons to the east and west, for here the foundation of the wall ended, and the sea is fordable, so that it was necessary to watch and defend it, so that the Turks should not cross there, and attack us in the rear. And on the walls of the city we ordered to be placed bombards, which would fire on them during an attack. And we prepared firepots to throw onto ships.[55]

Again it is Mary Dupuis who adds more details:

And also for the defence of this tower and mole, which was damaged, were built ramparts (*bastides*) all around and along the said tower and mole both of stone and wood, barrels and other vessels full of earth, because it was all rock, and he [d'Aubusson] placed and fixed there bombards, serpentines, cannons, coleuvrines, and other artillery on the said mole in appropriate and suitable places, so well and so properly that they did not have to be changed. And with them were placed all around the tower and mole a great quantity of small boats and old barrels which were all filled with incendiary material, so that if they were assaulted, they would be able to burn the galleys, *fusts* and other ships of the Turks which approached the tower and mole, and to be on their guard night and day.[56]

The Siege of 1480

D'Aubusson was not going to give up the mole and Tower of St Nicholas without a fight.

So Mesīh Pascha gave him one. 'About two hours before dawn', Dupuis remembers,[57] the Turks made a determined attempt to take the mole. They did not immediately attack it, however. After gathering a large number of 'boats, galleys, *fustes*, barks, and other similar instruments', they tried to frighten the Hospitallers placed on the mole and in the rubble of the Tower of St Nicholas: 'They began to make lots of noise and cry and call on their *Mahon*. And they made a very loud noise and a horrible and cacophonous sound with their large drums, gitterns, vielles and other instruments, often shouting and whirling in such a way that it seemed as if the entire sky had come crashing down and firing their cannons and bombards.'[58] This display caused 'a great amount of terror', writes Caoursin.[59]

The attack was then launched. Boats carrying the Turkish soldiers crossed the short distance between St Anthony's Church and the St Nicholas Mole. As they approached, the Hospitallers inside the tower and along the mole fired upon them with guns and bows; incendiaries were thrown on to the boats as they neared. Those who were able to land met fierce resistance – Mary Dupuis is enthusiastic in his use of 'valiantly' and 'courageously' – and were repulsed. They returned disheartened and unable to regroup for a second attack. Over 700 were killed with many more mortally wounded.[60] After their victory d'Aubusson, seemingly having fought among the defenders of St Nicholas, on horseback and carrying his banner, rode through the gates of the city 'in a triumphant manner' to the chapel, where he and other Hospitaller knights prayed before the Icon of the Virgin of Philerimos, which had been brought into the city from an outlying Byzantine church before the siege.[61]

Later, when d'Aubusson writes to Emperor Frederick III, he states that in this attack the Turks 'thought [the Tower of St Nicholas] easy to take with only moderate force'. It is also possible, however, that they were using the first attack as a means to probe the defences and ascertain the fighting willingness and capabilities of the Hospitallers. This would not be the case in their second attack.

For a few days the Turks continued bombarding the tower and the mole. During that period they also prepared to make another assault on St Nicholas. One of the clear problems of the first attack had been the need to cross the harbour between St Anthony's church and the Tower of St Nicholas, which left the transports vulnerable to missile attack from the tower, the mole and the town. To overcome this problem Mesīh Pascha had a bridge built that could reach between the two. It was quite an intricate structure: a simple, narrow pontoon bridge would not do. Mary Dupuis' account contains the fullest description:

> ... he made a bridge of barrels and tuns and other containments well secured together, and rowboats and rails, and they were attached one to another. Over the top of these were nailed tables, planks, boards, and other things. And it was made so long that it could stretch from the Church of St Anthony to the Tower of St Nicholas, and so wide

Rhodes Besieged

that six men could go freely side by side on the bridge and on both sides it was panelled and armed like a galley.[62]

In order to manoeuvre the bridge into position the Turks rowed over towards the Tower of St Nicholas and dropped an anchor to the seabed, attached to which was a strong rope. However, this was spotted by the Hospitallers, and, according to Dupuis, 'a sailor dived into the ocean and swam in the water to cut the rope, raised the anchor, brought it to the surface and carried it to the Grand Master'.[63]

When the Turks realised that the rope had been cut, they arranged for boats to pull the bridge into position as they began to launch their assault 'shortly after midnight' on 18–19 June. In comparison to the attack made a few days earlier, with its 'moderate force', this was a major assault. Not only had the Turks constructed the means to cross the water quickly and safely, they used their best men, including a number of military leaders, 'men of great reputation and authority', writes Dupuis, including the Captain of Sailors and Malerbay, the grandson-in-law of Mehmed II. Simultaneously they mounted a naval attack on the eastern or seaward side of the tower, using 'galleys, *fustes*, and other ships of great power', led by the Captain of the Galleys.[64]

But all of this careful preparation eventually came to nothing. The Ottomans attacked with their usual numbers and ferocity. Gunfire from the mole and the walls of the town were able to break up the bridge before too many reached the tower, and those Turks who made it across were beaten back. The 'noble and valiant' Knights fought tenaciously and skilfully, their training and devotion apparent with every blow. Dupuis and Caoursin could not praise their brothers enough. Only eleven or twelve were killed, but 'there were many wounded'. Dupuis relates the story of an otherwise unnamed Cordelier of St Francis who 'when the barks approached jumped into the sea all the way to the belt, and dragged them off their barks, cut off their heads or hacked them to pieces, and threw them into the sea'.[65] At the end more than 2,500 Turks lay dead, on the mole and in the water, with as many wounded. Despite all their careful planning, ingenuity and numerical superiority in men and ships, after ten hours of fighting the Turks were defeated in a straight hand-to-hand fight. The Knights Hospitaller had proved to be the better warriors on that day. Mary Dupuis concludes:

> and when the Pascha saw that his men had returned so badly beaten and that many had been lost, especially the best ones, he was taken with great sadness and melancholy, and he went into his tent where he stayed for the space of three days, not wishing to speak to anyone.[66]

The original sources naturally focus on the attacks of the mole and Tower of St Nicholas. The story is filled with action and heroism. Mary Dupuis may even have been there, although he never admits to it. He and Caoursin certainly heard of the attacks and the defiance of the Hospitallers in holding the tower and mole, while

The Siege of 1480

Grand Master Pierre d'Aubusson was either present – although no one reports this fact – or received the eyewitness accounts of those who were there.

But while these attacks were being made the Ottomans were also pressing the siege around the city. Dupuis recounts, for example, that Turkish bombards targeted the Grand Master's Palace and elsewhere. On one occasion:

> On the last day of May the Turks began to fire large courtaux and mortars into the city of which, among others, two shots fell onto the palace of the Grand Master, one of which penetrated three storeys and fell onto a stable and the ball burrowed itself deep into the ground. And the other, a courtau shot fell onto a vault of the brothers' dining room and destroyed the vault and broke two large marble pillars in the middle of the room holding up the vault. These two pillars were so large that two men could not reach around them. The stone went through everything and fell into a cellar underneath onto a tun of wine which was broken into pieces and the wine lost. And it also went into the ground. But by the grace of God none of the courtaux and mortars which were fired into the city did any harm to the people inside.[67]

At some point in the siege, possibly after the attacks on St Nicholas were proving to be more difficult than expected, Mesīh Pascha began to concentrate his forces against 'the other side of the town, close to the other strip of sea to the right of the Jewish Quarter because it was a very fair place, flat and linked to batter the city'.[68] But where exactly this was has been somewhat of a mystery. Brockman, following the lead of others, places this to the south-east of the city, approximately where the moat begins today and to the west of the current Tower of Italy.[69] At that time this was known as the Italian Post, a place referred to in d'Aubusson's letter and suggested by the current existence of a round bastion built by Fabrizio del Carretto after he became Grand Master in 1513. But d'Aubusson's complete reference to where the Jewish Quarter was is inside the walls, '*qui Judaeorum domos claudunt Orientamque spectant*', that is 'where the Jewish houses were enclosed and looking to the east'.[70] In other words, the Jewish Quarter was not south-east of the city but to the east.

This is confirmed when one studies the near-contemporary illustrations of the siege, the illuminations accompanying the manuscript of Guillaume Caoursin's *Gestorum Rhodi obsidionis descriptio* found today in the Bibliothèque Nationale (B.N. Ms lat 6067), and the painting, *The Siege of Rhodes by the Turks in 1480*, currently on display in the Hôtel de Ville in Epernay, France. Five of the Caoursin illustrations and the Epernay painting clearly show the attack taking place next to a small bay which comes up nearly to the wall south of the Windmill Mole – a feature which is still there today. The first illumination (f. 55) shows the Turkish commanders discussing the oncoming attack as their troops span crossbows in front of them. The Hospitallers stand behind a small breach in the wall that has been blocked by wood and prepare to defend the city. A second (f. 64) shows the Turkish commanders looking on as their batteries of gunpowder weapons attack the walls to the west (their left) across the

Rhodes Besieged

moat and to the east (their right) across the bay from a spit to the east of the Windmill Mole. At the end of this spit, identified in contemporary documents as the place where executions were carried out, are the gallows, next to which three cannon are mounted. The towers and walls have been clearly damaged but at this point no breach has been made. A third illumination (f. 70) shows that the wall has been breached close to the bay but repaired by the Knights, who are shown standing behind wood, baskets and barrels. The Ottoman leaders are seen discussing the forthcoming attack while their troops stand ready. The fourth illumination (f. 77) portrays the attack in progress, with soldiers attempting to enter the breach in the wall. Here they encounter a stiff resistance referred to in the Hospitaller narratives, while the banner of the Order also mentioned encourages the defence of the city. A few Turkish soldiers lie dead in the bay. The final illumination (f. 79) shows the aftermath of the failed attack. Large numbers of Turks lie dead outside the walls and towers and inside the bay. The Knights have exited the city and are burning the camp of the retreating Ottoman army. A sixth Caoursin illumination, a bird's-eye view of the entire city under siege but prior to the assault on the Jewish Quarter (f. 37), also shows the breach having been made in the eastern wall of the city, with the Ottoman cannon next to the gallows on the spit across from it. The Epernay painting is similar to this illumination in that the entire siege is depicted, but it shows the Jewish Quarter under attack, breaches made in the walls and Turks attempting to enter through them and over the walls. The Hospitallers fight valiantly to keep them out, the results of which can be seen in the large number of dead Turks lying in the water and on the shore. The scaffold mole, with its three large cannon, can also be seen; other cannon point at the Jewish Quarter from near the Ottoman camp.

The Caoursin manuscript and Epernay painting have been dated to 1482–83, making these illustrations the nearest contemporary artistic representations of the siege. While it is possible that the illuminator and painter were not present at the siege and simply painted them from the written descriptions, the details suggest eyewitness knowledge of the city, its fortifications and the siege action. The artists certainly knew where the Jewish Quarter of Rhodes stood, that its walls stood on the eastern side of the city next to the small bay south of the Windmill Mole.

The final proof comes from the placement of the Notre-Dame de la Victoire (Our Lady of the Victory) church by Pierre d'Aubusson after the siege. Commemorating the victory, d'Aubusson built the church in the ruins of the Jewish Quarter where the breach in the wall had been made.[71] In 1522, the Hospitaller Grand Master, Philippe Villiers de l'Isle Adam, was forced to tear down Our Lady of the Victory to open up a larger space between the town walls and the first building, and to use the stones and rubble to repair the walls and build temporary defences.

This means that the Ottoman Turkish attack was concentrated on the very eastern edge of the city between the Tower of Italy and the 'Harbour' Tower at the north-east corner of the city. In 1480 the modern Acandia Gate did not exist, and today the wall from the Tower of Italy runs north and then turns north-east for a short distance directly to a D-shaped tower – from where the wall runs due north straight to the Harbour Tower at the southern end of the Windmill Mole. From the Caoursin illustrations and the Epernay painting it appears that at the time of the siege the wall ran directly due north from the Tower of Italy to the Harbour Tower, and that there were no gates in this expanse of wall. The Turks focused their assault on this straight section of wall from 'a very fair place, flat and linked to batter the city', as Mary Dupuis says. Next to this plain was Dupuis' 'strip of the sea', which from the illuminations and painting is the modern Acandia (Akantia) Bay, lying east of the Windmill Mole – which on these artistic works is covered with windmills from the Harbour Tower to the Windmill Tower on its end – and west of a small peninsula of land that is always shown to have a scaffold at its northern tip.[72]

Mesīh Pascha ordered 'eight of the great bombards' set up there in an attempt to breach the wall and gain access to the city. According to Dupuis and Caoursin they seem initially to have been very effective:

> ...the Turks also were not hindered by the fact that the wall to the right of the Jewish Quarter was more than twenty-eight feet in height; they hit and battered the wall so hard and so sharply and for so long that there was no one in the city who was not very frightened of the fury of these bombards.[73]

Indeed, Dupuis claims that the sound of the bombards could be heard by the garrison of Hospitallers at Lango, 100 miles to the west, and at the Red Castle, 100 miles to the east.[74]

The destruction was massive and breaches began to appear in the wall. D'Aubusson quickly organised the population to make repairs and rebuild the defences every night. They used everything they could get their hands on to reinforce the wall: stones, wood and especially barrels full of earth. According to Caoursin, they also demolished houses in the Jewish Quarter near the walls and dug a ditch to act as a second line of defence if the Turks were to enter the city. Everyone responded to the Grand Master's plea: 'neither the Master, nor the stewards, nor the priors, nor the knights, nor the citizens, nor the merchants, nor the women, nor the brides, nor the girls avoided work. They carried stones and earth.'[75]

While the bombardment of the walls continued the Ottomans also began firing into the city, hoping to destroy houses and kill the population. Caoursin and Dupuis identify the guns used here as mortars, and thus provide one of the earliest descriptions of their use, 'firing stones so high in the air that they are lost to sight and fall so furiously'.[76] Few seemed to have been hurt in these initial mortar attacks, but d'Aubusson had to do something to keep people safe. Caoursin writes: 'He ordered all the women, children, and elderly to be gathered in cellars and protected by wooden roofs',[77] with the result that few were killed. Frustrated, Mesīh Pascha moved some of his guns to higher ground so they could be aimed more easily. He also began using incendiaries, according to d'Aubusson, 'guns firing fireballs and ballistae and catapults firing arrows which set fire to the buildings'. But, he continues, 'for the care of the city we chose men skilled in the art who extinguished the flames caused by the falling projectiles'.[78]

The Turks also tried to get close to the walls by digging trenches 'which they partly covered with wood and earth so that they approach the moat of the city under cover'. While doing this 'they built defences in many places from which they fired arrows continually, and they harassed and fatigued us with couleuvrines, serpentines and bombards'.[79] For the next thirty-eight days the Ottomans continued their preparations for an assault while the Hospitallers tried to counter these moves. D'Aubusson describes the activity:

> The tenacious enemy did not cease to collect stones and secretly to throw them into the ditch, so that part of the moat might be filled up until it equalled the *faussebraye* and form a pathway in the shape of a back, from which they could more easily enter the walls of the city. We, however, seeing their attempt, watched over the safety of the city, and throughout the town and castle repaired and armed and made ditches very diligently. The Turks, seeing this, turned in despair to the walls of the Jewish Quarter and elsewhere; and we made very strong defences and repairs from the breach caused by the Turks, fixing stakes of green wood into the ground, and covered them with roots and branches interlaced which, clinging together most tenaciously and firmly, withstood the power of their gunfire, and protected the breach so that the collapsed wall might prevent an easy descent into the city. And we filled our earthen defences with stakes and brushwood which protected our men and would be an obstacle to the Turks climbing up. We also prepared artificial fire and other incendiaries which might prove useful in repelling the attack of the Turks. Also it was thought to empty that part of the moat which the Turks had filled with stones. But as that could not be done openly, we secretly made for ourselves an exit beneath the stones, and in secret brought them into the town. The Turks nearest the moat thought that the heap of stones had diminished and that their opportunity for an attack was lessening, unless they rapidly carried it out.

Over 3,500 large stones were carried from the moat into the town, estimated the Grand Master.[80]

On 27 July[81] the Ottoman Turks intensified their bombardment of the walls of the Jewish Quarter, firing more than 300 shots, according to d'Aubusson and Caoursin.[82] It continued throughout the day and night without respite. But as dawn broke on the morning of 28 July the gunshot ceased. Then a single mortar shot was fired, the pre-arranged signal for the Turkish assault on the walls to begin.[83] While the Hospitallers seem to have been expecting a major attack, the initial onslaught of the Ottomans completely overwhelmed those guarding the walls of the Jewish Quarter. Without too much difficulty the Turks quickly mounted the walls, defeated the defending troops there – d'Aubusson uses the word *eradicare* to describe what happened – and planted their standards and banners.[84]

The Siege of 1480

Although caught somewhat by surprise, d'Aubusson and the Hospitallers responded quickly. In his letter to Frederick III, d'Aubusson sums up the retaking of the walls in short order:

> Suddenly, our men opposing themselves to the enemy, on the right and left of the walls, fought them in the highest places, causing great confusion and preventing them from advancing any further. Of the four ladders that were there which were used to climb down into the Jewish Quarter, with one broken by our order, we climbed up to the enemy, opposed them and we protected and defended the place. There were 2,000 very well armed Turks on top of the walls, crowded together with us and fighting hand-to-hand struggled by force of arms to drive us away. But by the persistence and constant valour of our soldiers we held on. Following those Turks who were already on the walls, was a huge number of Turks from their camp who filled the breach, the wall and the moat, so that it was impossible to see the ground. Deserters stated that 4,000 Turks had made the assault. Our men drove about 300 of the enemy who were on the walls into the Jewish Quarter, where they were killed to a man. In this conflict we raised the standard bearing the image of our most sacred Lord Jesus Christ, and that of our Religion, in the presence of the enemy. The battle was fought with great ferocity for two hours. Finally the Turks, pressed, fatigued and terrified, and wounded, turned their backs, and took to flight with such great haste that they became an impediment to one another, and added to their destruction. In the fight there fell about 3,500 Turks, whose corpses were found inside the city and upon the walls, in the moat, in the enemy's positions and in the sea, and which afterwards were burnt to prevent disease. The spoils of their corpses were taken by our men, who, following the fleeing Turks all the way to their camp on the plain, killed them vigorously and afterwards returned unharmed.[85]

But, as Mary Dupuis indicates, the Grand Master proved to be too humble in describing his own and others' heroic actions on the day:

> The said Grand Master, who was not far away [from where the Turks had broken through], accompanied by many knights and other soldiers, came to one of the stairs and was the first to climb. With great courage and marvellous feats of arms he climbed to the top; but in climbing he received great and awful blows, but he gave as well as he got. And he was thrown two or three times from the stairs to the ground. But he was valiantly aided and helped by the other knights who were with him, all of whom carried themselves so well and so valiantly that by force and in spite of all the Turks they climbed onto the walls, and there the Grand Master was wounded in two places.[86]

The Turks were repulsed.

This was their final action. The Ottoman Turks retreated, 'far from the city', writes Dupuis, 'out of range of the large bombards',[87] and then they left Rhodes. The

Rhodes Besieged

Hospitallers had survived, their walls relatively intact and their reputations made. But it would have been clear to all the Knights, as well as to the Rhodians, that the Turks would be back. Next time they would need to be just as well, if not better, prepared.

Notes
1 Guillaume Caoursin, *Opera* (Venice, 1496), p. 3.
2 Smith and DeVries, pp. 340–2.
3 Dupuis, p. 93. Caoursin (p. 6) and Giacomo Curti (*Ad magnificum spectabilemque* [Venice: Erhaldus Radtolt de Augusta, *c*.1510], f. 2v) use similar phrases in Latin to describe Master George: '*machinarum egregius artifex*' and '*maiximusque machinarum artifex*', with Curti also using the term '*bombarderius*'.
4 Franz Babinger, *Mehmed the Conqueror and His Time*, trans. Ralph Manheim, ed. William C. Hickman (Princeton: Princeton University Press, 1978) is certainly the best and most complete biography, but as a nice concise survey see Halil Inalcik, 'Mehmed the Conqueror (1432–1481) and His Time', *Speculum* 35 (1960), pp. 408–27.
5 The best study on the Fourth Crusade is Donald E. Queller and Thomas F. Madden, *The Fourth Crusade: The Conquest of Constantinople, 1201–1204*, 2nd ed. (Philadelphia: University of Pennsylvania Press, 1997), but see also Jonathan Phillips, *The Fourth Crusade and the Sack of Constantinople* (New York: Viking, 2004).
6 An excellent recent study of the walls of Constantinople is Stephen Turnbull, *The Walls of Constantinople, AD 324–1453* (London: Osprey, 2004).
7 National Library of Malta, Valletta, Section 5, Libri Bullarum, ff. 16v–17v, as translated in Brockman, p. 71.
8 Brockman, p. 64.
9 Caoursin, p. 3. The text states that it was 'twenty two thousand paces'.
10 Mary Dupuis identifies the Turkish launching site as Fusto.
11 Caoursin, p. 3.
12 Caoursin, p. 4.
13 Curti, p. 1r.
14 National Library of Malta, Valletta, Section 5, Libri Bullarum, ff. 13r–14r. See also ff. 1r–6r, 35r, 35v for other examples of d'Aubusson's petitions.
15 National Library of Malta, Valletta, Section 5, Libri Bullarum, f. 164r.
16 Curti, p. 1r.
17 D'Aubusson, in Brockman, p. 71. See also Setton, 1:351 n. 18, who gives the Latin of d'Aubusson's letter. Mary Dupuis numbers the sails at '100 or thereabouts' (Dupuis, p. 92).
18 Caoursin, p. 3
19 Caoursin, p. 6 and Dupuis, p. 93.
20 Caoursin, p. 3 and Dupuis, p. 93.
21 See Setton, I:348 n. 8.
22 Brockman, p. 65.
23 Curti, p. 1v.
24 Dupuis, p. 92.
25 Curti, p. 1v.
26 Caoursin, p. 6 and Dupuis, p. 92. Dupuis calls St Stephen a 'small, flat mountain'.
27 Caoursin, p. 6. Dupuis (p. 92) details the off-loading of the 'bombards, stones, and other engines necessary for them' but does not mention their being hidden behind the mountain.
28 Brockman, p. 66.
29 Caoursin, p. 6 and Dupuis, p. 92. The quotes are from Dupuis.
30 Dupuis, p. 92.
31 Caoursin, p. 6.

32 Caoursin, p. 6.
33 Dupuis, p. 93.
34 Pierre d'Aubusson, [Letter to emperor Frederick III] in *Scriptorum rerum germanicarum*, II (Berlin: n.p., 1602), p. 306. Dupuis (p. 93), Caoursin (p. 6) and Curti (f. 2r) also mention the placement of these bombards at St Anthony's Church, although Curti has four placed in the battery instead of three.
35 D'Aubusson, p. 306.
36 Caoursin, pp. 5–6 and Dupuis, pp. 93–4.
37 Dupuis, p. 93. Curti (f. 2r) also comments on George's eloquence.
38 Dupuis, p. 93.
39 Dupuis, p. 93. See also Caoursin, p. 6.
40 Dupuis, p. 93. Caoursin (p. 6) has only 100,000 men. Curti does not record the interrogation.
41 Dupuis, p. 93. Caoursin (p. 6) does not include the height of the bombards in his account nor mention the mortars or other firearms, but he does say that the stones were fired from the bombards '*vehementissimo velocissimoque*'.
42 Brockman, for example (p. 63).
43 Dupuis, p. 94. See also Caoursin, p. 6.
44 Dupuis, p. 94 and Caoursin, p. 6.
45 D'Aubusson, p. 306. The distance is measured using www.earth.google.com.
46 It has often been alleged that bombards were so large and generated so much heat when firing a ball that they needed to be cooled down for hours in between each firing so that the newly loaded gunpowder would not be set off. This is simply not the case. Gunpowder weapons, even the largest bombards, simply did not generate enough heat to need to be cooled down. Of course, it was always prudent to swab out a gun after it was fired but this was just to extinguish burning embers or unburnt powder and not to cool the barrel.
47 In just one Latin source, the letter of Pierre d'Aubusson to Frederick III, is mention of *colubrinis* and *serpentinis*, although no further details are given. By this time gunpowder weapons were very well developed and had an established typology in every European country. In France and Burgundy, apart from bombard, there were, for example, the terms *veuglaire*, *crappadeaux*, culverin and serpentine. For a detailed discussion of the names used in Burgundy in the fifteenth century, see Smith and DeVries.
48 Dupuis, pp. 93–4.
49 Caoursin, p. 6.
50 An illustration of a gun, dated 1452, that was destroyed in the eighteenth century shows this type of gun. See Essenwein, pl. AXXI–XXII.
51 Dupuis, p. 93. Curti, f. 2r, states also that the tower is round but gives it a height of 24ft.
52 An additional ring of fortifications was built around the re-constructed tower – see below.
53 D'Aubusson, p. 306. See also Caoursin, p. 7.
54 Dupuis, p. 94.
55 D'Aubusson, pp. 306–7. Caoursin (p. 7) is very similar to d'Aubusson here and seems to confirm Setton's claim that as vice-chancellor of the Hospitallers he also composed the Grand Master's letter to Emperor Frederick III (I:352 n. 22).
56 Dupuis, p. 94.
57 Dupuis, p. 94. The date of the first attack is somewhat in dispute. Dupuis dates it to 19 June, the date given by Caoursin (p. 9) and d'Aubusson (p. 307) for the second attack, which Dupuis does not date. Most historians, i.e. Setton (I:353) and Brockman (p. 78), accept Caoursin's dating.
58 Dupuis, p. 95.
59 Caoursin, p. 9.
60 Dupuis, p. 95; Caoursin, p. 9; and d'Aubusson, p. 307.
61 Dupuis, p. 95 and Caoursin, p. 9. The quote is from Caoursin.
62 Dupuis, p. 97. Caoursin (p. 12) claims that it was six horsemen who could cross the bridge side by side.
63 Dupuis, p. 97 and Caoursin, p. 12.
64 Dupuis, p. 97; Caoursin, p. 12; and d'Aubusson, p. 307.
65 Dupuis, pp. 97–8 and Caoursin, p. 12.

66 Dupuis, p. 98,
67 Dupuis, p. 94.
68 Dupuis, p. 95.
69 Brockman, p. 74.
70 D'Aubusson, p. 307.
71 Kollias, p. 102. Mary, whose image was on the banner unfurled by Pierre d'Aubusson at the defence of the Jewish Quarter, was given special credit for the victory there. See Michelangelo Bacheca, *Il prodigio mariano nell'assedio di Rodi del 1480 in due documenti pontifici inediti* (Assisi: Porziuncola, 1954).
72 Caoursin (p. 9) confirms this, saying that the Turks set up a gun on the mole where the condemned were hanged, also shown on the Caoursin illumination f. 48v and Epernay painting.
73 Dupuis, p. 95 and Caoursin, p. 9. See also d'Aubusson, p. 307.
74 Dupuis, p. 95. Caoursin (p. 9) also comments on the sound carrying far from the city, 100 miles away, but only mentions the Red Castle.
75 Caoursin, p. 9.
76 Caoursin, p. 9 and Dupuis, p. 96. The quote is from Dupuis. Caoursin suggests that 'no one had ever seen such large stone balls in the air'.
77 Caoursin, p. 9. See also d'Aubusson, p. 307.
78 D'Aubusson, p. 307. See also Caoursin, p. 10.
79 Both quotes are from d'Aubusson's letter to Frederick III (pp. 307–8).
80 D'Aubusson, p. 308. See also Dupuis, p. 96.
81 For a discussion of the dating problems for this attack see Setton, I:357 n. 37. Setton's conclusion that the main attack took place on 28 June – after a day and night of intense bombardment – is convincing.
82 D'Aubusson, p. 308 and Caoursin, p. 10. Dupuis (p. 100) says that it was more than 100.
83 D'Aubusson, p. 308 and Caoursin, p. 10.
84 D'Aubusson, p. 308. See also Dupuis, p. 100.
85 D'Aubusson, pp. 308–9.
86 Dupuis, p. 101.
87 Dupuis, p. 101.

The Uneasy Calm, 1480–1522

Defeating the Turkish army in 1480 must have seemed miraculous to the Hospitallers and Rhodians. The soldier Mary Dupuis, no doubt relieved at no longer having to fight, wrote of the rejoicing that took place in Rhodes following the Ottoman retreat from the island:

> And the victory came by the Grace of God, who fought for the city and defended those within. For which victory the Grand Master and all the noble knights and valiant people of the city, men, women and children, gave thanks to God, to Our Lady and to Saint John the Baptist. And they gave thanks again each day for the great grace that had been done to preserve and deliver them from the hand of the false dogs, the Turks, enemies of the Catholic Faith who by the Grace of God were entirely destroyed and confused. Amen.[1]

Celebrations and thanksgivings went on for weeks afterwards.

Although the siege was over, aid continued to arrive. Dupuis reports that two large ships sent from Ferdinand I, the King of Naples, 'completely filled with food and drink', and more than 1,000 reinforcements came to the city fifteen days after the Turks had left.[2] Although they arrived too late to fight, their assistance was not turned away. It must have been very clear to the Hospitallers that, although they had survived a long, hard-pressed and intense siege, it would probably not be long before the Turks tried again to wrest the island from their control. Pierre d'Aubusson and his Council were undoubtedly aware of the danger, as their actions immediately following the siege demonstrate. On 18 August, the day of the Turkish retreat, they assigned Hospitaller units preceptories, made vacant by deaths during the siege to Knights who had fought well against the Turks.[3] And just three days later, on 21 August, they sent the prior of Capua to Italy to report to the Pope and the King of Naples on their victory and to request further aid 'for it is of course assumed that the enemy proposes to come back'. They also authorised one of their brigantines to sail into the strait between Rhodes and Turkey to make sure that the Ottoman fleet was no longer blockading the island.[4] On 23 August they allowed those Turks captured during the siege to be sold as slaves and sent those who had deserted, and forsaken their religion, to Rome to ascertain whether their conversions from Islam to Christianity were genuine.[5] On 6 September they ordered the commanders of the Hospitaller galleys of the priories of Castile, Portugal, England, and the Castellany of Emposta to sail to Rhodes.[6] A little later, on 11 September, they voted to complete the destruction of St Anthony's Church begun by the Ottoman forces during the siege – and from where their bombards had attacked the Tower of St Nicholas – leaving only a small chapel for services to the dead, but with the proviso that 'if in the future the Religion came to a more peaceful and tranquil state' the church should be rebuilt.[7] On 20 September they assigned the defence of the preceptory and castle of Bodrum to Fra Edward de Carmandino, who had been bailiff of Cos prior to the siege, asking him to conduct a 'valiant defence' of that site against the Turks.[8] And on 23 September they wrote to all the members of the Order, summoning them to Rhodes as they were certain that the Ottomans were planning a new attack on the city.[9]

By November d'Aubusson began upgrading the defences of the city. On 16 November he ordered the Castellany of Emposta to send bombards to defend Rhodes;[10] a second letter that day to the same castellany also asked the Receiver of the Common Treasury there, Fra Dominico Salvatoris, to grant the Grand Master licence to collect money from brothers who had not been at the siege 'to rebuild the moat larger and deeper';[11] and a third letter the same day was sent to Fra Johanni Dargensolle, Receiver of the Common Treasury of the priory of Catalonia, asking him to allow d'Aubusson to do the same to brothers in that priory for the same reason.[12] The next year, on 3 February 1481, d'Aubusson ordered the trees and houses next to the walls to be destroyed.[13]

Then on 4 May 1481 Ottoman Sultan Mehmed II died. Although it had been doubtlessly known earlier, the news was publicly pronounced in Rhodes on 31 May. As one can imagine, the announcement was greeted with enthusiasm and rejoicing, as Guillaume Caoursin exults: 'If a pen could describe the joy of my mind, and speech expound the delight of my heart, today has provided the occasion.'[14] The succession to the Ottoman throne, never a straightforward process, was, this time, greatly complicated by two rival claimants, both sons of Mehmed – Bāyezīd and Cem (Djem).[15] Making things even more difficult was a Janissary corps that wanted their voices to be heard. They may have been the best soldiers in the world at the time, but Mehmed had driven them to the brink of rebellion by constantly calling on them to fight wars, not only far from home but throughout the entire year. Recent losses, such as the one at Rhodes, had also added to their discontent. Killing the Grand Vizier, Karamani Mehmet Pasha, whose job it was to ease the transition from Sultan to heir, the Janissaries determined to control whichever of the sons arrived first in Constantinople, giving him the support that would win him the crown but at the same time forcing their own will upon him. Bāyezīd arrived there before his brother and, with a huge payoff from the Treasury to placate the Janissaries, he ascended the throne.[16]

Cem, however, was not to be quickly deflected from what he thought to be rightfully his, and a brief war of succession followed, which, without any significant support, he lost. Ironically, and after a short dalliance with the Egyptian Mamluks, Cem made contact with d'Aubusson who, after consulting his allies, offered him a safe haven in Rhodes. The prince arrived on the island to much pomp and ceremony on 29 July 1482.[17]

Some in the West, such as Caoursin, wished to use the disunity of the Ottomans to regain some of the lands that had been lost over the past two centuries:

> A divided empire is easy to occupy ... For one ought not to neglect the opportunity presented ... If an army appeared from Hungary and a navy sailed into the Aegean Sea, the Hellespont and the Marmara Sea, bearing and showing the insignias of the life-giving cross, quickly the dragons would be destroyed by the troops of the faith. The East awaits European crusading soldiers and Latin inhabitants.[18]

However, most Europeans were not so enthusiastic to risk a fight against the Turks, no matter how disunited they were. Their formidability still frightened many, including it seems Pierre d'Aubusson and the Hospitaller Council. Although they clearly realised that this period of relative peace was very welcome, it did not mean that they would not face a similar threat at some time in the future.

A formal truce between the Ottoman Turks and the Knights Hospitaller in Rhodes was agreed on 26 November 1481, driven no doubt on the part of Sultan Bāyezīd by the necessity to secure his own throne and, on the Hospitallers side, by their need to recover fully from the recent siege.[19] It was renewed on 7 December 1482 and included payment to the Order to watch over Cem. The new treaty included a payment by the Turks of 35,000 Venetian ducats for Cem's maintenance, plus a further 10,000 ducats to the Grand Master for the Knights' willingness to play host. In addition, Hospitaller vessels were allowed to trade freely in Turkish ports. The Hospitallers, in turn, promised not to wage war against Bāyezīd on behalf of Cem.[20] Bāyezīd, according to the provisions of the 1482 treaty, must have wanted his brother to live in comfort, but at the same time he also must have been fearful of the potential threat he posed to the security of his Ottoman throne. So began a strange and confusing period in the history of the sultans of the Ottoman Empire. Bāyezīd II ruled while his brother, Cem, 'aspirant' to the throne, was in the hands of Christian powers.[21]

On 18 March and 3 May of 1481 another shock hit the Knights, this time from the ground, as earthquakes shook the entire Eastern Mediterranean region.[22] These especially affected the city of Rhodes and caused further damage to many of its walls and houses, on top of that caused by the Ottoman attacks of less than a year before. Caoursin discusses the effects of these quakes at length, revealing the added problems that they caused to the already weakened fortifications, especially with the anticipated return of the Turks to the island.[23] In doing so he also reveals something of a theological confusion: he knows there is a scientific explanation to the ground shaking – he waxes on for several sentences about this – but he cannot escape his belief in God's control over the elements ('God is omnipotent, the Creator and Governor of all things, he caused this to happen ... he also is the judge of all physical occurrences'). What could God mean by these earthquakes, especially when they followed so closely after the siege? Ultimately he limits God's responsibility, tying them to the death of Mehmed II:

> For we believe that the earth was unable to stomach a corpse so wicked, fetid and savage. Opening in a gigantic fissure, its viscera gaping, it despatched the body to its core and hurled it to the perpetual chaos of the damned. Its stench affects even hell, aggravating the sufferings inflicted on the damned. For it was around the time of his demise that there took place, in Asia, on Rhodes and the neighbouring islands, repeated tremors in the earth. Two were particularly violent, so powerful and terrifying that they brought down several fortresses, strongholds and palaces.[24]

Interestingly, the earthquakes seem ultimately to have been a good thing for the Knights at Rhodes, for they shook loose any weakened fortifications, which were then replaced along with those destroyed by the Turks. They also seem to have added to the sympathy those in Europe had for the Hospitallers, increasing donations for the repair and rebuilding of Rhodes' fortifications, and for the addition of new and better ones.[25]

Cem spent less than six weeks in Rhodes, leaving the headquarters of the Knights Hospitaller on 1 September 1482, even before payment for his protected exile was settled between the Knights and the Ottoman Turks. His destination was Bourganeuf, a Hospitaller commandery in Auvergne, close to Pierre d'Aubusson's home, which he reached after a lengthy tour of southern France. This was only one of several Hospitaller homes he would have over the next seven years, including Monteil-le-Vicomte, Morterolles and Boislamy. Although he was kept in great comfort – Bourganeuf even had special kitchens, a Turkish bath and quarters for his Muslim staff – there is no doubt that he was a prisoner. To the Knights, however, he was a symbol of their victory over the Turks in 1480 and they took every opportunity to show him off to prospective donors, the message being that Christians could defeat Muslims if they had determination and the necessary finances.[26]

On 4 July 1488 Pope Innocent VIII asked Pierre d'Aubusson to surrender the 'custodia' of Cem to his control, and, after one last tour through southern France, in March 1489 the brother of the Ottoman Sultan arrived in Rome.[27] Why the Hospitallers gave up control of such an important person and why the pope wanted him is a mystery.[28] Eric Brockman rather cynically states that the 'betrayal' of Cem was d'Aubusson's price for a cardinalship,[29] and certainly the dates correspond – the Grand Master was created cardinal deacon on 9 March 1489 and Cem arrived in Rome four days later (although d'Aubusson was not actually presented with his cardinal's hat until 23 March 1489). But that is hardly what the request for custodial transfer suggests,[30] and at least for Innocent's reign the Hospitallers were still responsible for Cem's protection and financial upkeep, while presumably the 45,000 ducats continued to be sent to them by Bāyezīd (at least there is no mention of a disruption in Turkish payments in 1489). So this may be too harsh a historical judgement.[31]

In fact, it was not until 1494 that the new Pope, Alexander VI, took complete control of Cem, and he and his sons, Don Juan and Cesare Borgia, allowed him to live in grand style, although he could not leave Rome.[32] Johann Burchard, a member of the papal court, observed the celebrity given to Cem:

> ... though Cem was not allowed to leave Rome, yet Alexander VI and his sons treated the Turkish Prince in very friendly and courteous fashion. He moved about the city with an escort and was accorded an honourable place in all the ceremonial functions. Don Juan Borgia in particular appeared to cultivate him and frequently dressed in the style of a Turk when accompanying Cem on his journeys through Rome.[33]

In 1494 Charles VIII was campaigning through Rome on his way to Naples and, as Pope Alexander VI had not supported his military action in Italy, the French king demanded hostages from him, one of whom was to be Cem. On 29 January 1495 he was sent to the king in Naples.[34] This was Cem's last European stop, however, as he died on 25 February – apparently of food poisoning, although more than one contemporary accused the Borgias of poisoning him.[35] His body was returned to a mourning Bāyezīd.

Why popes Innocent VIII and Alexander VI wanted Cem, to whom they referred to by the title 'Grand Turk', is difficult to determine. It may have been nothing more than having the famous and exotic brother of the Turkish Sultan in the court of the leader of Christendom. Certainly that was the allure for the Borgias, who egotistically enjoyed being surrounded by such symbols of their power. Innocent frequently spoke about conducting a crusade against the Ottoman Turks, and, at least in his plans, Cem was to have played a role, but no crusade ever advanced beyond the planning stages.[36]

No doubt Cem, at least at first, believed he would be aided militarily by the Hospitallers to gain the Ottoman throne; he even went so far as promising them that if they helped him he would remove the Turks from Europe, surrender Constantinople and cease attacks against Christians.[37] However, by the time he arrived in the Vatican it seems certain that he had given up any ideas of returning to Constantinople at the head of a largely Christian army. Guillaume Caoursin, who accompanied d'Aubusson to Rome in 1489, describes Cem at this time as a fat and lazy drunkard, while other observers claim he ate five meals a day, drank only alcohol or sugared water – although favouring the former over the latter – and, despite bathing and swimming often, was so heavy that he had the gait of an elephant.[38]

The Hospitallers certainly had no desire to go to war with the Turks, using Cem as a figurehead or not, especially if they were not to be aided by money and men from Europe. Instead, for them Cem represented a means whereby they could ensure peace with Bāyezīd, giving them time to rebuild both their shattered fortifications and their manpower.

There certainly were no major military activities between these two enemies for the thirteen years that the brother of the Sultan was in Europe. Nor were there even any threats of a new siege of Rhodes by the Turks, although the Hospitallers continued to worry that this would happen, and they constantly used this fear to raise money and bring recruits to the order. A letter written by Pierre d'Aubusson to the Pope in 1483 exemplifies this:

> We hope to gain many advantages of being able to live in peace while waiting for positive results. However, we will not abandon our work on the defences or fortifications but will remain on guard.[39]

It was of course a 'hope for peace, but prepare for war' attitude; one that proved very beneficial for the Hospitallers. Money was plentiful and the Knights used it not only for the construction of the fortifications mentioned above, but for the purchase of foodstuffs, ammunition and the upkeep of their fortifications in Cos and Château Saint-Pierre, among other places. On the other hand, new recruits were not so numerous: at times the Hospitallers used the threat of a new siege to recall their Knights to Rhodes, to press service from sailors who had come into harbour and to draw reinforcements from nearby islands.[40]

The damage to the fortifications of Rhodes caused by the Turks was considerable, as shown by both the written sources and the pictures in the Caoursin manuscript. After the euphoria of victory had died down, the Knights lost no time in preparing for the Ottomans' anticipated return. Rebuilding and strengthening the damaged walls must have been uppermost in the minds of Grand Master d'Aubusson and all the Knights Hospitaller. They had been tested to the very extreme and knew what and where the weaknesses of their defences were. Their reaction to the attacks of the Turks and the way that they rebuilt and adapted the walls can give us unique insights into the art of fortification. Here was the opportunity to react to the Ottoman attack and to incorporate new ideas in fortification construction and improvements in gunpowder artillery to make the city impregnable.[41]

But, although the opportunity presented itself to change the walls, the question the Knights needed to answer was what threat would they need to meet? Was it the same as before? Were there changes that were obvious? Were there changes that could be foreseen and what were they? What was the best way forward and what measures could be taken to ensure that the walls would be able to resist them? It was important that the changes they made to the walls would counter any threat that changes in artillery might pose. The walls of the city of Rhodes clearly show the interaction between fortifications and artillery – between creating walls that could provide the best defence and the development of artillery powerful enough to attack and defeat

The Uneasy Calm, 1480–1522

them. This is a very complex question and its solution relies not only on the development of fortifications and artillery, but on a whole range of factors such as financial constraints, geography, technology and knowledge.

One way to tackle the problem is to ask what came first: changes to artillery or changes to fortifications. Did new artillery and more powerful gunpowder initiate changes in fortifications and castles or did the need for better fortifications spur the makers of artillery and gunpowder to develop more powerful gunpowder and new and better gun barrels? Changes in one area may have led to changes in another, but before the modern era of scientific method – action and reaction, theory and experiment, something which is not usually accepted to have developed until the seventeenth century – the interaction is very opaque. That ideas and changes in one area interacted and influenced others is undeniable. It is the understanding of how this happened that is problematic.[42]

There are many extant guns that we know were used at the sieges of Rhodes and more that date from the same time as the sieges. Of these some twenty-two cannon belonged to the Hospitallers or are known to have been on the island of Rhodes and range in date from 1478 to 1522. These cannon show the development of artillery over the period from the 1470s to the second decade of the sixteenth century and an analysis of them is not only the way to understand this development in detail, but to see the backdrop against which the Hospitallers chose to rebuild the defences of the city.

From a first, cursory study of the collection of the surviving artillery, some of the developments are very obvious. The earlier pieces are essentially parallel-sided barrels of large calibre in which the bore of the barrel proper is of larger diameter than the bore of the powder chamber at the rear. Examples of this type of gun include N58 in the Musée de l'Armée and W572 in the Germanisches Museum in Nuremberg. What is very exciting is that three later cannon, all dated 1507, clearly show the next development. Two cannon, numbers N69 and N71 in the Musée de l'Armée, are clearly of this earlier form, while a third, W578, in the Germanisches Museum, is of a completely different form. Instead of being parallel sided from rear to front – albeit with changes in outer diameter – it has the long tapered form characteristic of barrels up to the nineteenth century.

To understand these changes one must look first in detail at the earlier pieces. Typical of these are N58, dated 1478, and N500, dated 1487, both of the Musée de l'Armée. Of crucial importance is the way that these were made. Just how copper-alloy cannon were cast in the fifteenth century is not known – there are no treatises, no illustrations and, as far as is known, no descriptions of how it was accomplished. Later on, from the mid to late sixteenth century, cannon were cast in moulds formed of baked clay set vertically with the cannon's muzzle up. The technique was to make an exact model of the cannon required over which a one-piece mould was formed. The model was then broken up and removed, leaving a hollow mould which was set vertically in a pit in front of a furnace. A bar or core, to form the bore of the finished cannon, was secured in position within the mould. This core was held in place by two frames usually made of iron. The upper one was set within the gun head and was removed when that was sawn off. The lower one was set near the base ring of the barrel, its position decided by the gunfounder. Molten bronze was then poured into the mould from the furnace. Crucially, the mould was made longer than was necessary. This was important as molten metal poured into a mould will contain a small quantity of undesirable impurities, as well as trapped air. These tend to accumulate in the later stages of the pouring and most end up floating on top of the molten mass of metal. By extending the mould these impurities and the trapped air were largely removed by cutting off this extension, called, in later sources, the gun head. The result was a finished casting, a cannon, in which the breech, the part which had to contain the full force of the exploding gunpowder charge, was the best casting, free from flaws, cracks and holes. This is doubly important for the performance of the gun as it is at tiny cracks and holes that castings start to break up. In essence, it was casting guns in this way that enabled the late medieval gunfounder to produce cannon which were able to withstand the force of the explosion of the gunpowder safely.[43]

This change was crucial to the development of artillery, producing the best possible barrel for the containment of the gunpowder explosion and allowing the use of larger charges of powder. It also meant that the thickness of the barrel could be reduced. Equally important, at this time, it was realised that the barrel only needed to be thick where the explosion of the gunpowder took place – in the rear portion of the barrel. The rest of the barrel could be made much thinner.

But when did gunfounders discover that this was the best way to make cannon? Close inspection of the earlier Rhodes pieces, particularly N78 and N500, clearly show that they were made in the muzzle-down technique. Around the rear, the breech, of each the metal is very pitted and full of holes and cavities. Both also have an inscription around their muzzle faces in relief, that is cast into the metal, and the only way that this could have been achieved was to have that part of the cannon at the bottom of the casting. So we can see that Western European gunfounders were using this technique at least until 1487. However, by 1507 barrels were cast muzzle up, as shown by the guns N69 and N71 of the Musée de l'Armée and W578 of the Germanisches Museum. As it is likely that the two techniques overlapped and that there was no sudden and dramatic change – as is shown by the two pieces cast for Grand Master d'Aubusson, catalogue number 4 dated to 1476–89 and number 9 dated to 1489–1503, as well as two very fine pieces that were also clearly cast muzzle up and dated to 1488 in Neuchatel, Switzerland – a date of around 1500 can be advanced as to when the muzzle-up casting technique had become the norm.

Having looked at the change in the design of the cannon barrel in the later fifteenth century, it is also necessary to examine what was also happening to gunpowder. Unfortunately, though the developments in cannon are relatively easy to see, the changes in gunpowder technology are far less obvious and more difficult to study. It is believed that the last significant development in making gunpowder was the process called corning – making the powder into uniform-size pellets, or corns. Earlier gunpowder makers produced a type of gunpowder called *knollenpulver* – powder formed into very large cakes which were then broken down into smaller pieces before use. Corning is different – once the powder had been produced it was wetted, usually with alcohol (brandy works very well), and then forced through a sieve to make grains of gunpowder of a uniform size, the same size as the holes in the sieve; *knollenpulver* was not a uniform size.[44]

When did this process become the standard way to make gunpowder and what difference did it make? Neither question is easy to answer. Although corning was definitely being carried out by the early sixteenth century,[45] it was developed much earlier than that. However, the evidence is confusing, with only rare direct references to corning. One of the earliest of these comes from the accounts of the dukes of Burgundy in 1420–21.[46] Perhaps the best evidence comes from the cannon themselves – by the late fifteenth century cannon technology had developed to be able to contain larger charges of this corned powder.

The usual reply to the second question – what difference did it make – is that corned powder is stronger than other forms of gunpowder. Sources state, for example, that is was twice as strong or 'two pounds of pressed and formed powder (*Knollenpulver*) develops more power than three pounds of meal powder'.[47] Recent work suggests, however, that this is an oversimplification and that it is less easy to quantify the difference in performance corned powder made. Corned powder obviously did make a difference, though, and was certainly more predictable and easier to ignite than older forms of powder.[48]

Gunpowder is an extremely complex material, its explosive properties depending on a set of interconnected variables, making it very difficult to understand even today. This is demonstrated by a conundrum. When the amount of powder used to fire cannon is studied something rather strange can be seen – much less powder per kilogram of ball weight was used in the earlier period, around 1450, than later. For example, Mons Meg, dating to 1449, fired a stone ball of about 150kg and used about 52kg of powder, which means that every kilogram of ball needed about 350g of powder – a ratio of roughly 3 to 1. A culverin, firing an 8kg ball, in 1580 needed some 6.5kg of powder – roughly 800g of powder were used for every kilogram of ball. In the early seventeenth century the amount of powder per kilogram of ball ranged from about 650g to 1kg – the weight of powder could be the same as the weight of the ball. If the later gunpowder was stronger, then why use more?

The answer goes a long way to explaining why cannon became so successful: guns were able to take a great deal more powder and they were able to withstand the enormous force of the greater explosion. This meant that they could achieve much higher muzzle velocities, which meant greater power and better range – no wonder they became so dominant on the battlefield, at sea and for sieges. This was possible because of the changes to cannon barrels in the 1480s: better castings and a more efficient design meant that they could contain this more powerful explosive.

It was this ability to increase the explosive power of cannon and increase the velocity of the ball fired that was crucial. To explain this, what happens when a projectile hits its target needs to be understood. Basically, the amount of damage done is relative to the energy that the ball has at the moment of impact. This energy, called the kinetic energy, can be calculated from the formula $E = \frac{1}{2}mv^2$, where E is the energy, m the mass (or weight) of the ball and v its velocity. What this tells us is that the energy is proportional to the square of the velocity – increasing it just a little increases the energy quite a bit more. As an example, if the impact velocity of a cannonball increases from 200 to 250m per second, an increase of just 25 per cent, the energy of the ball as it hits the wall increases by 64 per cent. It is obvious then that the best cannon will be one that fires the fastest cannonball.[49]

This leads to the next significant development in artillery, the change from using stone to cast-iron shot. Although it is clear that cast-iron shot were available from the early fifteenth century,[50] they were not universally adopted until almost the end of the century. For example, the accounts of the artillery of the dukes of Burgundy clearly show that it was not until the 1470s that cast-iron ammunition became common in the Burgundian artillery.[51] This change had two important consequences. The first was the fact that cast iron is some three times heavier for balls of the same size than stone shot. Smaller bore cannon could fire the same weight of shot and were lighter and easier to handle. Second, cast-iron ammunition could be made more uniform in size than stone balls, which were cut by hand. Once the mould for cast-iron shot had been made it could be used over and over again, turning out balls of regular size and weight with the result that cannon could be more accurate.[52]

There are two further areas of artillery that should also be considered. The first is the mounts and carriages on which the barrel was mounted and the second is the men who fired the cannon, gunners and their assistants. Over the period from about 1480 to 1522, carriages and mounts for cannon changed fundamentally, changing from complex and relatively immobile to simple and highly mobile. That they went through these changes in response to the developments in gun barrels is unmistakeable. When guns were large and heavy, firing large-diameter stone balls, they were moved around on large four-wheeled carts, requiring machines, *engin*, *gynne* or *gin*, to take them on and off these carts, and were set up in large solid frameworks on the ground.[53] Smaller pieces could and would have been moved on their own wheeled mounts, but were more for anti-personnel use than for battering down walls. With the developments in gun barrels that took place in the 1470s, '80s and '90s, carriages had to change as well.

The first mobile carriages for large pieces of artillery were similar to those of smaller pieces. The barrel was set into a trough formed in a large baulk of timber which extended backwards and angled downwards. A single axle was fitted beneath and the whole mounted on two large-diameter wheels. A removable second set of wheels could also be fitted to the end of the carriage. The way that the barrel was set into a trough of wood meant that its aim could not be easily changed except by raising or lowering the entire carriage. Some elaborate ways to effect elevation were also tried, for example, adding a second piece of wood underneath that carrying the barrel which was hinged so that the upper piece could be raised and lowered. Although this was probably not a bad solution, it was complex and still probably very heavy – especially for the larger pieces of artillery.

Changes to cannon barrels that occurred around 1500, resulting in reductions in their size and weight, seem to have altered the carriages too. Unfortunately, the details of these developments are not at all clear as there have been no thorough, in-depth studies of carriages and mounts for artillery that cover this period. However, the result, developed around the end of the fifteenth century, is known today as the trail carriage. This consisted of two long, angled sidepieces of wood held together by wooden crosspieces or transoms and supported on large-diameter wheels fixed to a transverse axle. What made the trail carriage so innovative was the way in which the barrel was secured. In the tops of the two sidepieces were semi-circular cut-outs into which the trunnions of the barrel fitted. The trunnions, set just behind the centre of balance of the barrel, supported the barrel, and their position was carefully worked out so that there was more weight behind than in front of them. Apart from a transom on which the rear of the barrel rested, no other support was needed. Elevation was effected by adding or removing blocks, quoins, between the transom and the breech of the barrel. The trail carriage enabled artillery to be more mobile and provided a stable platform from which to fire. Once the trail carriage was developed it remained the basic artillery mount on land for the next three and a half centuries.[54]

Just when the fully developed trail carriage first appeared is unclear but some time around 1500 seems most probable. Of course, the changes in artillery barrel design and the changes in carriages went hand in glove – as the long, tapered barrel design was being worked out, the carriage on which to mount it was also being developed.

Finally, the men who cast, operated and fired the artillery in this period must be discussed. Again, this is an area where too little is known. Other than a few of the names of cannon founders, and in one or two cases something of their background, little is known of their working practices, production methods or even how much they produced. Some names of cannon founders, such as Jorg Endorfer and Alberghetti, and where they worked is known, but nothing further. Of the gunners themselves there is very little, apart from scraps of information gleaned from the records. For example, other than the fact that Master George, the traitor of the 1480 siege, was a gunner and engineer, what else he did is not known. And in 1493, 'after long discussion on the practice of heavy artillery in the defence of the city of Rhodes and the attack of the enemy', it was decided to engage a certain Pierre de la Mote, 'a gunner of renown'.[55] Presumably the Hospitallers hoped that Pierre could teach them new methods of gunnery. Intriguingly, a Patrick de la Mote, likely the same person, had been appointed as a gunner and founder to the English king, Richard III, in 1484, and was reconfirmed in his post in 1485 by Henry VII.[56] The skills of a good gunner were obviously rare and

Rhodes Besieged

sought after all over Europe. However, just who laid and fired the guns on the walls of Rhodes or where and how they were trained is unknown.

It is clear then that the period from about 1480 to 1522 saw probably the most important changes in the development of artillery since the introduction of gunpowder artillery at the beginning of the fourteenth century. Though this seems an extravagant claim, it is worth remembering that the changes made in this period were those that were to define artillery for the next three and a half centuries. The long, thin shape of the cannon barrel, tapered from rear to front, corned gunpowder, cast-iron ammunition and the trail carriage were all largely developed in the last twenty years of the fifteenth century – after that changes were, by and large, minimal and confined mostly to refinements. It is also crucial to realise that these changes did not take place rapidly, nor were they universally and quickly taken up. In the late fifteenth century change and its adoption was much slower to take effect – most developments took many years or even decades to become widespread. This is especially true in the field of artillery. Gun barrels were not only expensive in terms of raw materials, manpower and money terms, they lasted a long time. Few, if any, rulers in late medieval Europe could or would be able to renew their artillery quickly. All would rely on the gradual replacement of guns as they wore out, were damaged or lost. Older guns would be used alongside pieces of the most up-to-date type. This is apparent in both of the sieges of Rhodes. In 1522 the Knights were still using guns that had been cast before the first siege alongside ones that had been made just the year before.

Although there are a large number of cannon belonging to the Hospitallers, there is nothing comparable for the artillery used by the Turks. Yet, there is no reason to believe that their artillery was vastly different. While there are no extant examples that are dated from the period between the two sieges, there are a number of guns that date to the 1520s and 1530s. These show that, like the artillery of the Hospitallers, they were long, tapered pieces firing cast-iron shot. These include two pieces in the collections of the Royal Armouries, Leeds, and a further example in the Museum of Artillery in Woolwich. The earliest (XIX.243), dated 1524 and just two years after the second siege of Rhodes, has been shortened by the removal of the end of the muzzle but is still 485cm long with a bore of 19cm. Outwardly it is sixteen-sided with a flat cascable. The second (XIX.94), dated 1530–31, is similar, though circular in cross section. Like that of the 1524 example, the barrel tapers evenly from back to front and has a flat cascable. It is 523cm long with a bore of 23cm. The third piece (II.191), dated 1530, almost identical to the second in shape, is 568cm long with a bore of 25cm.[57]

Changes and improvements in cannon design and gunpowder, and the introduction of cast-iron ammunition around 1480 resulted in the greater destructive power of artillery and, in turn, initiated developments in the construction of fortifications to contain the new power unleashed against them. The changes to the fortifications of Rhodes after 1480 indicate how these developments were worked out in the fast-changing environment where the threat from the Turks was very real. The existing thin walls became even more vulnerable – not only were guns more powerful, but they could be fired more often, thus making it more difficult to effect repairs. With the new forms of artillery, attackers were increasingly able to create breaches in and demolish walls – especially the older, thinner ones.

The final manifestation of these changes was the development of effective fortifications consisting of mutually supportive strong points called 'bastions'.[58] However, the bastion did not appear overnight. It took decades for the ideas to be developed and the best solutions found. A detailed study of the changes to the defences of the city of Rhodes after the 1480 siege allows the prevalent ideas for countering the new threat to be seen.

Unfortunately, there is no detailed picture of the state of the fortifications immediately after the siege, but it is clear that d'Aubusson initiated a vast programme of refortification and building work that would totally transform the walls of the city. The changes in the fortifications from 1480 to his death in 1503 centred on keeping the Turks further away from the walls and gates while simultaneously protecting them from a sustained artillery barrage. His most important contribution was to increase greatly the width of the moat surrounding the landward side of the city and to create *tenailles*, defences in front of the walls and called *terrepleins* by contemporaries, made of solid earth and therefore able to provide an excellent defence against gunpowder-propelled projectiles.[59] D'Aubusson does not, however, appear to have increased the thickness or the height of the walls.[60]

It is impossible to know the exact chronology of d'Aubusson's works, at least before he became cardinal of Asia in 1489 and the cardinal's hat was added to his customary arms. Thus in the following discussion the changes made to the city will be described clockwise from east to the west.

From the Caoursin illuminations, the Epernay painting and narrative descriptions of the destruction following the siege, the wall to the east, usually described as that of the Jewish Quarter, was very badly damaged. In many places the walls had been breached and largely destroyed. For d'Aubusson, the repair of this stretch was clearly a high priority, but there is no surviving evidence of when the wall was repaired. The northern stretch of walls seems to have been returned to its previous condition: a thin, high wall crowned by crenellations, and were not further fortified or strengthened. However, as a thanksgiving for the victory, d'Aubusson built the large church, Our Lady of Victory, on the internal north-east corner, adding its eastern wall to the fortifications there.[61]

The southern stretch of the eastern wall was also restored to its original size and thickness, but here d'Aubusson added a large *tenaille* to further protect the wall from attack. Today, this construction is in three pieces to accommodate modern roadways, though originally they were all joined together to form one structure. The northern section is a long, narrow rectangle work, running in a north–south parallel to the wall between it and the sea. Unlike d'Aubusson's other *tenailles*, it appears to have been built from the ground as an earthwork faced by stone blocks.[62] A spur-shaped extension at its southern end extends to the south-east with wide artillery embrasures around its rim, providing fire along the moat and out to sea. The southern two sections originally formed a single large triangular work turning from the northern section south-west to protect the city wall. This *tenaille* was created by digging out around it, leaving the earth and rock in place – the inner face was likely the original counterscarp of the moat which existed in 1480. Subsequently the *tenaille* was faced in stone and given a parapet and embrasures around its outside rim. The Grand Master then had the counterscarp faced with stone. In this way d'Aubusson accomplished two things: by greatly widening the moat, from some 10 to between 50 and 70m, the enemy was kept further away from the walls; and the *tenaille* protected the original city wall by preventing an enemy from hitting it, especially at its base, where the greatest damage could be done.[63]

D'Aubusson widened the moat from that *tenaille* to the Tower of St John, as shown by three shields bearing his arms on the counterscarp; it now measures between 30 and 50m in width. Interestingly, on this stretch of fortifications no *tenaille* was created to protect the wall, although he did add a large artillery outerwork or gallery to the existing square interval tower, which today is to the west of the Tower of Italy.[64] Why d'Aubusson did not form a *tenaille* here is unknown.

In 1480 St John's Gate was protected by a square tower and spur-shaped bulwark (or boulevard), with the entrance to the city via a bridge over the moat which was roughly 10m wide. Although it appears to have mostly escaped damage in the siege, d'Aubusson added significantly to its defences. As at the south-east corner, he increased the width of the moat to a distance of around 75m, leaving an arc-shaped *tenaille* around the gate. Again, the counterscarp of the 1480 moat formed the inner face of the *tenaille*. The new gate was placed on the outside of the *tenaille* and, one assumes, was reached by a wooden bridge that could be destroyed if the city was attacked. Because the *tenailles* were formed by leaving large blocks of earth and rock standing which were then faced with stone, gunports could not be made in them at low level. Here perhaps the solutions that the Hospitallers put in place after 1480 created further problems – they were not able to provide defence at moat level. They were not creating early bastions which provided covering fire along walls as some have suggested.[65] Instead, d'Aubusson's solution was to create separate 'firing galleries' either in the moat or at low level, which could provide the necessary protection.[66] One, on the east side of St John's Gate, consists of a series of tiered defences, part of the city walls, while the other, on the west, is a small building incorporating gunports which enfiladed the moat towards the Tower of the Virgin, and though undated was probably also built by him.

From St John's Gate to the Tower of the Virgin d'Aubusson created his largest *tenaille*, 280m in length, parallel to and covering almost the entire length of the wall. The excavation to create the *tenaille* widened the moat to between 60 and 70m.

The Tower of the Virgin guarded an entry into the city known as the St Athanasios' Gate. Here again, d'Aubusson added a *tenaille* to encircle the earlier tower, like that at St John's Gate, and is dated securely by inscription to 1487. To this a firing gallery similar to that on the east side of St John's Gate was also added to provide covering fire down the moat on both sides of the long *tenaille*. A single-storey firing gallery was built on the west of the *tenaille* to enable the defenders to fire along the moat westwards. As there is no coat of arms on this latter structure it cannot be determined who was responsible for its construction, although it is highly probable that it was d'Aubusson. The creation of the *tenaille* and the widening of the moat increased its width from about 10 to around 50m.

The wall from the Tower of the Virgin to the Tower of Spain is protected by a long, triangular-shaped *tenaille*, once more cut from the previous glacis. The shape of the *tenaille* was determined by the earlier moat, the original counterscarp forming its inner face which here bears the coat of arms of Grand Master Orsini. The distance between the city wall and the new counterscarp was increased to almost 60m.

The Tower of Spain, at the end of the *tenaille* to the north-west, was built by d'Aubusson after 1489; his arms adorn one wall and bear the cardinal's hat, which he received in that year. Unusually, the bulwark which he created around an earlier small tower is not a *tenaille*, but a structure built from the ground up. As he also widened the moat here, as almost everywhere else, he must have first excavated the moat completely before building it. Why did d'Aubusson not use the same method here as before – creating a *tenaille* from the original glacis and counterscarp? Perhaps it was the difficulty in providing fire along the moat that the *tenailles* presented. Elsewhere the answer had been to construct firing galleries to either side of the *tenaille*. Is it possible that these were thought to be too weak and difficult to man? By building the Tower of Spain from the ground up, gunports could be incorporated at low level. These could be manned more easily from the city as the whole structure provided a more secure position for the defenders – it was, in fact, a more effective way to defend the moat. It is interesting to note that two of d'Aubusson's later defences, this and St George's Tower, were built in this way. The Tower of Spain has twelve gunports at the base which could provide enfilading fire down both sides and across the moat.

The moat has been widened between the towers of Spain and St George, probably by d'Aubusson, although none of his coats of arms are to be found on the counterscarp. Prior to 1496 the Tower of St George consisted of a small square tower to which had been added a spur-shaped bulwark very like that at the Gate of the Virgin. In that year d'Aubusson completely transformed it, building a vast structure around the older defences. As at the Tower of Spain, the Tower of St George was built completely from masonry and was not a *tenaille* cut out of the older counterscarp. Also like the Tower of Spain, St George's lower levels had gunports and were integrated into the city walls. For its size it has very few positions from which guns could be fired at low level – just seven on its south side, two on the north and none at all facing the counterscarp.

B.J.St.J. O'Neil has suggested that the Tower of St George was an early form of bastion, concluding that d'Aubusson was one of the originators of this anti-gunpowder fortification.[67] There is no doubt that it is a forward artillery platform designed to enable the Hospitallers to bring a very large barrage to bear on an enemy attacking from the moat and on either side of or across from the tower. It was also one of the few places in the fortifications of Rhodes at this time that could take large-calibre gunpowder weapons, as witnessed by the numerous artillery platforms which remain in place on its top. But was this the sole purpose of this extraordinary, very expensive fortification? It must be.[68]

D'Aubusson probably also increased the width of the moat north of St George's Tower to between 50 and 70m, although again his arms do not appear on the counterscarp before it turns to the east. This corner, the north-west of the city, was significantly changed by d'Aubusson, probably in response to the severe attacks on and destruction of the walls here.[69] As elsewhere, he widened the moat and left behind a mass of rock and earth. He also connected this to the previous walls, turning what had been a fortification which ran in sharp angles towards the east – and the Grand Master's Palace – and the north and then east again, to one which continues in a straight line all the way to the north-east corner and then turns east. He thus enclosed the older walls entirely behind this defensive structure. In effect, this was another *tenaille*, but one which became part of the city walls rather than remaining separate and in front of them.[70] This would remain a solid earth and stone structure until the rule of d'Amboise, when he penetrated the *tenaille* to make a gate, as will be discussed below.

Along the northern walls d'Aubusson also made some changes, including the widening of the moat, although not to the same width as elsewhere. However, the modern reconstruction of this area, including the 'fantastic' rebuilding of the Grand Master's Palace in the twentieth century, makes it difficult to fully understand his changes here. D'Aubusson's refortification plans also included two of the fortresses built on moles into the harbour. His coat of arms appearing on the south face of the Naillac mole probably indicated that he carried out repairs on the fortifications there. Fort St Nicholas was far more damaged, virtually destroyed on its western side by intensive Turkish gunfire from St Anthony's Church. The strategic importance of this fort and mole, proven by how much effort the Turks had expended trying to capture it during the siege, was not lost on d'Aubusson or the Knights Hospitaller. First, d'Aubusson rebuilt the central tower and its curtain wall to their original size and shape. Then he encased these in a massive outer bulwark: the western part extremely thick and solid, with embrasures for artillery; the eastern part, which could only be threatened from the sea, less thick with smaller embrasures.[71]

The costs of d'Aubusson's fortification programme, both in terms of materials and manpower, must have been extraordinary. Unfortunately, no detailed expense account has survived, although the numerous appeals for money from the Grand Master to the Christian powers in the West for the rebuilding of the walls of Rhodes, in anticipation of another Turkish attack, suggests that he was fully aware of how expensive the project would be.[72] That such an extensive rebuilding took place also indicates that the money and manpower was found and used.

The Uneasy Calm, 1480–1522

Peace with the Ottoman Turks was necessary during the reconstruction of the Rhodes' fortifications. However, neither Pierre d'Aubusson nor the Hospitaller Council stood against small-scale military activities against Ottoman lands or ships. Piracy was condoned, as were raids and even a small invasion or two. Even before Cem fell into their hands the Hospitallers had begun to raid Turkish, Arab and Egyptian vessels, while on 23 May 1481 the Order's Council discussed the invasion of Mytilene.[73]

That the raiding of Ottoman ships and lands would be considered acceptable activities by the Hospitallers, especially after they had barely survived a Turkish siege, seems strange to the modern historian. It is certainly difficult to understand what d'Aubusson was thinking when he not only allowed but encouraged it. Nor did the peace treaties of 1481 or 1482 put an end to this type of military activity, although it seems to have been significantly diminished on both sides, especially as the Hospitallers were able to trade freely in Ottoman and Egyptian ports.[74]

However, once the Knights Hospitaller had surrendered Cem to Alexander VI and especially after Cem's death, tensions began to increase. Accusations of Ottoman piracy were recorded in 1494, 1495, 1496, 1497 and 1500, while Hospitallers were also involved in numerous acts of piracy during those same years. Most of the Christian pirate ships carried the imprimatur of the Hospitaller Council and Grand Master (which promised 'safe-conduct'); some had official licences granted to them and some were actual Hospitaller vessels. All paid a portion of their booty to the Knights on Rhodes.[75]

By this time no one in Europe was more famous than the Knights Hospitaller and their Grand Master, Pierre d'Aubusson. They were Christianity's heroes; for a religion that was still smarting from the loss of the Holy Land in 1291 and the inability to hold back the Ottoman Turks at Nicopolis in 1396, Varna in 1444 and Constantinople in 1453, among other places, it was a very difficult period. Nobody accepted that Allah could be more powerful than Jesus, of course, but Christian propagandists were hard-pressed to come up with anything or anyone to hold up as an example of their religion's superiority over Islam. The valiant Hungarians who had been fighting the Ottoman Turks throughout the fifteenth century, the citizens in Belgrade who waged a tenacious defence against the siege of their city in 1456 and the Hospitallers' victory in 1480 were all held in high esteem in Western Europe.[76]

Pierre d'Aubusson and other Hospitallers took as much advantage of this popularity as possible. D'Aubusson himself travelled widely throughout Europe, visiting imperial, royal and princely courts. He was well known in Sicily, France and the Holy Roman Empire, and a frequent visitor to the Vatican. He was a favourite guest of Pope Innocent VIII, who in the consistory of 9 March 1489 created him cardinal deacon, awarding him the red hat and the deaconry of St Adriano two weeks later, on 23 March. He was named 'Legate *a latere*' to all Asia, a new responsibility which recognised not only d'Aubusson's geographical location as the furthest eastern prelate in Christianity, but also celebrated his effectiveness as a Christian warrior against the Ottomans. In 1495, Innocent's successor, Pope Alexander VI – who seems not to have liked d'Aubusson – named him Captain-General of all Christian forces fighting the Turks.[77]

From this time until his death d'Aubusson's speeches and letters took on more of a crusading rhetoric. He called openly for an attack on the Turks, who for so long had been at peace with the Hospitallers, as shown in a letter directed at the Papacy and royalty of Europe on 17 July 1501:

> It is most imperative that His Holiness, His Royal Majesty [the King of France] and the other Christian sovereigns encourage and persuade the most serene king of Hungary to wage war manfully against the Turks and to persist in it with constancy. For the Hungarian people are bellicose by nature, and thanks to their proximity to the Turks and their expertise in fighting them, they can do a good deal to hold the Turk's attention, causing him to divert large numbers of troops to resist them. There is even a hope that the tyrant himself [the Sultan] will take the field against them. That would give the fleet an opening and a splendid chance to achieve great things to the honour of the Christian name.[78]

Later that year, perhaps to set an example for those princes he was calling to crusade, d'Aubusson led his Hospitallers and a mob of other volunteers – it is incorrect to describe them as an army – in an attack of the island of Lesbos and a siege of its capital, Mytilene.[79] It was a miserable failure. Dissension among the motley group, who could not perform even the most minor of tactical manoeuvres, meant that d'Aubusson was not able to repeat his earlier success and in only a few days the siege failed.

From then on, for the last two years of d'Aubusson's life, the Grand Master, cardinal of Asia and Captain-General of the Christian forces, could do little more than expound at great length about the Ottomans. He called for and planned crusades, questioned the expediency of attacking and occupying Eastern Mediterranean islands when the Sultan's army was amassed on the Hungarian border and his navy in the Sea of Marmara, and refused to meet with Ottoman ambassadors who wanted to make peace. On Rhodes he pressed for greater discipline among his Knights and he fought for improved conditions for the inhabitants of the city. That is except for the Jews. In what may be called the most hypocritical move of d'Aubusson's career, and at the very end of his life, on 9 January 1503 he banished them from the city unless they would convert to Christianity,[80] casting out the very people who had stood by him so zealously in the 1480 siege when their section of the city had been overrun by the Turkish soldiers who had breached the walls. In an effort to improve the Christian 'spirituality' of Rhodes the Grand Master had seemingly forgotten the very reason for his success, the people. He died on 30 June 1503 and was buried in a bronze mausoleum which he had constructed in the Church of St John, next to the Grand Master's Palace.[81] It was a monument built to last the centuries, but it did not last another generation, as the attack which d'Aubusson had so long anticipated finally came in 1522. In the wake of it he was disinterred twice: once when his body was borne around the town during the siege as a means of exciting the citizenry to repeat what had taken place in 1480, and a second time, after they had failed, when the Ottoman conqueror, Suleyman, removed his corpse from its tomb and disposed of it.

Bāyezīd II remained on the Ottoman throne for almost another decade after the death of Pierre d'Aubusson. Most modern historians describe him as a peaceful ruler. In fact, he was not peaceful, but he was less militarily successful than other fourteenth-, fifteenth- and sixteenth-century Turkish rulers.

One thing that does differentiate him from other sultans, however, is how he treated his half-brother, Cem. Despite Cem's continual desire to unseat Bāyezīd from the throne, he was not hunted down and slain. On the contrary, as already seen, his comfortable maintenance – in far better conditions than most of his hosts – was always assured by the Ottoman crown. While it is true that Bāyezīd kept him under fairly constant surveillance, by known staff and hidden spies, and must have known of his recurrent talk of leading an army to unseat him,[82] the Sultan basically left Cem alone. Cem was a prisoner to be certain, but it was an imprisonment for which most contemporaries would have willingly surrendered their freedom.

Does this mean that Bāyezīd loved his brother and would have done anything to preserve his life, or would his death have elevated Cem to a sufficient height that his memory – and the numbers of others willing to profit from it – would have fomented rebellion sufficient to bring the Sultan down? It will never be known. One thing is certain, Bāyezīd never attempted to dispose of Cem, and while his brother lived, as promised, he never attacked those who protected him.

When Bāyezīd came to the throne he was immediately confronted not only with the loss to the Hospitallers in Rhodes, but also with the loss of Otranto in southern Italy. With hindsight, the conquest of Otranto was either the boldest or the most stupid campaign ever waged by the Ottoman Turks. In the midst of their siege of Rhodes and seemingly in a truce with the rest of Christianity, on 28 July 1480 a sizeable Ottoman fleet sailed to the coast of Apulia and unloaded a large army equipped with a large number of gunpowder weapons to attack a city of relatively little importance, Otranto. After one day the city fell and on 11 August so too did its castle. The depredations that followed became legendary and, no doubt, grew in their retelling. The French chronicler Thomas Basin's account is but one example:

There was a bishop of irreproachable conduct and old age. These savage barbarians (more like dogs than humans, one might say) subjected this man to a most horrible death, without consideration of his dignity or his age, without any pity or fear of God whatsoever. They impaled his body from his groin all the way to his head so that his entrails were completely pushed out of the body. And they exacted the worst violences on many women and virgins of the town, and then they humiliated them by making them wear very short garments to cover their genitalia.[83]

Rhodes Besieged

All those who would not convert to Islam were beheaded.

Using Otranto as a base for further raids on Italy, the Turks then attacked Lecce, Taranto and Brindisi in the months that followed. But logistical support and reinforcements at such a distance from home were difficult to provide and it became apparent by the winter that the Ottomans would be hard-pressed to hang on to their Italian beachhead. A Christian army, led by Ferrante, King of Sicily, began a relieving siege in May 1481 and in September the city was recovered, and its garrison massacred in retaliation.[84]

By this time Mehmed II was dead and Bāyezīd was the Ottoman Sultan. Otranto was thus lost during his reign and he has come under criticism by some historians for his inaction in trying to relieve his soldiers there, or failing to have tried to bargain for their release.[85] However, in September 1481 Bāyezīd's concerns were closer to home, and it was not until Cem was securely out of reach that he planned new campaigns. The first of these was against Moldavia where, in 1484, he led an army and captured the Black Sea ports of Akkerman and Kilia.[86] The second was directed against the Mamluks of Egypt, who had long been a bane to the Ottoman control of the Eastern Mediterranean, certainly exercising far more influence and sponsoring much more piracy than the Hospitallers in the region. Yearly, between 1485 and 1491, Turkish armies attacked Egypt, although they gained few victories and little benefit.[87] Egypt remained out of his grasp. For his third campaign, Bāyezīd once more turned towards Europe, waging war against Venice from 1499 to 1503. As expected, most of this conflict was fought at sea, with the Ottoman navy showing that it could compete with the renowned Venetian fleets for the first time. At the Battle of Zonchio, fought over four days in August 1499 (12, 20, 22 and 25), Turkish ships outnumbered Venetian ones, Turkish shipboard guns outperformed Venetian guns – including registering what was perhaps the first sinking of a ship by shipboard gunfire – and the Turkish admiral, Kemel Reis, out-manoeuvred the Venetian admiral (and later Doge) Antonio Grimani.[88]

Zonchio was not a decisive naval defeat for Venice, however, and in December 1499 a Venetian fleet attacked their former colony of Lepanto, which had been lost to the Ottoman Turks at the time of Zonchio. Lepanto was retaken, only to be lost again the following February. Once more in August 1500 the Venetians tried to recover Lepanto – the colony deemed central to trade in the Eastern Mediterranean – but ran into the main Turkish fleet off the fortress of Modon and were defeated; as the Venetian fleet fled, the fortress was bombarded and the town captured.[89] Coron was also taken, with the result that two significant trading colonies had been lost.

During these months Turkish ships had also been raiding the coasts of the Adriatic Sea. The Turkish army followed its naval victories by securing the land, capturing and garrisoning its fortifications and towns. Pope Alexander VI called for a crusade to assist the Venetians against the Turks, but few responded positively. The war lasted until a tentative peace agreement took effect in 1503.

The Uneasy Calm, 1480–1522

Bāyezīd II reigned until 1512, but from 1503 until his death the Turks were unable to make any significant military progress in south-eastern Europe or the Middle East. Halil Inalcik suggests that his 'mild administration encouraged dissatisfied elements in Anatolia . . . to rebel against Ottoman authority', and it is difficult to argue against such a conclusion when the Turks were forced to drain off military revenues and frontier forces to face local uprisings and, more significantly, a Persian/Turcoman rebellion led by Shah Ismaîl Safavî.[90] Ultimately, faced by opposition from his son, Selim, and the Janissaries, on 24 April 1512 Bāyezīd resigned as Sultan and a month later, on 26 May, he died.[91]

In the eight years that Selim I ruled the Ottoman Empire after his father, he waged war. His armies pushed out from every frontier, but his primary concentration was on the Middle East. By his death he had increased Turkish land holdings by two-and-a-half times, from 2.5 million to 6.5 million square km. Undoubtedly his ruthlessness helped. At his ascension to the Sultanate Selim executed all his brothers and nephews, as well as any other relative who might potentially threaten his power. He dealt equally harshly with those who resisted his armies. In 1514 he decisively defeated Ismaîl's rebellion at the Battle of Chaldiran and by 1516–17 he had received the obeisance of all Ottoman potentates.[92]

By 1516 Selim was ready to wage war on the Mamluks, who for more than 250 years had controlled Egypt and Syria. His campaign was swift. By summer 1516 Aleppo surrendered and on 24 August he defeated a Mamluk army at the Battle of Marj Dâbik. Damascus and Jerusalem fell shortly thereafter. The following year, on 28 January 1517, an attack from both land and sea conquered Cairo, and soon after the rest of Egypt fell. On 17 July the holy cities of Mecca and Medina were surrendered to Selim.[93]

Sultan Selim I was present on all of these expeditions. Returning from Egypt to plan further conquests, no doubt to include Rhodes, he became sick and died on 22 September 1520. His successor was his son, Suleyman, later to be called 'the Magnificent' in the West – his Turkish nickname was 'the Lawgiver' – who immediately began to follow his father's bellicose example. It was not long before Suleyman surpassed him.

Suleyman's first two targets were the cities that had eluded his great-grandfather, Mehmed II: Belgrade and Rhodes. Belgrade had withstood two Ottoman sieges, in 1440 and 1456, the latter with a marvellous display of resistance from the townspeople and sundry poor peasant Crusaders brought there by the popular preacher and later saint, John of (Giovanni da) Capistrano.[94] To Suleyman this city, an island of Christian sovereignty in a sea of Ottoman military control – every bit as much as Rhodes was a real island in an Eastern Mediterranean Sea of Ottoman naval control – had to be conquered. Mustering a vast army which he led himself, the new Sultan marched on Belgrade. Attack upon attack was sent against the walls, more than twenty according to original sources, in between which the city was bombarded by the numerous Ottoman cannon. Finally, without hope of relief, on 28–29 August 1521 the citizens of Belgrade surrendered to Suleyman.[95] Rhodes was next.

Rhodes Besieged

As long as Cem was alive and in the custody of the Knights Hospitaller, the Ottoman Turks kept away from Rhodes, even during the period when he was with the Borgias and King Charles VIII in southern Italy. Nor did Cem's death in 1495 have an immediate effect on the peace between Rhodes and Turkey. But the Ottoman-Venetian War of 1499–1503 did. Although the Hospitallers attempted to remain outside this conflict – in fact, in 1499 Grand Master d'Aubusson personally warned the Doge Augustino Barbarigo that Venetian aggressiveness against the Turks would threaten Rhodes[96] – they were forced into it when Pope Alexander VI personally named Pierre d'Aubusson commander of the Christian fleet in February 1501. Undoubtedly this was meant to boost the confidence of a navy that had suffered substantial recent defeats, but, despite it being in their best interest to remain neutral in the war, the Hospitallers joined the fray with exuberance. On 24 April d'Aubusson, then 78 years old, accepted the position and added four Hospitaller galleys and four *barzes* to the fleet.[97]

The Knights also prepared for an attack on Rhodes, anticipating that the Ottomans would use the Hospitallers' participation in the Venetian-Ottoman War as justification once again to besiege the city. Six days after accepting Alexander's request, d'Aubusson wrote to the Pope:

> ...the Turk himself was getting ready a huge fleet of about three hundred sail to lay siege to the city of Rhodes where he was expected to arrive sometime in May; [d'Aubusson] suspected that the siege would be a long one, because the Turk was coming in person to the nearby province of Lycia, where vast preparations were being made of all things essential to a siege.[98]

The answer came with the arrival in early July of a Franco-Venetian fleet commanded by the famous warrior Philippe de Cleves et la Marck, Lord of Ravenstein. His intention was to attack the city of Mytilene, and he wanted to have Hospitaller naval assistance which d'Aubusson granted him. The siege of Mytilene began on 17 October 1501 and lasted until July 1502, when an Ottoman Turkish fleet, led by their capable admiral, Kemel Reis, relieved the town.[99] Distracted by this conflict, and the pursuit of peace by the Venetians after it had failed, Bāyezīd II let whatever plans he had for invading Rhodes drop.

On 30 June 1503, at age 80, Pierre d'Aubusson, fortieth Grand Master of the Hospitallers (for twenty-seven years), cardinal of Asia *a latere* (for fourteen years), commander of the Christian fleet, builder and rebuilder of the fortifications of Rhodes, and victor of the siege of 1480, died. He was buried in full armour, cardinal robes and hat, his Grand Master's baton, spurs and his personal coat of arms and that of the Order, in the Church of St John the Baptist near the Grand Master's Palace.[100] His body would disappear sometime after Suleyman's victory, the mausoleum undoubtedly melted down for its bronze. Neither are recorded to be still in the church in 1856, when it was destroyed by an explosion of gunpowder stored inside.

D'Aubusson's successor was Emery d'Amboise, who was then serving the Order as Grand Prior of the *Langue* of France. He was Grand Master until 1512. Interestingly, as soon as the change in leadership was made the Hospitallers decided to announce it to the Ottomans in a letter addressed to Sultan Bāyezīd II. Nicolas Vatin asserts that this should not be seen as a gesture of defiance, however. Instead, by this the Knights 'had made the choice to renew a more conciliatory diplomacy'.[101] This has astonished some historians as it had only been in August 1503 that sixteen Ottoman galleys raided the coast of Rhodes and were chased off by Hospitaller ships; eight Turkish vessels were sunk and two captured, with the Knights losing one galley.[102] But maybe the Hospitallers felt that it was more prudent to push for peace than to wage war. If nothing else, peace would give them a chance to improve their defences.

Following the changes made in the walls by his predecessor, d'Amboise does not seem to have done much. The most impressive construction he was responsible for was cutting an opening through the north-west *tenaille* to allow for entry into the city from that direction. Exactly why this was done cannot be determined from the sources, although the closing of the gate where the Tower of St George had been built by d'Aubusson was no doubt an issue.[103] The gate, named after d'Amboise, has two semi-circular towers to defend it and is dated by his arms to 1512.[104]

The previous year, again dated by his arms, Grand Master d'Amboise had also constructed a battery on the northern side of the same *tenaille*, now called the Battery of the Olives. This complex two-storey structure contains eleven gunports facing north and north-east along the moat. Only one gunport faces north-west, but others may have been obscured by the *caponier* later built by Carretto.[105]

D'Amboise's coats of arms also appear on three places to the south-east of the city, near where the Tower of Italy now stands. One on the counterscarp probably indicates nothing more than repairs carried out, while the other two, on the back of the wall inside Rhodes, dated 1506 and 1507 respectively, may indicate nothing more than further repairs to this stretch of the walls, but their proximity to each other is curious.

The Turkish response to the Hospitaller peace overtures was positive and in 1504 Bāyezīd sent an ambassador, Korkud Çelebi, to Rhodes to negotiate a truce, to which the Knights quickly agreed. Both sides would respect the other's trade and not threaten their lands or people. Surprisingly, this peace held for many years, although at times it seemed on the brink of collapse. In summer 1506, for example, a Turkish fleet landed men and artillery on the island of Lerro seemingly to besiege the Hospitaller castle there, although nothing seems to have come of the attack.[106] Also in 1507 d'Amboise summoned the Order's fleet on a couple of occasions to face what he perceived as an Ottoman threat to Rhodes, but which did not materialise.[107] That the Hospitallers remained nervous can be seen in a letter written on 10 October 1510 by d'Amboise to Fra Louis de Solerio, chaplain in the *langue* of Provence, which asks him to come to Rhodes 'to do service in the conventual Church of St John to defend Rhodes against the Ottomans'[108] and in the fact that d'Amboise continued to build and adapt the city's fortifications. But no attack on Rhodes came.

The reason for this may be simple: the Ottomans were as interested in peace as the Hospitallers at this time. In fact, when Selim I replaced his father as Sultan in April 1512 he sent word to Rhodes that he wished to continue the peace treaty of eight years before. Again the Hospitallers agreed, although this did not come officially into effect until 1 April 1514 due to the confusion following the deaths of d'Amboise on 22 November 1512 and his replacement, Gui de Blanchefort, on 24 November 1513 – en route to Rhodes from France.[109] Fabrizio del Carretto, who had ably commanded the defence of the Fort of St Nicholas in the 1480 siege, was elected as his replacement and served as Grand Master from 15 December 1513 until his death on 10 January 1521.

The main reason for peace, however, may have been the mutual hatred the Hospitallers and Ottomans had for the Mamluks.[110] This hatred, which had certainly continued since they had defeated the Crusaders at Acre in 1291, intensified for the Knights in 1500 when a ship carrying twenty-nine Hospitallers took refuge in Alexandria harbour after duelling with an Ottoman galleon. These men were accused of piracy – piracy that Hospitaller sources claimed was perpetrated by Ottoman vessels – and detained. Only after a number of letters were sent from Grand Master d'Aubusson to the Alexandrians were his Knights released.[111] In 1510 a fleet of Hospitaller ships, commanded by Philippe Villiers de l'Isle Adam (later to be Grand Master of the Order), destroyed a Mamluk fleet loading timber and other cargo at Ayas, capturing eleven *naves*, four galleys and a *galiot*.[112] This last incident happened just as Venice and the Papacy were attempting to make peace with Egypt, thwarting their efforts and creating discord among the Eastern Mediterranean Christian powers.[113] Other, smaller incidents between the Mamluks and Hospitallers occurred frequently during this time. Nor did a peace treaty in 1516 help much as the Knights seem to have been involved in piracy against Mamluk/Egyptian ships in 1517, 1518, 1519 and 1520, and Egyptian ships in 1520, 1521 and 1522.[114]

By 1517, though, the Mamluks had been defeated by the Ottomans, who had not been at all displeased with the Rhodes-Egypt conflict before this time. Selim I had seen this as a way to build his forces to contend against both. Perhaps it is only coincidence that just as the Hospitallers decided to change their military attitude against the Mamluks, and the signing of a peace treaty in 1516, the Turks launched their final assault on Egypt. By 1517, Cairo, Damietta and Alexandria (and soon the rest of Egypt) had fallen, the conquest of which was announced to the Knights by the victorious Ottoman fleet which visited Rhodes on its return to Turkey.[115]

Was this visit of Rhodes by the Ottoman fleet in 1517 a taunt?[116] Was Selim saying to the Hospitallers that they were next in line for conquest? Certainly the Knights seem to have thought so, although some historians believe that Selim I, like his father, Bāyezīd II, had no desire to encounter such a fighting force as the Hospitallers, who to a man seem to have been willing to lay down their lives to preserve their Eastern Mediterranean headquarters. The Ottomans were more interested in facing enemies who saw their occupation less in religious terms and hence were more likely to surrender to preserve their lives and livelihoods.[117] Other historians have suggested that the Hospitallers' fear was justified, that the Turks' targets for conquest were only to surround Rhodes more completely and thereby to cut off any potential relief when they did choose to attack the island.[118] Carretto, an experienced Knight who had lived in Rhodes for almost his entire life as a Hospitaller, was not ready to risk the security of the city on a bet that Selim would remain at peace with them.

So he too added to the fortifications constructed since the siege of 1480; in fact he added significantly to them, making more changes during his rule than any since the time of d'Aubusson. His major work was the widening of the walls around the land circuit from the Tower of Italy to the north-west corner. The Caoursin illuminations and the Epernay painting show the earlier wall-walk to be of traditional size for medieval castles and city walls, large enough to allow men to fight behind the parapet with bows and handguns, but certainly not large enough to accommodate cannon of any significant size. Today the Rhodes wall-walks measure from 5 to 10m and have wide embrasures and artillery platforms, wide enough for large cannon to be fired from them.

Construction of these widened walls would not have been easy or cheap. Houses and other dwellings close to the walls would have had to be demolished and cleared away, and the people compensated. By building to the inside of the walls he increased their thickness to their present size. At the same time, strangely, Carretto also raised the original city wall by some 3 to 4m, the former crenellations filled in as can be seen in several places. On top of the new, widened city wall he then created a *terreplein*,[119] which not only allowed the positioning of large cannon on top of the walls, but also enabled the easy movement of these cannon around them. From dates on inscriptions with Carretto's arms the widening of the walls was completed in some places by 1517.

Carretto was also responsible for the impressive round artillery tower on the southeast of the city, known as the Tower of Italy or the Tower of Carretto. It consists of an interior round tower which carries Carretto's arms and may either have been completely built or extensively repaired by him. Illustrations of the 1480 siege, Caoursin's illuminations and the Epernay painting, show the tower there to have been destroyed or badly damaged, although it is difficult to believe that nothing replaced it between then and Carretto's construction. Embrasures are placed on the top of this tower. Surrounding it is another round tower, shorter and apparently thicker, a bulwark or boulevard with gunports on the level of the moat and embrasures on the top. The entire Tower of Italy was finished between 1515 and 1517.

Carretto was also responsible for rebuilding two parts of the *tenaille* on the northwest corner of the city which had fallen down, apparently from the earthquake which shook the city in 1513. On both of these under Carretto's coats of arms is an inscription which translates as, 'Fra Fabrizio del Carretto rebuilt this collapsed tower from its foundations', one of which also contains the date 1514.[120] He also built a *caponier* on the same corner, extending out into the moat and containing gunports enabling the defenders to fire along the moat both to the south and north-east.[121]

Grand Master Carretto added a large number of cannon to the Knights' arsenal, gathered large amounts of victuals and war materiel, and petitioned Pope Leo X, a personal friend, and other Christian leaders for continued support.[122] He also allowed Hospitaller ships to participate in, or at least turned a blind eye toward, piracy. With the large number of Turkish and Mamluk accusations of Hospitaller piracy during Carretto's rule it is difficult to believe that their ships did not raid other ships in the Eastern Mediterranean, or that permission was not given from the highest level of the Hospitaller leadership to do so. Indeed, piracy was so frequent that Venice, France and Egypt asked the Pope to order the Knights to stop these activities.[123] And while one man's piracy may be another man's trade during the sixteenth century, one must wonder why the Knights would constantly provoke their potential attackers. Did they so badly need the goods they pillaged from their opponents' vessels that the risk of provocation was worth it, or did they somehow believe that such piracy would so cripple the Turks that they could not wage war against the Knights Hospitaller? We may never know the answer.

Neither Selim I nor Carretto would live to see the next siege of Rhodes. Selim died in November 1520 and Carretto in January 1521. Selim was succeeded as Sultan by Suleyman, Carretto as Grand Master by Philippe Villiers de l'Isle Adam, admiral of the Hospitaller ships at Ayas. Both were extremely capable military leaders. L'Isle Adam did his best to continue his predecessors' preparation for an Ottoman attack. He built or repaired some fortifications, his coats of arms evident in a few places. Among these was work on St George's Tower where his arms are found on the northern face; however, what he actually did there is unclear.[124] His coats of arms also appear on walls at the north-west corner, but again it is difficult to know exactly what work seen today was his.

As Grand Master, l'Isle Adam also added cannon, gunpowder and other arms for the defence of the city, and gathered provisions.[125] However, what had been only a potential threat to his four predecessors became the inevitable for l'Isle Adam and the Knights Hospitaller when Suleyman personally led the siege of Rhodes in June–December 1522.

For forty-two years the Knights of Rhodes had been an example to the rest of Christianity. In 1480 they had defeated the Ottoman Turks by a tenacious and effective defence of their city. And as the Turks had not returned in the intervening period it must have looked to those in Western Europe that the Hospitallers were invincible, that perhaps the Turks were so afraid of being defeated again that they had decided to forego another attack on the island. As Cardinal Giustinian wrote to the new Pope Leo X in 1513, hopeful of inciting a crusade against the Ottomans:

> The bravery and military experience of the Knights of Rhodes are not to be overlooked, for they are the inveterate foe of the Turks, and are accustomed to victory: If all the other Christian Princes, each in accordance with his strength, had shown themselves as tireless in their hostility to the Turks as the single island of Rhodes has done, that impious people would not have grown so strong![126]

In 1522 it all changed.

Notes

1. Dupuis, p. 102.
2. Dupuis, p. 102. On 11 October these reinforcements were allowed to return to Italy; undoubtedly mercenaries, they were too expensive to keep around when other defensive priorities were more pressing (see Setton, II:361). Other reinforcements arrived from the priory of St Gilles in January 1481 (National Library of Malta, Libri Bullarum, ff. 33v–34r).
3. National Library of Malta, Valletta, Section 5, Libri Bullarum, ff. 53v (liiib)–55v (lv b). D'Aubusson also reassigned some vacant commanderies on 13 October 1480 (National Library of Malta, Libri Bullarum. f. 62v [lxii b]).
4. Setton, II:361, citing National Library of Malta, Reg. 76, f. 35v.
5. Setton, II:361, citing National Library of Malta, Reg. 76, f. 36r.
6. National Library of Malta, Valletta, Section 5, Libri Bullarum, ff. 17v–18v.
7. Setton, II: 361–2, citing National Library of Malta, Reg. 76, f. 37.
8. National Library of Malta, Valletta, Section 5, Libri Bullarum, ff. 18v–19r.
9. National Library of Malta, Libri Bullarum, ff. 19r–v, 23r–24.
10. National Library of Malta, Libri Bullarum, f. 64v.
11. National Library of Malta, Libri Bullarum, f. 64r (lxiiii a).
12. National Library of Malta, Libri Bullarum, ff. 73v–74r (lxiiiib–lxxiiiia).
13. Vatin, p. 149, citing National Library of Malta, Reg. 76, ff. 62r–v.
14. Caoursin, p. 33. See also Setton, II:362–3.
15. Cem's name is spelled in several ways, with Cem and Djem appearing most frequently. In using the spelling Cem we are following the lead of Halil Inalcik and other prominent Turkish historians.
16. Inalcik, *The Ottoman Empire*, p. 30 and Setton, II:381.
17. Inalcik, *The Ottoman Empire*, pp. 30–1. D'Aubusson had corresponded with Cem before the siege, as evidenced by a letter preserved in the Hospitaller archives in Malta and dated 7 March 1478 (National Library of Malta, Libri Conciliorum, f. 182.
18. Caoursin, p. 37. See also Vatin, p. 151 and Vatin, 'The Hospitallers at Rhodes', p. 151.
19. Vatin, pp. 156–60.
20. Vatin, pp. 161–80 and Setton, II:384.
21. Vatin, pp. 153–5, which summarises his more lengthy study, *Sultan Djem: Un prince Ottoman dans l'Europe du XVe siècle d'après deux sources contemporaines: Vâki 'ât-I Sultân Cem / Oeuvres de Guillaume Caoursin* (Ankara: Société Turque d'Histoire, 1994). See also John Freely, *Jem Sultan: The Adventures of a Captive Turkish Prince in Renaissance Europe* (London: HarperPerennial, 2005).
22. Anthony Luttrell, 'Earthquakes in the Dodecanese, 1303–1513', in *Natural Disasters in the Ottoman Empire*, ed. E. Zachariadou (Rethymnon: Crete University Press, 1999), p. 149. There were also several aftershocks, although how many were felt in Rhodes cannot be determined from the original sources (Caoursin says seven but indicates that only the two major ones had consequences, pp. 27 8).
23. This inspired, in the 1496 printing of his *Opera*, a dramatic woodcut of the shaking of the city, with almost all of the towers breaking off and falling to the ground. As with most of the woodcuts accompanying this volume the accuracy is suspect.
24. Caoursin, p. 34. We are using Vatin's translation (Vatin, 'The Hospitallers of Rhodes', p. 151) with a few modifications. On the earthquakes see Nicolas Vatin, 'Les tremblements de terre à Rhodes en 1481 et leur historien, Guillaume Caoursin', in *Natural Disasters in the Ottoman Empire*, ed. E. Zachariadou (Rethymnon: Crete University Press, 1999), pp. 153–84.
25. Setton, II:363 n. 52, identifies two unpublished letters written by Pope Sixtus IV requesting added funds for the isle of Rhodes 'because of the earthquakes which shook it'.
26. Setton, II:385–6.
27. Vatin, pp. 220–7.
28. Both Ferrante, King of Sicily, and Matthias Corvinus, King of Hungary, had previously asked for Cem but had been turned down. Vatin, pp. 209–19, discusses this very question.
29. Brockman, p. 99. Neither Setton (II:386) nor Vatin, pp. 226–7, share Brockman's cynicism here.

30 A transcription of this can be found in Setton, II:386 n. 16.
31 Although Vatin (pp. 221–2) contends that the transfer of Cem to Rome did concern the Turks greatly.
32 Alexander also received a payment of 90,000 ducats from Bāyezīd for the care of his brother (Setton, II:442), which likely means that the Hospitallers received no further funds from the Turks for Cem once control of him was taken over by the Papacy.
33 Brockman, p. 99, quoting from Johann Burchard, *At the Court of the Borgia* (*Johanni Burckardi Liber Notarum ab anno MCCCCLXXXIII usque ad annum MDVI*), trans. Geoffrey Parker (London: Folio Society, 1963), p. 60.
34 Vatin, pp. 232–5.
35 Setton, II:481–2. The French accused the Borgias of Cem's poisoning, although Setton does not see why they would have done so. Brockman, p. 102, on the other hand, accepts the possibility.
36 Setton, II:410–6.
37 Setton, II:412.
38 Caoursin, p. 68 and Setton, II:409–10. One of these observers was the painter Andrea Mantegna.
39 Vatin, p. 182, quoting from a letter published in Paoli, II:430ff.
40 Vatin, pp. 181–2.
41 On changes in fortification construction to face increased use of gunpowder weapons in the fourteenth and fifteenth centuries, see Kelly DeVries, 'The Impact of Gunpowder Weaponry on Siege Warfare in the Hundred Years War', in *The Medieval City Under Siege*, ed. Ivy A. Corfis and Michael Wolfe (Woodbridge: The Boydell Press, 1995), pp. 227–44; Kelly DeVries, 'Facing the New Military Technology: Non-*Trace Italienne* Anti-Gunpowder Weaponry Defenses, 1350–1550', in *Heirs of Archimedes: Science and the Art of War through the Age of Enlightenment*, ed. Brett Steele and Tamara Dorland (Cambridge: The MIT Press, 2005), pp. 37–71; and Simon Pepper and Nicholas Adams, *Firearms and Fortifications: Military Architecture and Siege Warfare in Sixteenth-Century Siena* (Chicago: University of Chicago Press, 1986).
42 Where, when and how did gunfounders and engineers learn their trade? What were the mechanisms that drove change? How were innovation and developments communicated? Was there any form of experimentation? The answers to these questions are well outside the parameters of this book – in fact answering just one of them would probably need another book on its own – but they would greatly enhance our knowledge of the developments to gunpowder weapons at the end of the fifteenth century. What the study of the sieges of Rhodes can do is shine a powerful light in a period which was crucial in the development of artillery and fortifications.
43 John Francis Guilmartin, Jr., *Gunpowder and Galleys: Changing Technology and Mediterranean Warfare at Sea in the Sixteenth Century* (Cambridge: Cambridge University Press, 1974), pp. 284–91, has suggested that the muzzle-down method of manufacture was used by the Turks, while in Western Europe the muzzle-up technique was used. He goes on to suggest that this 'explains' deficiencies in the Turkish artillery. The evidence of Western European guns does not bear this out – both in Western Europe and Turkey the muzzle-down technique was being used.
44 For an excellent discussion of this see Bert S. Hall, *Weapons and Warfare in Renaissance Europe: Gunpowder, Technology, and Tactics* (Baltimore: The Johns Hopkins University Press, 1997), pp. 79–87.
45 Hall, p. 103.
46 Hall, p. 88.
47 'The Firework Book: Gunpowder in Medieval Germany. Das Feuerwerkbuch c.1400', ed. Gerhard W. Kramer, trans. Klaus Leibnitz, in *the Journal of the Arms and Armour Society* 17.1 (March 2001), p. 25.
48 Medieval Gunpowder Research Group, Report number 2, August 2003: 'The Ho Experiments' on www.middelaldercentret.dk/pdf/gunpowder2.pdf.
49 If the mass of the cannonball was increased by 25 per cent, for example from 40 to 50kg, the energy at impact would only increase by 25 per cent. Thus it was far more important to increase muzzle velocity by increasing the amount of powder or quality of powder than the weight of the shot fired.
50 Hall, pp. 93–5.

The Uneasy Calm, 1480–1522

51 Smith and DeVries, p. 254.
52 However, it must be stressed that round shot in flight are never accurate due to the effects of air pressure acting on a randomly spinning ball.
53 It is a mistake, however, to assume that this meant that early guns were always very slow to move. Modern calculations have demonstrated that they could be moved around at much the same pace as the army – not that mobile itself – and daily average movements of around 10km were normal for both. See Monique Sommé, 'L'armée Bourguignonne au siège de Calais de 1436', in *Guerre et société en France, en Angleterre et en Bourgogne XIVe–XVe siècle*, ed. Philippe Contamine et al. (Lille: Centre d'histoire de la région du Nord et de l'Europe du Nord-Ouest, 1991), pp. 197–219.
54 This development can be seen in the illustrations in August von Essenwein, *Quellen zur Geschichte der Feuerwaffen*, 2 vols (1877; rpt. Graz: Akademische Druck – u.Verlagsanstalt, 1969).
55 Vatin, *L'order de Saint-Jean-de-Jérusalem*, p. 182.
56 *Calendar of Patent Rolls, Henry VII, vol. 1: 1485–94* (London: Her Majesty's Stationery Office, 1914), 15 December 1485.
57 H.L. Blackmore, *The Armouries of the Tower of London, I: Ordnance* (London: Her Majesty's Stationery Office, 1976), pp. 173–4, and Kaestlin, J.P., ed., *Catalogue of the Museum of Artillery in the Rotunda at Woolwich. Part I: Ordnance* (London: Her Majesty's Stationery Office, 1963), p. 28.
58 The standard definition of bastion is that of Sir John R. Hale in 'The Early Development of the Bastion: An Italian Chronology', in *Europe in the Late Middle Ages*, ed. J.R. Hale, J.R.L. Highfield and B. Smalley (Evanston: Northwestern University Press, 1965), pp. 466–94 and *Renaissance Fortification: Art or Engineering?* (London: Thames and Hudson Press, 1977).
59 In modern architectural parlance a *terreplein* is a wide platform on top of a wall and behind a parapet.
60 This clearly has been done to the Rhodes walls but, judging from the coats of arms placed on the inside of the walls, was not accomplished until the Grand Mastership of Fabrizio del Carretto (see below).
61 Elias Kollias, *The Medieval City of Rhodes and the Palace of the Grand Master*, 3rd ed. (Athens: Archaeological Receipts Fund, 2005), p. 102.
62 The other *tenailles* were created by digging around them, leaving the earth and rock to form the *tenaille* which was then faced with stone (see below).
63 Gabriel, II:56–7, notes the construction of this *tenaille* but does not realise that it was formed by digging out the enlarged moat and leaving the earth in place in between.
64 On this square tower see Gabriel, II:54.
65 For example, B.J.St.J. O'Neil, 'Rhodes and the Origin of the Bastion', *Antiquaries Journal* 34 (1954), pp. 44–54.
66 It is possible to speculate that the combination of the *tenaille* and the firing gallery might have led to the idea of the bastion, which after all is very like the *tenaille* with a solid base on which to mount artillery. The 'firing galleries' that d'Aubusson added can be seen as the forerunner of the loops in bastions which provide enfilading fire.
67 O'Neil.
68 This is also the suggestion of Athanassios Migos, 'Rhodes: the Knights' Background', *Fort* 18 (1990), p. 15. Gabriel (II:34–42) has a very confusing discussion of the Tower of St George and is unwilling to accept the entire work as that of d'Aubusson despite no strong evidence to the contrary.
69 The attack of these walls is not only attested to in the narrative accounts of the 1480 siege, but also appears in the Caoursin illuminations and the Epernay painting, as does the extensive damage caused there.
70 Gabriel's discussion of this corner (II:31–2) is important, as is a study of all the coats of arms and the constructions they are a part of. Note especially the two shields of Carretto which indicate that he 'rebuilt' parts of two walls damaged by earthquake that had previously been built by d'Aubusson.
71 Gabriel's description of this fort (II:79–90), especially inside it, is indispensible.

72 See below.
73 Vatin, 'The Hospitallers at Rhodes', p. 150.
74 Vatin, *L'order de Saint-Jean-de-Jérusalem*, pp. 183–4. Licences were issued by the Council twice in 1484 for piracy against Arab and Turkish ships. Other, more unofficial piracy, undoubtedly occurred.
75 Vatin, *L'order de Saint-Jean-de-Jérusalem*, pp. 184–7.
76 See Kelly DeVries, 'The Lack of a Western European Military Response to the Ottoman Invasions of Eastern Europe from Nicopolis (1396) to Mohács (1526)', *Journal of Military History* 63 (1999), pp. 539–59 and Setton, II:392–3.
77 A biographical record of those elevated to cardinals in the consistory of 1489, including Pierre d'Aubusson, can be found in 'The Cardinals of the Catholic Church Biographical Dictionary' at www.fiu.edu/~mirandas/bios1489.htm. See also Brockman, p. 105.
78 We have used Vatin's translation of this letter (Vatin, 'The Hospitallers at Rhodes', p. 152) which is otherwise unpublished. Vatin's article from which it is taken, 'The Hospitallers at Rhodes and Ottoman Turks, 1480–1522,' in *Crusading in the Fifteenth Century: Message and Impact*, ed. Norman Housley (Basingstoke: Palgrave Macmillan, 2004), pp. 148–62, 231–5, is a brilliant discussion of d'Aubusson's and other Hospitallers' crusading efforts.
79 See Nicolas Vatin, 'Le siège de Mytilène (1501)', *Turica* 21–3 (1992), pp. 437–59.
80 Vatin, p. 33. The banishment had only a limited effect, however, as not many Jews had left Rhodes before d'Aubusson's death, and afterwards there was little interest among the Knights to enforce the expulsion order.
81 Brockman, p. 105 and Vatin, p. 273.
82 Vatin, p. 209.
83 Thomas Basin, *Histoire de Louis XI*, ed. Charles Samaran (Paris: Société d'Édition 'Les Belles Lettres', 1963–72), pp. 118–9. On the attack of Otranto see Babinger, pp. 387–408.
84 Setton, II:364–75.
85 For example, Andrew C. Hess, 'The Evolution of the Ottoman Seaborne Empire in the Age of the Oceanic Discoveries, 1453–1525', *American Historical Review* 75 (1970), 1904.
86 Inalcik, pp. 30–1.
87 Inalcik, p. 31.
88 The Battle of Zonchio has not been well researched and certainly deserves more study. For limited coverage see Sidney Fisher, *The Foreign Relations of Turkey, 1481–1512* (Urbana: University of Illinois Press, 1948), pp. 61–7; Kelly DeVries, 'The Effectiveness of Fifteenth-Century Shipboard Artillery', *The Mariner's Mirror* 84 (1998), pp. 389–99; and Frederic C. Lane, 'Naval Actions and Fleet Organization, 1499–1502', in *Renaissance Venice*, ed. J.R. Hale (Totowa: Rowan and Littlefield, 1973), pp. 152–3.
89 Fisher, pp. 68–9. This battle is sometimes called the Second Battle of Lepanto.
90 Inalcik, pp. 31–2. Inalcik sees this as the cause of Turkish peace with Venice in 1503.
91 Inalcik, p. 32.
92 Inalcik, p. 33; Andrew C. Hess, 'The Ottoman Conquest of Egypt (1517) and the Beginning of the Sixteenth-Century World War', *International Journal of Middle Eastern Studies* 4 (1973), p. 65; and David Morgan, *Medieval Persia, 1040–1797* (London: Longman, 1988), pp. 112–23. Ismaîl is generally credited for establishing Shi'ism as the dominant form of Islam in Persia.
93 Inalcik, p. 34 and Hess, 'The Ottoman Conquest of Egypt (1517)', pp. 70–6.
94 R.N. Bain's 'The Siege of Belgrade by Muhammed II, July 1–23, 1456', *English Historical Review* 7 (1892), pp. 235–52, is now somewhat outdated. Better descriptions of this siege are in Babinger, pp. 138–44 and Setton, II:173–84.
95 There is a need for a more detailed study of this siege. Setton, III:199 is uncharacteristically short on the siege itself but does write more about the reaction in Western Europe to the fall of Belgrade (III:199–200).
96 Setton, II:516.
97 Vatin, pp. 255–7 and Rossignol, pp. 237–8. Although *barze* is normally translated as 'barge' it is difficult to see how this type of ship would be used in warfare. Simon Pepper, 'Fortress and Fleet: The Defence

of Venice's Mainland Greek Colonies in the Late Fifteenth Century', in *War, Culture and Society in Renaissance Venice: Essays in Honour of John Hale*, ed. D.S. Chambers, C.H. Clough and M.E. Mallett (London: Hambledon, 1993), pp. 29–55, calls these 'round ships' following the lead of the great naval historian, Lane, 'Naval Actions', p. 149.
98 Translated in Setton: II: 516–7.
99 Vatin, pp. 261–4 and Rossignol, pp. 238–43. See also Vatin's more detailed study of the siege: Nicolas Vatin, 'Le siège de Mytilène (1501)', *Turcica* 21–3 (1992), pp. 437–59.
100 Rossignol, p. 246 and Brockman, p. 105.
101 Vatin, p. 279.
102 Brockman, p. 106.
103 Kollias, p. 85.
104 Gabriel, II:32–3.
105 Surprisingly Gabriel (II:34) says very little about either the Battery of the Olives or the *caponier*.
106 Palmira Brummett, 'The Overrated Adversary: Rhodes and Ottoman Naval Power', *Historical Journal* 36 (1993), p. 530.
107 Brummett, 'The Overrated Adversary', p. 530.
108 National Library of Malta, Libri Bullarum, f. 26v.
109 Vatin, p. 284.
110 For a more in-depth discussion of the Hospitaller-Mamluk conflicts at this time see Vatin, pp. 316–23.
111 Vatin, pp. 256 n. 5, 316–7.
112 Brummett, 'The Overrated Adversary', pp. 534–5; Setton, III: 24; and Palmira Brummett, *Ottoman Seapower and Levantine Diplomacy in the Age of Discovery* (Albany: State University of New York Press, 1994), p. 40. This was apparently in response to an anticipated joint Ottoman-Mamluk raid on Rhodes. See Brummett, 'The Overrated Adversary', p. 534.
113 Brummett, *Ottoman Seapower*, pp. 40–4.
114 Vatin, pp. 301, 321–3.
115 Brummett, 'The Overrated Adversary', p. 540, and Brockman, p. 109.
116 During the 1517 attack on Egypt a Turkish naval captain had sent an insulting and taunting letter to Carretto, but whether this was done on his own or with the permission of the Sultan is not known. The letter is in Sanudo, *Diarii*, 24:440–1. See also Setton, III:172.
117 For example, Vatin. That Selim had also left Belgrade alone may add evidence to this idea.
118 Brummett, for example, especially in 'The Overrated Adversary'.
119 This is not to be confused by the use of term *terreplein* in 1522 by Jacques de Bourbon, and repeated by Gabriel, which in modern architectural terminology is a *tenaille*.
120 Luttrell, ' Earthquakes in the Dodecanese', pp. 150–1 and Gabriel, II:94–5.
121 As with the Battery of the Olives on the same corner, Gabriel (II:34) dismisses with little discussion the *caponier*, a very interesting gunpowder artillery fortification.
122 For example, Setton, III:181.
123 Brummett, *Ottoman Seapower*, pp. 101–3 and Setton, III:24, 37.
124 Gabriel (II:34–42) believes that much of St George's Tower was constructed by l'Isle Adam, with little responsibility for its enormous size being d'Aubusson's.
125 Vatin, pp. 345–7; Setton, III:204; and the various articles in Bernard Baray, ed., *De Rhodes à Malte: Le grand maître Philippe de Villiers de L'Isle-Adam (1460–1534) et l'ordre de Malte* (Paris: Musée d'Art et d'Histoire Louis-Senlecq, 2004).
126 B. Paulus Justinianus and Petrus Quirinus, 'Erimatarum Carmaldulensium Libellus ad Leonum X Maximum', in G.B. Mittarelli and Anslemo Costadoni, ed., *Annales Carmaldulenses*, 9 vols (Venice).

The Siege of 1522

Fear of invasion became reality on 26 June 1522, the Feast of Corpus Domini (Our Lord), when the advanced fleet of Ottoman ships anchored in Kalithas Bay, some 6 miles to the south-west of the city of Rhodes.[1] Troops began disembarking immediately, with slaves and labourers put to work unloading victuals, arms, armor, gunpowder, cannon, tents and all the other habiliments of war. When a ship was emptied it pulled away from shore, making way for another vessel, while the unloaded ship probably returned to Turkey for more supplies and men. This process would be repeated over and over again between 26 June and 10 July.

Estimates of the number of ships taking part in the invasion vary widely among historians, both contemporary and modern. Jacques de Bourbon, the most trusted of Hospitaller eyewitnesses, says that the fleet consisted of 103 galleys, as many *sutille que bastards*, not counting 25 or 30 *galleres*, which came first to lay the siege and which blockaded the passages during the siege. There were after 35 galleasses, good and large, 15 *mahonnes* and 20 *tafforees*, these ships being only a little different from galleasses. There were 60 *fusts* or more and many brigantines, and among barques, galleons and horse transports there was 10 or 12 ships which carried the munitions and the great artillery to batter the town. At its arrival the fleet numbered around 250 vessels.[2]

However, the accuracy of such numbers does not really matter. The proximity of the mainland, which on a dull day can be easily seen from the port or walls of Rhodes – on a bright day the rays of the sun reflecting off the sea between Rhodes and Turkey obscures the view – allowed transports to make as many journeys as necessary. Nor does it really matter that a secondary fleet joined them from Syria some time at the end of June or beginning of July, bringing the number of ships to a total of 400 according to Bourbon.[3] (Bourbon's numbers seem to compare nicely with the tally of Ottoman ships in Jacob Fontanus and Marino Sanudo's *Diarii*, which numbers the fleet at 300, including 70 light galleys, 40 heavy galleys, 50 transports and unnumbered *fustes*, brigantines and other vessels.[4]) Indeed, what may be more important in Bourbon's reckoning here is that Suleyman was bringing together two fleets, his Turkish one as well as one from Syria, which left the Middle Eastern coast largely unprotected from enemies or pirates. Clearly Suleyman meant business!

Rhodes Besieged

How many troops were transported to the siege on these ships? Eyewitnesses, Jacques de Bourbon, Gabriel Taragon and Piero da Campo, say 200,000 and Sir Nicholas Roberts 165,000 (100,000 soldiers, 15,000 sailors and 50,000 'labourers with spades and pikes'), although these are undoubtedly exaggerations.[5] Certainly Bourbon, Taragon, da Campo and Roberts, although they were in Rhodes, had no real idea of how many Ottoman soldiers besieged their city. Looking out from the walls to the counterscarp, which at all times was covered by cannon, tents, fires, horses, carts and men, it must have seemed as if the whole Turkish nation had descended on to Rhodes – 165,000 or 200,000 was merely their way of saying that the numbers of soldiers opposing the Hospitallers was huge. No doubt Suleyman knew the exact number, although Ottoman sources are silent on this, as it seems doubtful that he would let a lack of soldiers be the cause of failure. When he needed them, as in early December, reinforcements – also not numbered – were readily available. Besides, only so many men were necessary to surround the walls of Rhodes. More than that number, 165,000 or 200,000 for example, would simply eat up the victuals, drink up the potable water and foul the campsites. Disease, and the lack of foodstuffs and fresh water, ended more pre-modern sieges than military failure.

While the size and composition of the whole Ottoman army and its supplies cannot be determined, one surviving document gives us a glimpse of just what the besiegers at Rhodes took with them. An inventory of Mustafa Pasha's fleet lists cuirasses, coats of mail, helmets, gauntlets and shields in large numbers, pikes and javelin 'handles', cannon, handguns, bows and crossbows, projectiles to be fired – balls, arrows, crossbow bolts – bombs, powder flasks, linstocks, paper for cartridges, matches, sulphur, saltpetre, charcoal, pitch and products derived from petrol. There was also steel, tin and perhaps copper, tools and material for carpenters, stonecutters, masons and diggers. Also included were 3,700 wicker baskets.[6]

The planning for this campaign had begun at least six months before the fleet and the army arrived in Rhodes. This was the first major military operation of Suleyman's lengthy reign and it showed all the hallmarks of what modern historians might call his 'grand strategy'.[7] To the Sultan known as 'the Magnificent', the first emphasis of any conquest was planning. Every soldier and artisan who was needed was called up, every victual, weapon, crossbow bolt, armour, tent, animal, rope, drum and horn, chisel, piece of metal, even every wicker basket was brought together. Ships, carts and pack animals were requisitioned. Nothing was left to chance or luck.

The campaign that led to the siege of Rhodes in 1522 started out in Constantinople. On 18 June Suleyman sent part of his invasion force by sea, including an estimated 40,000 mariners and 20,000 Azab or irregular soldiers, while he led the remainder of his army overland, leaving two days earlier than the fleet.[8] The fleet was commanded by his Second Vizier, Mustafa Pasha, who sailed first to Gallipoli (roughly 250km), where he was joined by more ships led by Pilaq Mustafa, the Qapudan of

The Town and the Port of Rhodes Besieged by the Turks, by an anonymous French artist in about 1485. This incredibly detailed painting was given to the city of Epernay in northern France by Claude Chandon in 1916 and may be the painting of the famous victory commissioned by Louis XI for Notre Dame Cathedral in Paris, but there is no documentation to support this. The amount of very accurate detail strongly suggests that the artist either had been present at the siege or had, at the very least, visited Rhodes. Its similarity to the images in the Caoursin manuscript leads to the conclusion that the same artist might have been responsible for both, although it is also possible that the Epernay painting was painted using the illuminations of the Caoursin manuscript as the artist's source. Many incidents of the siege are depicted in this painting, including the attacks on the Tower of St Nicholas, the wooden bridge built by the Turks to attack the Tower and the attacks on the Jewish quarter and the south-east corner of the city. The view of the painting is from the north looking south.

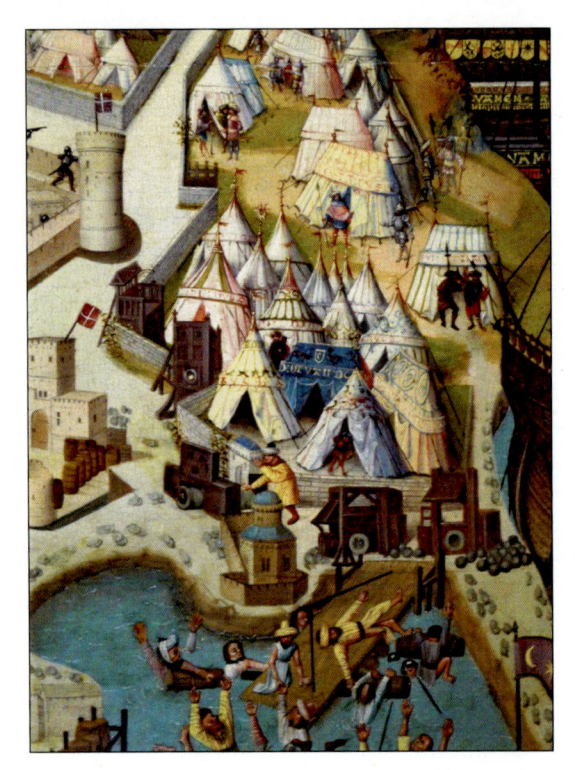

The Turkish camp and the gun positions around the church of St Anthony. Four large guns, possibly bombards, are shown mounted in wooden emplacements. The two on the left are firing at the city while the two on the right are bombarding the Tower of St Nicholas across the Mandraki harbour. At the bottom is the bridge the Turks used in an attempt to storm the Tower of St Nicholas. It has been broken by the attacks of the Hospitallers.

The Tower of St Nicholas. The attacks by the Ottoman Turks from the sea are shown at the bottom. The broken bridge, made from planks of wood secured to empty barrels, is shown at the top. This bridge, reported by Mary Dupuis to have been wide enough to allow six men to walk abreast, was floated across the Mandraki harbour from St Anthony's Church. However, prompt action by the Hospitallers thwarted this attempt to take the Tower.

This detail shows the south-west part of the city with the Turkish camp beyond. The Hospitallers on the wall are using both long bows and hand firearms – possibly matchlocks. There are a number of guns in the Turkish camp, including pieces mounted in large wooden structures and what appears to be a mortar in the upper centre of the picture.

etail of the city. The wall across the lower right corner is the collachium wall around the Hospitaller headquarters.

The Grand Master's Palace as it appeared in 1480.

Detail of the fighting on the Jewish Quarter at the north-east corner of the city.

Detail of the fighting on the walls east of the city, with the figure of St John assisting the Hospitallers from atop one of the towers.

Detail of the spit beside the Windmill Mole showing the city scaffold and three bronze Turkish guns. The painting shows this spit running parallel to, and almost as long as, the Windmill Mole.

The fighting on the Jewish Quarter on the eastern side of the city.

etail of the fighting on the east of the city showing Turkish bombards. Most are of wrought iron, but the bronze piece, loured orange, is similar to four existing Turkish bombards (see Appendix 1, Cannon Catalogue, nos. 25 to 28).

The eastern side of the city with the Windmill Tower, also showing the attack on the walls to the east of the city.

The Siege of 1522

Gallipoli, and Kortoglu. They then sailed to Chios (roughly 200km) and then on to Marmaris (300km) and Rhodes (55km). In the meantime, Suleyman had marched from Constantinople across the Bosphorus Strait to Scutari (about 5km), to Yenişehir (165km) and to Kütahya (120km). This seems to have been the intended spot for the gathering of his armies. Qasim, the Beylerbey of Anatolia, Bali Pasha, the Agha of the Janissaries, and Ali Bey, the Agha of the Azab, joined him there on 1 July; Ayas Pasha on 2 July and Ferhad Pasha on 11 July. The whole force then marched on to Marmaris, a further 320km. Suleyman, traveling at the rear of his army, arrived there on 28 July.

The movement of such a large fleet and army meant, of course, that the Hospitallers suspected they were being targeted for attack. The only possible doubt was whether the Ottomans were actually planning to go elsewhere, as they had been in 1517 when it must have seemed to the Knights that they were about to be attacked, but Sultan Selim I had gone instead to Egypt. However, in 1522 Rhodes was indeed the target.

Philippe Villiers de l'Isle Adam had been elected Grand Master of the Knights of St John of the Hospital on 21 January 1521. At the time he was in Paris, serving the Order as the Grand Prior of the *Langue* of France. He had been a Hospitaller since 1478, when aged 18 he was received into the Order. In 1480, when he had fought with Pierre d'Aubusson and the other Hospitallers against the first besieging force of Ottomans, he was just 20, a young and inexperienced Knight. How many others in 1522 could remember that victory forty-two years earlier is not known, but it cannot have been many.

By the time of his election as Grand Master l'Isle Adam had been a Hospitaller for forty-four years. He began making preparations to travel to Rhodes immediately after his election as Grand Master, although he was certainly still in France on 13 July 1521, and had met with King Francis I in the time between his election and that date.[9] He had also spent time buying supplies in France, and it is possible that the cannon which bear his arms as Grand Master were made at this time and travelled with him to Rhodes.

When l'Isle Adam arrived on Rhodes is not recorded, but it was certainly before 28 October, when he wrote to Francis from there and relayed his fears about possible Ottoman invasion. This had been prompted by a letter he received, written by Suleyman at Belgrade on 10 September, informing the Hospitallers of the Turkish victories over Belgrade, Šabac, Semlin and five other towns. L'Isle Adam writes: 'Sire, since he has become the Grand Turk, this is the first letter which he has sent to Rhodes, which we do not take for an expression of friendship, but rather for a veiled threat ...'[10]

In February 1522 the Council of the Hospitallers, led by l'Isle Adam, ordered the requisition of three-quarters of all non-domestic slaves to assist in checking and repairing the walls of the city. The walls, even though they had been extensively remodelled and, presumably, maintained since the end of the siege of 1480, still needed to be thoroughly gone over once more. Any vegetation was removed and chipped or broken stones replaced. Not only did the walls have to be strong, they had to appear to be invulnerable. Fortification was as much psychological as physical. If a besieger faced a fortification he thought was too strong to fall, it probably was. Although this was not likely, especially as the Sultan was to be present, the Hospitallers did all that they could to ensure that the changes they had made in the walls since 1480, together with the memory of their tenacious defence, might dishearten those attacking them. L'Isle Adam also named two commissioners to take care of the needs of the peasants who were on the island of Rhodes so that they would not be frightened by the appearance of Suleyman's fleet.[11]

From then, until 2 April, the sources are silent as to the activities of the Knights, although there must have been many, with undoubtedly the gathering of supplies and bringing of peasants into the safety of the city given high priority. On 2 April l'Isle Adam sent out the first of many reports and letters. Fra Johannes de Yseray reported to Pope Adrian VI, who had been elected to the Papacy on 9 January 1522, about what the Hospitallers had done to protect their Eastern Mediterranean headquarters.[12] This was followed, in the first week of May, by two letters to the Hospitallers in Candia, suggesting that there was some doubt as to whether the Ottomans would attack Rhodes and that they instead might wage a campaign against Hungary.[13] In hindsight this seems an odd letter to send to his brothers on Crete. Why not ask them for reinforcements, even if they were not ultimately necessary? L'Isle Adam must have thought that the Turks were planning an attack on Rhodes. Indeed, he continued to work on the defence of Rhodes, as seen in the general review of the Rhodian Hospitallers he ordered on 7 May. Each Knight was to possess 'a helmet, a bevor, arm defences, and a brigandine or breastplate with its *fauld* or *brachis* and *corsalettos*. They were also to have their sharp sword or polearm or two handguns or two crossbows or one handgun and one crossbow or two English longbows.'[14]

Sometime before the Turks' arrival – Bourbon does not give a more accurate date than this – the Grand Master also sent out ships to try to buy grain from anyone who would trade with the Hospitallers. There was some positive response to these voyages, with Bourbon mentioning specifically the wheat shipments arriving from Naples and Rumeli, which he remarks 'gave great consolation to those in the town'.[15] L'Isle Adam also sent a Brother Sergeant, Antony of Bosus, 'a man of good spirit and wisdom', to Crete for a load of wine. This was a dangerous task, comments Bourbon: 'for the Candiotes dared not to sail to Rhodes with wine, as they were accustomed, for fear of the Turkish army. And also those of the town were not willing to send ships to Candia fearing that they might be surprised and intercepted on their route by the same army.' But Brother Antony was more than up to the task as he returned not only with his ship laden with wine, but with fifteen other vessels – called *grips* by Bourbon – also loaded with wine. He brought soldiers with him as well, although they seem to have hidden among the wine 'because the Lords of Candia did not allow men to go to the aid of Rhodes for fear of the Turk'.[16]

Another ship, owned by a rich Venetian merchant, Jehan Anthonio Bonaldi, delivered 700 bottles of wine. Bourbon reports that Bonaldi was initially planning to take his wine to Constantinople, but when he heard of the potential attack on Rhodes, he refused to take anything to 'the enemy' and sailed his ship toward the island. After selling his wine there, at a lower profit than he could have had at Constantinople, Bourbon asserts, he put himself, his ship and its crew in the service of the Hospitallers:

> And during the siege, the said captain carried himself very honourably in his person, and found himself in places that good men should find themselves, and not sparing his goods, but it is true spending largely without demanding any payment or recompense of the Religion.[17]

Another ship, a Genoese carrack, laden with spices bought in Alexandria, and its captain, Dominico Fornari, also decided to stay and fight with the Hospitallers.[18] Finally, in preparation for the siege l'Isle Adam also had all of the grain on the island harvested and brought into the city.[19]

Because almost all of the sources for the siege of 1522 were written by Hospitallers it is much easier to arrive at a more accurate number of the besieged than of the besiegers. Grand Master l'Isle Adam wrote to Venice reporting that he had some 16,000 men: 8,000 stationed at the four corners of the city, 2,000 to serve as mobile forces and 6,000 to serve as a reserve with him in the centre of town.[20] Venetian 'spies' confirmed these numbers,[21] while Jacomo Crispo de Naxos says that there were just 14,000.[22] However, an eyewitness chronicler of the siege, Jacobus Fontanus, states that only around 5,000 free men were able to carry arms, among whom were 600 Hospitallers and 500 Cretans. The remainder were sailors, rowers and mariners. (Of the latter Fontanus mentions only three who were good soldiers, a Frenchman, Michel Vidal, a Sicilian, Seringus Vandalus, and a Rhodian, Nicolaos Mego, while others, mostly peasants, were 'more useful in digging and transporting dirt than they were in fighting', and still others, the citizens of Rhodes, were 'neither honourable in working or in danger. They were more ostentatious than courageous.'[23])

It is difficult to dismiss l'Isle Adam's tally of the total number of men as he actually had no reason to inflate the numbers when writing to the Venetians. After all, his letters at this time always sought reinforcements – if anything he would have underestimated the number. Yet, of these 16,000 certainly not all were skilled warriors. There was perhaps a core of around 600 Hospitaller knights and sergeants, while others – maybe the 5,000 described by Fontanus – who 'could carry arms' were a mixture of mercenaries, mariners, pioneers, etc., including Vidal, Vandalus and Mego. The rest were unskilled irregulars who could defend the city if necessary but otherwise were better at 'digging and transporting dirt'.

On 18 July Bourbon reported:

Rhodes Besieged

> The enemy set up a mantlet under which they put three or four medium-sized pieces, that is to say *sakers* and *passevolans*, which they shot against the posts of England and Provence but the mantlet and the pieces were soon destroyed by artillery on the wall. And those who shot them were all killed or wounded.[24]

Sakers and *passevolans* at this time were small guns firing iron shot of around 2.7kg. They could hardly have even dented the walls, and this implies that the first batteries of the Turks were set up simply to find range and test the defences (and perhaps the will) of the city. As the text indicates, a Turkish battery was more than just guns. It also consisted of wooden palisades, gabions – wicker baskets or drums filled with earth – and mantlets, behind which the guns were placed. As shown in illustrations of the time, just before the firing of the cannon, in this case the small *sakers* and *passevolans*, an operator raised the mantlet only far enough to provide space for the gun muzzle and only as long as to allow sighting and firing. Of course, like any defensive structure in warfare, especially one set up on an open field or siege position, there was some risk involved. In this case, the mantlet was hit and destroyed by gunshot from the Hospitallers and the gunners slain, perhaps by splinters of the wood that was supposed to protect them. But it is likely that only a direct shot could do such damage, with the structure protecting the Ottoman gunners from any glancing or missed shot. Indeed, in this case it is the Hospitaller gunners who must be applauded as the accuracy of their initial fire was impressive.

Bourbon writes about other batteries set up the following day, with equally impressive Hospitaller results:

> ... [The Turks] set up two other mantlets ... one beside a church called Saint Cosmos and Saint Damian and the other a little higher toward Ponent. And from these mantlets were fired great pieces, such as coulovrines, double cannons and bombards against the walls of England and Spain, which mantlets the artillery of the town fired good shots and often destroyed them during the day, but at night the enemy rebuilt them. And to do more damage to the city and to hit us the enemy set up many other mantlets in diverse places and as if to surround the town. And at the beginning there were 64 of these, which number was well diminished by the artillery fired from our side, and there remained only 34. And each mantlet held three pieces of artillery.[25]

Here Bourbon mentions coulovrines, double cannon and bombards. These were European terms for gunpowder weapons and one might wonder then how this Knight might have applied them to the Turkish guns he saw from the walls. Fortunately, he goes on to give some details of the guns used by the Turks, which he claims he took from a Hospitaller spy in the Turkish camp:

The Siege of 1522

> First, there were six great *cannon perriers* of bronze firing stone of approximately three palms and a half or thereabouts, and fifteen other pieces of iron and of bronze that fired stone of five or six palms. After there were twelve great bombards firing stone of nine to ten palms, and two other great bombards firing stone of eleven palms in size. Also there were twelve basilisks but they only fired from eight, of which four fired against the posts of England and Spain and two against the post of Italy, the others firing sometimes against the Tower of St Nicholas. Also there were fifteen *double cannons* firing iron balls like basilisks. The medium-sized artillery as *sakers* and passevolans were in great number, the handguns, innumerable and incredible. Also there were twelve mortars of bronze which shot into the air, eight of which were placed behind the church St Cosmos and St Damian and two others behind St John de la Fountain toward the post of Italy, one broken, and the others in front of the post of Auvergne and fired the pieces night and day to murder the people. And the stone which they fired were three sorts, which the largest were of seven or eight palms and were a thing very inhumane and disheartening. But thanks to the grace of our Lord and evident miracle, the said pieces were not too bad and killed only 24 or 25 people.[26]

Just what were these guns like? How big were they? What damage could they do? The first pieces mentioned by Bourbon are the six 'cannon perriers' which fired stone shot of 'three palms and a half' – some 26.5cm in diameter – weighing in the region of 25kg.[27] Looking at the surviving Turkish cannon that were used on Rhodes, there is a piece which is very close to this size, W571, in the Germanisches Museum in Nuremberg, Germany – see cannon 30 in Appendix 1. This piece, which has a bore of 29cm and is 3.22m in length, has a roughly parallel outer form. Internally the bore is some 29cm in diameter for much of its length, but the rear section, where the charge of gunpowder was put, is of much smaller diameter, giving the barrel a larger wall thickness – just where the explosion occurs. This form of cannon is relatively common throughout Western Europe in the last decades of the fifteenth century and the beginning of the sixteenth century. It is possible that this type of gun was developed in the late fifteenth century as a compromise between the weight of the actual barrel and the size of the ball it could fire.

The second group mentioned by Bourbon, the 'fifteen other pieces of iron and of bronze that fired stone of five or six palms', thus a calibre of 38 to 45cm and would have fired stone shot of between 75 and 125kg. Without any further details is impossible to know, for certain, what these guns looked like. However there are some later pieces, which survive in the collection of the Naval Museum in Istanbul, which could be of similar form. The first is 389cm long with a bore of 52cm; the second, bearing the *tuğrasi* or signature of Suleyman, is 332cm long with a bore of 39cm; and the third, again with Suleyman's *tuğrasi*, is 327cm long with a bore of 40cm. Internally these are like the cannon perriers with a bore that extends some two-thirds of the length of the barrel with a powder chamber of smaller diameter.

The 'twelve great bombards firing stone of nine to ten palms, and two other great bombards firing stone of eleven palms in size' provided the main bombarding force. The bombards of nine to ten palms had a bore of some 68.5 to 76cm and fired shot of between 435 and 595kg, while the largest pieces were some 84cm in calibre and fired balls of 800kg. While there are no surviving examples as large as the latter bombards, there are bombards, both Turkish and from Western Europe, that have bores of around 65 to 70cm.[28]

No contemporary sources report the size or shape of a gun with such an evocative name as a basilisk. However, modern research has determined that the basilisk was a very long gun with a fairly small bore, such as the Turkish bronze gun, dated 1530, and now in the Rotunda at Woolwich (II.191), which is some 568cm long with a bore of just 25cm.[29] Similar to the Woolwich bronze basilisk are two further bronze guns in the collection of the Royal Armouries: XIX 243 is 485cm long with a bore of 19cm and is dated 1524; while a second, XIX 94, is 523cm long with a bore of 23cm.[30]

What is also likely is that the basilisk fired cast-iron shot, approximately three times heavier than stone of the same size, about 45kg. These guns would probably have done the most damage to the walls of the city because, as a consequence of their length and the likelihood that they were using far more powder in proportion to the weight of shot than the cannon perriers or bombards, the cannonball was travelling at far greater speed. A number of Turkish basilisks, apart from that noted above, also survive and provide a vivid picture of just what the Turks were using to attack the city in 1522. The most impressive is a wrought-iron basilisk, 747cm long with a bore of 25cm, currently standing in the square between the Naval Museum and Barbarossa Hayreddin Pasha's tomb in Istanbul, and another is 700cm long with a bore of 24.5cm, again made of wrought iron, and located today in the Naval Museum in Istanbul. Both are attributed to the attack of Cairo by Selim I in 1517. The former would have fired an iron ball in the region of some 48kg (allowing for 2cm windage) while the latter about 45kg.

Next Bourbon lists 'fifteen double cannons casting iron balls like basilisks'. Unfortunately, although these are described as being like basilisks, and firing iron shot confirming that basilisks also fired iron, just how large a calibre they had or how long they were is not given.

Finally, there were 'twelve mortars', the firing of which is described as 'so inhumane and disheartening', probably because their primary effect was against the population of a besieged site, the non-combatants. Mortars were angled at high elevation, usually 42–45 degrees, and were able to fire over the walls of the town, their shot landing on the houses and their inhabitants. Bourbon writes that there were 'three sorts' of shot for this gun, the largest firing a ball some 7 to 8 palms in size, 21 to 24in or 53 to 61cm, weighing from 200 to 300kg.

Table summarising the guns listed in Jacques de Bourbon's description of them:

	Quantity	Shot diameter		Shot type	Shot weight kg
		Palms	cm		
Cannon Perrier	6	3½	26.5	Stone	25
'pieces of iron and bronze'	15	5–6	38–45	Stone	75–125
Bombard	12	9–10	68.5–76	Stone	435–595
Bombard	2	11	84	Stone	807
Basilisks	12		[25]	Iron	[45]
Double cannon	15		[25]	Iron	[45]
Mortars	12	7–8	53–61	[Stone]	200–300
TOTAL	74				

Note: Information in brackets is inferred from the text

In all, Bourbon lists seventy-four great pieces in addition to smaller guns, sakers and passevolans, 'in great number' and handguns 'innumerable and incredible'. It is therefore quite clear that the Turks brought a considerable arsenal of gunpowder weapons to the siege. There is no detailed information as to how these were set up in batteries, but it is likely that they were a mixture of the large guns and smaller pieces, the sakers and passevolans, together with handgunners to provide covering fire when the mantlets were opened and to protect the gunners and those operating the guns.

Finally, some comment or estimate is required as to how far from the walls the Turkish batteries were. At the minimum the batteries might have been set up close to the edge of the moat, although here they would have come under severe fire from the Hospitaller guns. At the maximum it is unlikely that the Ottoman guns were more than 200m from the actual walls of the city – further than this and the guns would have been both inaccurate and far less effective. Taking into account the large amount of damage that the Turks inflicted on the walls, this would strongly suggest that they were closer rather than farther from them.

Ranged against the Turkish batteries was the artillery of the Hospitallers, mounted both upon the walls and within the various boulevards, towers and *tenailles* of the city. Bourbon, who includes a lot of detail about the Turkish pieces, is silent about the actual details of the artillery of the Knights. And while Fontanus does include an intriguing description, it is difficult to understand exactly what he means as he is without military training and is writing in Latin, a language at the time in which there was no satisfactory vocabulary for gunpowder weapons:

Rhodes Besieged

> There stood in several places twelve bronze siege guns of d'Aubusson, not a few of which have their mouths pointing into the sky and their base very closely on the ground (*quintam numerum haud superantes ore in coelum erecto, base arctiori versus terram*), firing ... stone balls of seven palms onto the tents and temples [of the Turks] day and night continually ... They also fired from thin (*digitalis*) bombards copper balls filled with incendiary material, bitumen, sulphur, pitch ... but the more savage force came from forty bombards which fired balls some of nine palms and some eleven ...[31]

Fortunately, many of the pieces used by the Hospitallers remained in Rhodes until the nineteenth century, when they were finally dispersed – to France, Germany and Turkey. This collection of pieces, nineteen in number, provides a unique opportunity – a snapshot in time as it were – to see both the guns and fortifications as one interdependent unit.

As might be expected, the guns on the city walls were, in many ways, very similar to those ranged against them. The Hospitallers had cannon perriers, long basilisk guns, as well as a range of smaller pieces. The first and largest group, the cannon perriers, are a type of cannon with a large bore in relation to their outer diameter and with a smaller diameter powder chamber. Two surviving pieces are especially interesting in that they date from 1482[32] and 1487 – just after the first siege. Yet, their survival on Rhodes shows that they were still in use in 1522. The first, called LA BUSSONA, bears the arms of Grand Master Pierre d'Aubusson and is 328cm long with a bore of 27.5cm. The second, called DIE KATERI, bears a number of inscriptions showing that it was made by Jorg Endorfer for the Archduke of Austria, Sigismund. Just how it came to be at Rhodes is not known, but it was probably a gift to the Hospitallers. It is 363cm long with a bore of 39cm. Both of these are cannon perriers and very much like those of the Turks.

A number of other Hospitaller guns are similar to these two pieces, but of later date. What is especially interesting about them is that they show the development of more modern features while retaining the basic form of the gun – a large bore barrel and smaller bore powder chamber. These later pieces have trunnions, and there is a move towards a more tapering shape and away from the parallel-sided barrel. This change can best be seen in three cannon, all dated 1507 and made in Lyon, France. The first, called LE FURIEUX, bears the arms of Grand Master Emery d'Amboise and is 190cm long with a bore of 26cm. The second has both the arms of the Hospitaller Order and those of the Bourbon family and is 300cm long with a bore of 23cm. Externally the barrels of these two pieces are divided into two sections. The rear is a slightly tapering smooth cylinder while the front, of smaller diameter, is divided by small raised mouldings – much like the barrels of LA BUSSONA and DIE KATERI. Interestingly, the front of the barrel of the longer piece is also facetted longitudinally. The third piece has a very different form, tapering from the rear to the front, much like all later cannon, but the entire length is divided into sections by small raised mouldings.

There are at least six further cannon perriers surviving from the walls of Rhodes, including two with the arms of Grand Master Philippe Villiers de l'Isle Adam, which, with the five mentioned above, indicates that this type of cannon was a major part of the Hospitallers' armament during the 1522 siege. For those of l'Isle Adam to have reached Rhodes in time for the siege, they must have been made in 1521.[33]

Among the other surviving Rhodes guns are a number of long cannon with relatively small bores and similar to the Ottoman basilisks noted above. Of these, a bronze gun in the Musée de l'Armée in Paris (N68), with a length of 540cm and a bore of 16.5cm, is the closest in length and calibre to what is now thought to have been a basilisk. Three other cannon – 482cm (Nuremberg W579), 405cm (Paris N70) and 402.5cm (Nuremberg W574) in length with bores of 22cm, 17.5cm and 17cm – are also probably basilisks.[34] Unfortunately, until the middle of the sixteenth century, cannon names and types tended not to be well defined, with considerable latitude in the dimensions of each type of cannon. What is clear though is that both the Hospitallers and the Turks saw the need for these long, thin weapons which gave them extra range.

Taken together, this group of surviving guns indicates that the walls of the city were armed with many artillery pieces that were long or of a larger calibre. Whether these were the only guns is impossible to know as there is no indication of just how much this sample is representative of the entire arsenal of the Knights – did the Turks remove guns after the siege as seems likely? Also likely is that the walls were armed with both these larger guns and smaller pieces in the same way as the Turkish batteries. For example, preserved in the Grand Master's Palace is a small piece which was probably used during the siege. It bears the arms of Grand Master Fabrizio Carretto and was certainly used as an anti-personnel weapon. This is confirmed by the existence of many smaller artillery positions where guns of this size could have been used, the caponnier on the north-west corner of the walls and the 'shooting galleries' attached to the boulevards of England and Provence, for example.

Although there are cannon from the 1522 siege, no mounts or carriages survive – these, being made primarily of wood, have long since perished and disappeared. This is true for all the carriages and mounts for cannon of this period, so that illustration and pictorial evidence must be relied on to see what they were like. These sources show large wooden carriages supported on large wheels on which the cannon were fitted. This meant that the artillery pieces, even the largest ones, were reasonably manoeuvrable and, with the wide ramparts built after 1480, they could be moved from one position to another relatively quickly and easily.

Unfortunately, where any of these cannon were sited on the walls, boulevards and towers of the city is not known, and the narrative sources do not help – Fontanus writing that they were simply placed *per muros et torres*, for example.[35] However, it is certain that at least the larger pieces must have been mounted on the wide ramparts at the top of the walls. Nothing shows the change in fortifications and artillery in the period from 1480 to 1522 as clearly as the thickening and widening of the walls at Rhodes. The walls were adapted so that not only were they much thicker, stronger and able to withstand the force of the 'new' artillery, but the very widening enabled the mounting of these guns on their carriages behind the parapet. This placing of the artillery high up so that it commanded the counterscarp and glacis meant that the Hospitallers were able to take the fighting right to the Turks – destroying their batteries and causing death and destruction.

On 28 July, in Bourbon's words, 'which day was *mal fortunee* for Rhodes',[36] Suleyman, 'the Great Turk' in contemporary Hospitaller sources, arrived at the siege.[37] The siege camp had been set up and the siege begun, although without much intensity. Undoubtedly, Suleyman had planned to arrive just at this point, his presence not needed to establish the Ottoman camp but essential for carrying out any major tactics, such as attacking the walls with men or guns. This may have been why a letter written from the Ottoman camp to Istanbul on the day of Suleyman's arrival indicates that his generals were 'wait[ing] to set up [their] own artillery and to complete [their] own means of combat'.[38]

Suleyman's arrival was announced with great fanfare. As his galley came into view, all the other Turkish ships in the fleet at Kalithas Bay hung banners from their tops and unfurled their sails. As he alighted and rode to camp, he was surrounded by a unit of Janissaries, who, accompanied by their band, sang loudly and fired salutes from their handguns. The pageantry and theatre of the display must have been marvellous. Certainly it could be seen and heard from the walls of Rhodes and was meant for the eyes and ears of the Hospitallers as much as for the Turks.[39]

Suleyman's pavilion had been set up at Megasandra, 7 to 9km south of the city, 'out of the danger of the artillery', Bourbon derisively notes.[40] But there was no doubt as to the Sultan's bravery the following day when he began to take personal charge of the siege. He inspected every unit of the army and the batteries of guns. The disposition of these forces is revealed in a letter probably written the day of Suleyman's arrival to his Grand Vizier in Istanbul, Lutfi Pasha. Pir Mehmed Pasha, the Grand Vizier on site, commanded those facing the eastern part of the walls from the sea to an undetermined location, possibly the Tower of Italy, where the walls slope to the south-west. Next to him was Qasim Pasha, called in the letter 'pioneer to those of Anatolia', who probably faced the walls from the Tower of Italy to St John's (Koskino) Gate, where the walls turn slightly to the north before carrying on to the west. Next were the soldiers of the Second Vizier, Mustafa Pasha, whose position can be better determined as he is described facing a 'difficult and unsurpassable locality, of difficult access to the walls and boulevards that fortified it', certainly meaning the walls from St John's Gate to the Tower of Spain, which were protected by lengthy *tenailles* and large boulevards. Finally, on the west and north sides all the way to the sea were the forces of Ahmed Pasha and the Beylerbey of Rumeli, Ayas Pasha. The Janissaries, led by Bali Agha, described in the letter as 'principal commander of the soldiers of the religion, so valorous that he is like a roaring lion', appear to have been positioned among all of the other soldiers, no doubt to inspire them when they grew weary or discouraged during the siege.[41] Kortoglu commanded the fleet of warships that would attack from the sea when Suleyman desired.[42]

On 29 July Suleyman ordered his men to begin digging approaches and trenches protected by a barrage of small arm fire from *hacquebuttes*.[43] Bourbon describes this work:

And also they worked to make their trenches and approaches with more diligence than before, at the same time making greater effort than before to carry the earth with spades and picks right to the moat. And they dug a great arc all around the town. And although there were infinite shots of artillery of the town against the said earth being moved, of which an innumerable quantity of men who were hiding behind it were killed. Nevertheless they never stopped taking the said earth all the way to the edge of the moat. And since that which was day by day raised higher and higher and higher and reinforced at the back. And at the end the said earth was higher then the walls of the town by ten or twelve feet, and at the end they made a mountain of this earth between the post of Spain and Auvergne.[44]

This was an interesting tactic: its intention was clearly to bring the Turkish gunfire as close to the walls of the city as possible and to protect the gunners while doing so. It is also clear that they intended to attack that part of the wall unprotected by *tenailles*. The Ottomans used this earth to construct 'mountains', probably some form of wall along the edge of the counterscarp which Bourbon says rose 10 to 12ft (3–4m) above the height of the city walls. The Hospitallers constantly fired on the workers while these were being built, causing considerable damage and loss of life. However, presumably by sheer weight of numbers and determination of the labourers, the Turks managed to complete the work. They then fired from the hills, so effectively, Bourbon writes, that they 'battered our people who were on the posts of the wall and boulevards, so that no person could get up there, but we made repairs of tables to protect our men in their batteries'.[45]

While building on the hills across from the walls between the towers of Auvergne and Spain, the Ottomans also dug a trench along the edge of the counterscarp completely around the city walls. Once completed this was immediately filled with Turkish soldiers. Bourbon provides their disposition, interestingly matching that written in the letter to Lutfi Pasha at Istanbul above:

The pashas and captains entered into the trenches and they each chose their place, according to their degree and authority: that is, Mustafa Pasha as principal captain chose the trench directed to the boulevard of England with his men and many captains under him. Pir Pasha, the oldest of the four pashas, went to the trench firing against the post of Italy with his band of men and many captains under him. Ahmed Pasha was in the trenches of Spain and Auvergne and the Aga of the Janissaries with him and the other captains under him. The Beylerbey of Anatolia was in the trenches of Provence and the Beylerbey of Romania with his band across from the gardens of St Anthony with his *tremontane* band and many men under him.[46]

The Turks also set up seven batteries 'close to the mills near *Ponent*', from which they bombarded the walls for 'eight or ten days'. Just where *Ponent* was is not at all clear today, nor whether it was a specific place or just a direction. These batteries are reported to have caused much damage against the walls opposite them, putting the Hospitallers there 'in great doubt', but l'Isle Adam ordered repairs, which he personally

Rhodes Besieged

supervised, and remained at the spot 'from morning until night, so that the work was done more quickly'. At the same time the Knights' guns at the post of Alamain and the Grand Master's Palace returned such fierce fire on the Ottoman batteries that eventually they dismantled them and 'took them away'.[47] This was certainly a victory for the Hospitallers, but it came at a cost, for the Turks were able to destroy the tower of St John's church, next to the Grand Master's Palace, which had been used as a lookout tower to locate their artillery and troops and to sight the Hospitaller guns on them. The significance of the loss of this tower is seen in the fact that it is recorded in every source on both sides, including Suleyman's daily record of the siege.[48]

It is also in Suleyman's 'Journal' where the skill of the Hospitaller gunners is attested. Whenever the Ottomans fired a cannon, the Sultan asserts, thirty Hospitaller pieces were aimed at it and destroyed it. The Grand Vizier, Lufti Pasha, confirms this, reporting that the Knights could 'fire many shots at the same time'.[49]

After being repulsed at Alamain Gate, Bourbon states that the same Turkish mantlets were moved and placed against the Tower of St Nicholas, presumably firing from the same position used by the Ottomans in 1480, located at the Church of St Anthony. From here they bombarded the harbour fortification for ten to twelve days, but the return gunfire from the Hospitallers was 'so good and vigorous, that there was not one mantlet of the enemy that lasted an entire hour'. So severe was this response that they reduced the Turks to only firing at night 'while the moon did shine'. Eventually Suleyman recognised the futility of these attacks and he withdrew the batteries to elsewhere.[50]

What a turnaround in tactics between the two sieges. At the siege of 1480 the capture of the Tower of St Nicholas had been seen as vital to the capture of the city of Rhodes, and the Turks had made a great effort to achieve it, with the futile expenditure of large amounts of time, men and gunshot. Perhaps as a consequence of this, in 1522 Suleyman made only a token attempt to take the fortress and, when this did not succeed, turned back to his assaults on the walls south of the city. The harbour, and its relatively weak walls, escaped further attack.

The Ottoman navy had been trying to blockade the island since it first arrived in June. But this was not highly successful, as shown by the number of messages that the Hospitallers were able to deliver by boat to waiting parties in Europe and Crete. In fact, they seem to have been able to come and go into Rhodes' harbours at will. The Mandraki Harbour (the military harbour since ancient times) was covered well by Hospitaller batteries in the Tower of St Nicholas, as has been seen, while the commercial port, lying directly in front of the city, was protected by a chain running between the Naillac Tower and the Tower of the Windmills as in 1480, and also by another chain which stretched between the Tower of Windmills and the Tower of St Nicholas, a distance of nearly a kilometre.[51] So ineffective was this blockade that at one time during the siege the commander of the Ottoman fleet, Kortoglu, was bastinadoed on the deck of ship in the presence of his sailors.[52]

Elsewhere in the siege the Turkish bombardment continued. Heavy attacks were made on the walls of England and Spain, against which, Bourbon writes, were fourteen

The Siege of 1522

Ottoman mantlets 'from which many sakers fired incessantly to kill men and firing of great bombards of which some of the stones were six or seven palms around and some of nine or ten'. So fierce was this fire that they 'destroyed the new wall of the *terreplein* of the post of England, although the old wall which was below the new one was untouched or only a little damaged'. Suleyman then turned his attention to the boulevard and wall of Spain, where they made 'breaches and they levelled the defences of the boulevard, and by the earth and stones that fell into the moat they were able to climb onto the *terreplein* of the wall of the town'. Batteries were also set up facing the walls of Provence and Italy where similar breaches were made.[53]

During this time the Hospitallers had been busy firing their own guns against the Turkish batteries. They were very accurate and succeeded in breaking up many of these, but the Ottomans repaired them during the night and replaced the crews so that each day the bombardment began anew. Even the death of their Master Gunner, Mehmed, whose legs were blown off by a gunshot from the walls of England, did not discourage them.[54]

The walls of Provence were unprotected by exterior fortifications, beyond a *fausse-braye*, so breaches being made there are easy to visualise. However, at Italy, England and Spain far more extensive defences protected the inner wall. Just what the Turks managed to do, or even what they hoped to accomplish by targeting these sites, is difficult to understand. Bourbon writes that breaches were made, but it is unclear exactly where they were. The *tenailles* in front of Spain and England were attacked but not destroyed. They are, after all, solid earth and rock – the remains of the ground left in situ when the moat was widened after 1480. Nor is it likely that the thick boulevard in front of Italy was breached. One interpretation may be that the Turkish guns reduced the upper wall down to the height of the older structure on the *tenaille*, the rubble from the wall filling up the moat between it and the counterscarp, thus allowing the Turks to climb on to the *tenaille*, as Bourbon indicates.

The man overseeing the Hospitaller defences against the Turkish attacks was Gabriel Tadini di Martinengo, a Brescian military engineer previously under Venetian employ on Crete. With the impending siege of Rhodes, the Grand Master had written to the authorities in Candia requesting Tadini's assistance. Although this was officially denied, he was spirited away and arrived in Rhodes on either 22 or 23 July.[55] Tadini proved to be of enormous value to the Hospitallers, advising on everything from making new defences and repairing the damaged walls to countermining. He was rewarded by being made a Knight Hospitaller two or three days after his arrival.[56]

When the breaches were made in the walls of Spain, England, Provence and Italy, Tadini put his engineering skills to work. Bourbon remarks that he:

> ... caused to make the traverses and repairs on the wall at the places where there was a breach, and the said traverses were mounted with large and small artillery which not only shot to the breach but also towards the trenches. And the said traverses daily killed many and other of the traverses the said captain made to place small artillery, as

hacquebuttes, and handguns were put on certain houses of the town that were in front of the breaches of Spain and also of Provence with some repairs. And from the said houses our men killed many of the enemy in the assaults.[57]

The traverses Tadini built seem to have been defences at right angles to the wall on both sides of the breach from which the besieged could fire at the Turks if they tried to break through. These were obviously large enough to mount a range of artillery and handgunners who not only were able to fire into the breach but also into the Ottoman trenches. He also placed hand-held gunpowder weapons on the roofs of houses inside the city in preparation for attacks through the breaches.

As mentioned, Suleyman had with him a very large number of pioneers and miners. So far they had been used primarily to dig the approaches and trenches up to the edge of the moat. They had also built the 'mountains' which stood above the counterscarp. Now it was their turn again. With the walls breached in several places and the moat filling with rubble from the bombardments, the miners started their digging towards and under the city walls. They seem to have cut many mines, although the exact number is not known. Each original source has its own estimate of the number of mines that the Turks dug during the siege.[58] Bourbon refers to two specifically: one between the towers of Spain and Auvergne and the second under the boulevard of England, in front of the Tower of the Virgin. These two mines, filled with gunpowder, were set off on 4 September. The first seems to have done little damage, but the second, according to Bourbon, 'was so furious, that a large part of the town shook and blasted about six holes in the wall'.[59]

At the detonation of these mines the Turks made their first assault on the walls, at the boulevard of England. Bourbon reports that the Ottomans began to cross to the boulevard by using the earth and stones that had been cast down into the moat by the explosion of the mine. But Tadini had built repairs and traverses there which did not fall, and from them the Hospitallers fired down on to the approaching men. Many made it through the barrage, and hand-to-hand fighting ensued 'with picks and fire-lances, with shots of bows and handguns from both sides seeming as if they fell like rain'. Eventually the Turks were driven back by the Hospitallers.[60]

On 9 September Suleyman ordered another assault, again preceded by the detonation of mines, one under the walls of Provence, which Bourbon writes 'had no effect'. A second, again at the boulevard of England, struck 'a measure or more of the wall of the boulevard next to where the first mine had broken the first wall'. This caused great confusion among the defenders of that part of the wall, with Bourbon alleging that 'all the men in it ran away'. However, when the standard of the Knights was raised, they rallied and repulsed the attack, joined by the artillery from the Koskino boulevard and 'other places' – seemingly firing along the moat.[61]

It was now the Turks' turn to lose heart. As they fled to the safety of their siege lines, their leaders rallied them 'with great strokes of swords and scimitars', and hand-to-hand fighting resumed. For three hours, Bourbon writes, the battle raged until 'the enemies were beaten on all sides with large and small artillery'. Only one Ottoman banner was taken, however, he laments, 'for as soon as a man climbed onto our repairs, he was slain by handguns from the trenches', although he is consoled in the fact that 2,000 or 3,000 Turks were killed.[62] Yet the Turks did not give up easily and on 17 September made another assault, again against the boulevard of England, and were again beaten back. This was part of a three-pronged attack ordered by Suleyman, the others made against the walls of Spain and Auvergne. These, too, were driven back because of the 'large and persevering artillery firing from the traverses on both sides and from the small artillery on the house next to the breach', Bourbon claims. This time he calculates 3,000 Turks killed in the assaults.[63]

On 22 September the Turks exploded another mine at the boulevard of England, but did no damage because Tadini had made 'vents by countermining' which dispersed the force of the blast.[64] This is the first time that Bourbon specifies the 'venting' of Turkish mines. The Hospitallers were able to dig shafts down to where the gunpowder had been placed. When it was set off, the pressure of the explosion was vented out by the shafts and its force was dissipated.[65]

On the following day, 23 September, two more mines were detonated, one under the walls of Spain and the other near St George's boulevard. Nothing is said about the Spanish mine, but that at St George's boulevard 'was so terrible that it made all the town tremble and made the wall to open from the top to the bottom and inside joined the *terreplein* and on the outside remain whole and entire, and no other damage by God's mercy because the said mine was vented by the countermines and also because of a rock which was under the barbican was blown out and by the opening of the rock the fury passed'.[66]

There was now less time between Turkish assaults. On 24 September they launched their largest attacks on the walls to date, against four separate locations, 'all at the same hour and time', says Bourbon.[67] These were at the breach in the walls of Spain, the boulevard of England, the breach of the walls of Provence, and the *tenaille* of Italy, next to the sea on the far east of the city, as confirmed later in Bourbon's account. It is the fighting against the walls of Spain on this day that Bourbon focuses on, recounting his experience there in helping to retake the boulevard. Under the cover of the smoke produced by bombards, an attack was led by Bali Pasha, the Agha of the Janissaries, commanding a company of his elite Turkish troops into the breach that had been created by earlier bombardment and mines. Quickly, thirty or forty Ottoman banners and insignia were planted into the earth of the breach before much of a Hospitaller response could be made. A six-hour skirmish followed. Several Turks reached the boulevard in front of the Tower of Spain, captured and held it for 'three hours or more'.

When l'Isle Adam, who was leading the defence of the boulevard of England, heard that the boulevard of Spain had been taken he rushed there with the 'banner of the Crucifix', one of the most sacred emblems of the Hospitallers, a reminder to them of their origins and purpose, to fight the enemies of Christianity. Its presence rallied the beleaguered defenders and they pushed the Turks back, enabling the 'artillery of the post of Auvergne, to the right of the boulevard of Spain' to fire upon them with the result that the attackers were 'so well scattered that all were killed'. By the time the

Rhodes Besieged

Knights had recovered the boulevard only a few Turks were still alive and were soon disposed of. All the Ottoman banners were captured.[68]

The success of the Hospitallers at the walls and boulevard of Spain was due to a number of factors, not the least of which was the presence of the Grand Master and the sacred banner of the Crucifix. Bourbon justly praises his leader's bravery in this action, but he also gives credit to the artillery fire from the walls of England and from the traverses of Spain and Auvergne, which Tadini had constructed a few days earlier, and to the small arms fire from the roofs of the houses nearby.[69]

The other three assaults had also been repulsed, although there is little detailed information about this. The Turks paid a heavy price for their failed efforts. Bourbon estimates that by the end of the day 12,000 or 14,000 were killed and that 'the quantity was such that a man could not perceive nor see the ground'. The bloodshed at the *tenaille* of Italy was so great that 'their blood made the sea red'.[70]

These defeats and the heavy loss of his soldiers' lives did not sit well with Suleyman, who had watched the entire battle from a specially built vantage point. The Great Turk was furious and dismissed Mustafa Pasha from his command, preserving his life only on the pleadings of the other Pashas as they worried that the execution of such a high-ranking military leader would give heart to the Hospitallers.[71] As a final gesture of loyalty to the Sultan, Mustafa was allowed to participate in the construction of mines, some of them to the boulevard of England. However, these were countermined or, if fired, did marginal damage to the walls.

The Turks were growing weary of the siege. Their bombardments and mining had not succeeded, while their assaults on the walls had been repulsed at the cost of the lives of a large number of their fellow soldiers. They also may have been running low on gunpowder and ammunition. Bourbon writes that spies in the Ottoman camp reported dissatisfaction to the point of rebellion, even by the Janissaries, and that some were beginning to abandon the siege camp for their ships.[72]

But the defenders, too, were fatigued and beginning to run low on supplies. There were also spies in their camp, or at least it was rumoured that traitors within the city were reporting the perilous state of the Hospitallers to the Turks. Bourbon mentions two in particular. One, a Jewish physician, Apella Renato, had been placed in Rhodes as a spy during the reign of Selim I – even being baptised as a Christian – and had been inactive since. During the siege he once again became an active spy for the Turks. After supplying information on weaknesses in the walls and the demoralised state of the Rhodians he was eventually discovered and executed.[73] The second was an unnamed Albanian who later in the siege went to the enemy's camp and warned them 'that most of the soldiers were dead or injured in the last assault', that they should continue the combat and that another assault would take Rhodes.[74]

Clearly, paranoia fed by fatigue and xenophobia had begun to affect the judgement and morale of both sides. This occurred in many lengthy sieges and often coloured the objectivity of sources, especially those of eyewitnesses, and the historical interpretation of them. At Rhodes it was the suspected treason of the Chancellor of the

Order, Andrea d'Amaral, which is blamed, at least in part, for the loss of the city. Bourbon goes into great detail on the charges laid against d'Amaral in an effort to prove his guilt, but for a modern reader the evidence is flimsy and circumstantial.[75]

On 30 October d'Amaral was supposedly implicated in treason when his servant was caught attempting to send messages to the Sultan. He was arrested and imprisoned in the Tower of St Nicholas. A number of people came forward to accuse the Chancellor, certainly indicating that he was very much disliked by the local population, possibly due to his arrogance and overbearing nature. Interrogated about these charges, d'Amaral claimed his innocence, even under torture, but was found guilty. On 7 November he was stripped of his Hospitaller membership and, the following day, executed. His head was mounted on to the Tower of St George facing the Turks, who, if he was innocent, must have recognised that the besieged Knights and citizens were nearing the end.[76]

The problems in the Turkish camp caused by the dismissal of Mustafa Pasha were quickly cleared up, for shortly afterwards, Bourbon reports, the Turks returned to the siege, 'and began anew to fire artillery more heavily than ever, for new munitions had been brought there'. The Sultan had apparently received new supplies, although Bourbon also credits Mustafa Pasha – who had not yet left for Egypt – with sustaining morale by his continual assaults on the city.[77] Mustafa led three assaults on three successive days all on the boulevard of England, in which the Turks used 'stones which fell like rain or hail' and 'bags full of artificial fire', incendiary devices like grenades. However, these failed to make any immediate difference in the siege, although many of the besiegers were injured by the 'artificial fire'.[78]

So far, the Knights had held on to their city through nine weeks of intense bombardment, numerous mines and many assaults. The walls had been severely beaten and breached in several places, although Tadini's engineering skills had saved them on numerous occasions. No doubt many had suggestions for the Grand Master on how to further defend the city. One which may have seemed a good idea at the time but turned out to have unforeseen detrimental consequences was to clean the moat around the boulevard of Spain of the stones and earth that had fallen into it. Bourbon claims that 'by great diligence, night and day' mines were constructed and 'the most part of the earth that lay in the moat was brought into the town'. Why the Hospitallers suddenly wanted to clear the moat of debris is puzzling until one reads the reasons given by Bourbon. Removing the earth and stones certainly kept the Ottomans from using them to climb on to the walls and breach, but it also appears that the Rhodians needed the earth 'to make repairs inside the town'.[79]

The Turks, seeing that the moat was cleared, took advantage of the situation by digging trenches across it to the base of the boulevard. At times their progress was slowed by Hospitaller handgun fire from the nearby walls, which the Ottomans countered by covering their trenches 'with tables', and eventually they reached the wall, becoming, in Bourbon's words, 'lords of the barbican'. Once gaining the foot of the wall the Turks began to 'pick' at it, 'sleeping not' – obviously rotating work crews. The Knights tried a number of counter-measures but were hampered by their lack of soldiers. They tried to

Rhodes Besieged

drive the Turks away 'with barrels full of powder and with engines of artificial fire', but while this killed many, 'it availed nothing for the quantity and multitude of labourers and others were so great that the captains did not care even if they lost 500 or 1,000, for continually they changed and renewed'. To protect themselves from the fire the Ottomans built a wooden roof covered in ox hides.[80]

With the Turks on the edge of breaking through the city wall, Tadini came up with an innovative, but somewhat counter-intuitive, plan. Knowing that there were too few defenders of the city to prevent the breaching of the wall adequately, he recognised:

> ... that there was no other remedy except to cut the wall at the bottom so that they could see and discover them, and beat them with artillery. Then our men began to cut the wall, and made some holes to fire their handguns on the enemy who did the same from their side. And by these holes, they slew and injured many of our men and we did likewise.[81]

While this was going on, Tadini continued to build defences within the town in case the Turks succeeded in breaking through the wall.[82] Traverses were constructed on each side of an expected breach and filled with 'large and medium artillery'. During this work the great engineer 'by putting his eye to a hole to look out, a handgun shot from the enemy trenches burst through his eye and came out from behind his ear and put his life in danger'. He recovered, but it put him out of action for six weeks.[83]

The Turks continued to work at breaking the wall. On 20 October they attempted to explode more mines, but they failed. They also tried to bring down the wall using ropes and grapples,[84] but the Hospitaller fire from the boulevard of St George 'broke their ropes and they did nothing'.[85] On 23 October another mine was exploded, which the Turks 'thought would knock the wall down to the ground, but all the mine did was to leave the wall hanging over the enemies, which was more to their disadvantage than to our damage'. Evidently the mine lifted the wall but left it leaning, so that it became dangerous to continue to hack at it from below as the Turks had been doing. However, it was badly damaged by the explosion and, after firing their artillery at it for a few days, 'it was broken down and there was a way and an opening into the town'.[86]

Although they seem to have opened a large breach in the walls, the Turks made no immediate attempt to storm the city through it. Indeed, Bourbon states that the Hospitaller artillery 'sitting at the two mills of the gate of Koskino, that is to say a basilisk, a double cannon and a coulovrine ... looked right onto the breach', implying that the Knights' artillery was what kept the Turks from attacking.[87]

The Hospitallers anticipated an attack now 'day by day and hour by hour'. L'Isle Adam, who had moved to the Tower of Spain during the assaults of 24 September and had not left since, stood with a group of knights opposite the breach, 'his life in great danger', and awaited the onslaught.[88]

Suleyman now 'sought other means' by attempting to enlarge the breach his troops had made. Trenches were dug across the moat from which handgunners attacked those attempting to make repairs. At the same time, earth was piled up between the city wall and the *faussebraye* between the posts of England and Auvergne and the gap into the city was enlarged until it was 'ten or twelve feet wide', and new covered trenches were dug leading up to the breach. The Hospitallers were unable to repair the damage caused by the Turks, as Bourbon notes: 'because we did not have any more slaves nor other labourers to repair what was broken day and night.' At the same time, assaults on the Koskino Gate and the *tenaille* of Italy continued, unhindered by the Turkish activity at the Tower of Spain.[89]

Soon, however, the *tenaille* of Italy, which was being shot at by 'seventeen great guns', as numbered by Bourbon, began to give way. Here the Knights were outside the city walls, upon the *tenaille* that had been built by Pierre d'Aubusson in the wake of the 1480 recovery. Gradually the Turks began to wear down both the fortification and the will of the Hospitallers there to hold out against them. Finally, only a third of it was left defensible, 'which was towards the sea', with most of the defenders having retreated back into the city.[90] Ultimately the Turks 'cut to the town wall' and began 'to pick and cut as [at the walls of] Spain', again trying to dismantle the wall.[91]

Realising that the Turks might also break through there, l'Isle Adam ordered the demolition of part of the churches of Our Lady of the Victory – erected in celebration of the defence staged on that section of the wall, the Jewish Quarter, during the earlier siege – and St Panteleemon. The Rhodians used the stones to make repairs and construct traverses similar to those built earlier at the walls of Spain. But the work did not progress very quickly 'because there were no labourers', once more confirming that the casualty rate among these people had been very high.

The attack on the boulevard of England had also been progressing. The Turks continued to pick at the wall and were actually able to take the boulevard itself. But the Hospitallers had placed 'certain incendiaries and barrels of powder well hidden and covered there' which they set off as the Ottomans entered the boulevard, killing 'a good number of the enemy'. It turned out to be only a temporary victory, though, as these men were quickly replaced and held the boulevard for the rest of the siege. The gate of the city controlled by the boulevard was now open to attack.[92]

At the breach in the walls of Spain the Turks continued their dismantling of the walls. This progressed at a slow pace, but by now the Hospitallers were so few in number that they could but stand by as onlookers. Their repairs and traverses were attacked constantly by artillery and handgun fire, while Ottoman labourers moved through covered trenches to cut into the wall and 'grate the earth below it'.[93]

By 28 November, Bourbon writes, 'the Ottomans had significantly weakened the city walls near the Tower of Spain, where the wall was actually breached, as well as the walls of England and Italy. They now planned to make assaults on all locations. Throughout this day and the night following, the Turks ceased not to fire large artillery both from the edge of the moat with those large pieces, firing stones of nine to eleven palms of size, and from the mantelets without. And by count were fired the same day and night 150 shots or more against the repairs and traverses of the wall.'[94]

Rhodes Besieged

Suleyman launched his last big attack at dawn the next morning. Bourbon, once more to be found at the Tower of Spain, focuses on what occurred there. Making a frontal assault on the breach, the Turks entered the city only to be cut to pieces by the Hospitaller artillery and handguns waiting for them on the traverses and houses nearby. According to Bourbon, more than 2,000 were killed in this initial attack. The survivors attempted to return to their own lines only to be riddled with gunfire again. Rain that had been falling heavily throughout the morning hindered the Turks further as the ground on which they were attacking became muddy, slowing their movement, forward or back. Nor was the attack at the *tenaille* of Italy any more successful:

> The said day also the enemies made an assault on the *terreplein* of Italy which was well received, but when they heard at the breach of Spain that their companions were repulsed so lively, they tried to retreat with great loss of men. Seeing also that it was a bad time, they returned to their trenches without doing anything else.[95]

It is clear that during these assaults the Turks lost large numbers of soldiers. Sir Nicholas Roberts, an English Hospitaller at the siege, testifies to those killed at the breach near the Tower of Spain and at the *tenaille* of Italy: 'Upon St Andrew's eve last was the last battle between the Turks and us; at that battle was slain 11,000 Turks.'[96] This must have been a significant blow to their morale, yet neither the Ottoman leaders nor their men seem to have given up.

Ahmed Pasha, who had been in overall command since the disgrace of Mustafa Pasha, appears to have decided not to make further direct assaults on the breaches for the moment. However, sometime at the end of November the Turks entered the moat and attacked the *tenaille* between the Tower of Spain and the boulevard of England. The Knights positioned there fought valiantly but ultimately could not hold the fortification and abandoned it.[97]

In hindsight, one can see that this was the final blow to the defence of Rhodes by the Knights Hospitaller. But at the time there was still some fight in them, at least in one faction. Others, however, began to look for solutions to the siege that might preserve their lives and those of the remaining townspeople. On 3 December, an envoy from Suleyman, a Genoese or *Cyou*, according to Bourbon, approached the Auvergne Gate and asked to speak with the Knights about surrender. When questioned about his intentions, he:

> said that he was astonished by us, why we had not surrendered, seeing the piteous state the town was in. And he as a Christian man counselled us to surrender with some agreement, and that if we wished to listen, that some expedient could be found that there was some other way.

He was sent away, the Hospitallers responding that 'the enemies did have great advantage, but they were still outside the town by the grace of God, that they could still receive them and feast them well, if they made other assaults'.[98]

The Siege of 1522

He returned two days later, wishing to speak with a Genoese merchant living in the city named Mathieu de Via, whom he was told was ill. His request to deliver a letter from Suleyman to the Grand Master in person was refused and he was again sent away, this time with a gunshot in defiance. A day or two later, a different envoy, identified as an Albanian, approached the city and was also sent away. Although none of these envoys had actually been allowed inside the city, rumours of the Turks' offer of surrender spread throughout the population. While there was no immediate outburst of support for surrender, the citizens secretly persuaded their Metropolitan and some Knights to intercede with l'Isle Adam on their behalf. He was steadfast, responding that 'no such thing ought to be done or thought for anything in the world, but rather he and they should die'. The Knights left but returned a short time later asking him to reconsider the citizens' petition and to convene a full Council of the Order.[99]

The Council met, allowing two or three of Rhodes' leading citizens to put their case forward. They asked the Hospitallers to consider negotiating with Suleyman. Before delivering an answer to the townspeople, the Council asked the Lord of Saint-Gilles – 'who was in charge of the munitions' – and Tadini for reports of the state of 'munitions, men-at-war, and of the batteries'. Saint-Gilles answered:

> saying and affirming upon his honour and his conscience that the slaves and labourers were almost all dead or wounded, and that it was very hard to find men to move a piece of artillery from one place to another, and that it was impossible without more men to make or set up the repairs which every day were broken and crushed by the great and furious batteries of the enemies. As for munitions the said lord said that all that was in the town was used up long ago, and that brought [to the guns] would be at great pains to respond to one assault.

Tadini then reported:

> ... seeing and considering the great batteries that were attacking the town, and after seeing such a large breach and that the enemies threatened to enter into the town by their trenches more than a hundred feet in length and in traverses seventy or more. Seeing also that in two other places they were hacking at the wall, and that the largest part of the men-at-war, Knights and others, were dead or injured, and the munitions failing, and there were less labourers, that it was impossible to resist them any more, that without any doubt the town was lost, if there came no strength to raise the siege.

L'Isle Adam then spoke, opposing any surrender. He asked them to consider whether it was not better 'for all to die or to save the people and the relics'.[100]

The Council debated the issue for a long time. But in the end they decided to accept the treaty offered by Suleyman.[101] Negotiations between the Turks and Hospitallers began. It was agreed that ambassadors would be exchanged and a truce of three days declared. Sir

Rhodes Besieged

Nicholas Roberts, who claims to have been one of the Hospitaller ambassadors, although his name is not mentioned by Bourbon, describes meeting the 'Great Turk':

> I was one of those that the Lord Master [of the] religion sent to the Great Turk for [ ] such time as the pact was made between the Turks and him. The Great Turk is of the age of [28] years; he is very wise, discreet and much [ ] both in his words and also in his [ ] being of his age. I was in his court [ ] at such time as we were brought first to make our reverence unto him. We found [ ] a red pavilion standing between two [ ] lines, marvellous, rich and sumptuous. [He was] sitting in a chair, and no creature sat in the pavilion, which chair was of [ ] work of fine gold, his guard standing near his pavilion to the number of 22.[102]

Suleyman's offer was unconditional: the Hospitallers were to surrender the town and its people and in turn they could leave with their possessions. If they refused, he threatened not to depart until he had captured the town, 'that all the Turks would die there, rather than he would fail, and that nothing would escape, small or large. But all the way to the cats they should be cut to pieces.'[103] They had three days to decide. The ambassadors on both sides returned to camp, the Hospitallers reporting to the Order's Council. The Council decided to accept the terms, but was met by another delegation of townspeople who demanded that they not surrender as they did not trust that the Turks would keep their word. L'Isle Adam, now accepting that Rhodes was lost, answered that he would gain assurances from Suleyman that he would preserve the lives of the citizens. He sent two further ambassadors to ask for this and for an extension to the truce to enable the Hospitallers to discuss the terms of surrender with all the citizens of Rhodes.[104]

Suleyman refused and ordered a resumption of the bombardment of the city. The truce was broken and the enemy shot 'more sharply than before'. The Knights made no reply to this, Bourbon insists, because they wanted to preserve what little gunpowder they had left for 'some assault or need'.[105] L'Isle Adam met again with the faction of the townspeople who had objected to surrender, telling them that he would fight to the death, but he also had it announced that:

> ... all those who were assigned to be at the posts were not to leave, and not to move either day or night on pain of death. And those who were not assigned to the posts and who were not otherwise helping were to come to the breach of Spain where the said Lord was continually.[106]

Spurred on by this decree, the citizens manned the walls for a while, but gradually they returned to their homes and families. Even the execution of one young Rhodian for leaving his post could not keep them where they were supposed to be to defend the city. Eventually even those citizens who had initially opposed surrender realised the futility of continuing the struggle. They once more approached the Grand Master of the Hospitallers and suggested that they were now willing to accept the Sultan's terms.[107]

Negotiations began again with the exchange of letters between l'Isle Adam and the Turks. After a few false starts and misunderstandings, terms were agreed and, on

20 December, the city of Rhodes was surrendered by the few remaining Knights of the Hospital who were still there.[108] On Christmas day the Janissaries entered the walls of the city, not by force of arms but by negotiation. Bourbon and Fontanus suggest that some sacking of homes and churches did take place, but other sources deny that this happened. Suleyman would keep his word. A smooth transition from Hospitaller to Ottoman control took effect. On 1 January the Knights and all those who wanted to leave sailed out of the harbours. The Sultan had allowed them their naval guns – in fact he said that he would provide them with artillery for their ships if this was needed, no doubt in order to ensure their safe arrival – but the big guns on the walls were to stay, and there they remained until the nineteenth century.[109]

Sir Nicholas Roberts, writing on 15 May 1522 from Messina, Sicily, to the Earl of Surrey, recalls the destruction of so much and the death of so many:

During the siege the Lord Master had been found in every battle, often as the worst[110] knight of the religion [Hospitaller] knights there were slain 703, of the Turks 103,000, they gave us 22 battles the twenty [fourth] September was the general battle, from the beginning of the day to hie[ ] without ceasing; they gave us battles in five places of the town, and there were slain by their own confession, at that battle 22,000; the Great Turk was there in person, and in the battle we had slain three score [ ] upon our walls, or ever he were ready to [ ] them; there were slain of our part 6,000 [ ] during the siege time.[111]

Notes

1   Brockman, p. 125.
2   Jacques de Bourbon, *Relation de la grande et merveilleuse et trés cruelle expugnation de la noble cite de Rhodes (Paris, 1527)*, as reprinted in Abbé de Vertot, *The History of the Knights of Malta, by Mons l'Abbé de Vertot. Illustrated with LXXI heads of the Grand Masters, &c*, vol. 1, Proofs section (London, 1728), pp. 118–9.
3   Bourbon, p. 119 and Brockman, p. 125.
4   Fontanus, p. 14r and Sanudo, 33:359–64. See also Setton, III:205.
5   Vatin, p. 350 and Roberts, p. 713. See also Setton, III:205.
6   Vatin, pp. 481–91.
7   See Inalcik, pp. 35–40; Imber, pp. 48–61; articles in Metin Kunt and Christine Woodhead, ed , *Süleyman the Magnificent and His Age: The Ottoman Empire in the Early Modern World* (London: Longman, 1995).
8   Setton, III:205.
9   Setton, III:203–4.
10 This letter is contained in E. Charrière, *Négociations de la France dans le Levant*, 4 vols (Paris: Imprimerie Nationale, 1848–60; rpt. New York: Burt Franklin, 1965), I:85–90. The excerpt quoted is translated in Setton, III:204.
11 Vatin, pp. 345–6.
12 Vatin, p. 346.
13 Vatin, p. 346.
14 Vatin, p. 346 and footnote: *Que quidem monstra fiet hoc modo videlicet quod omnes domini fratres predicti habeant dicta arma vestita super se et in propria persona hoc est celatum bavoram braccialetos bergantinam sive alecuetum cum suis faldis sive brachis aut corsalettos. Item quilibet ipsorum habebit suum ensem accinctum etiam arma inhastata etiam duas spingardas vel duas arbalestras vel unam spingardam et unam arbalestram aut duos arcus pro angliciis.*

Rhodes Besieged

A *bevor* protected the lower half of the face; a *brigandine* is body armor made from small overlapping plates of iron riveted to a textile garment; a *fauld* is the lower plate of a breastplate; *brachis* are arm defences; and *corsalettos* are front and back armour plates. For a discussion of some of the remaining armour from Rhodes see Walter J. Karcheski, Jr. and Thom Richardson, *The Medieval Armour from Rhodes* (Leeds: Royal Armouries and Higgins Armoury Museum, 2000).

15 Bourbon, pp. 112–3.
16 Bourbon, p. 113.
17 Bourbon, p. 113.
18 Bourbon, p. 113.
19 Bourbon, p. 113. Strangely, the English translation of Bourbon, which was made from the first French edition, reports that almost all of the island's crops were unripe, but whatever was edible, even if only 'half ripe', was taken into town. Peasants and labourers worked for several days to do this but were unable to harvest everything before the arrival of the Turks, leaving 'the most part' in the fields (*The begynnynge and foundacyon of the holy hospytall, [and] of the ordre of the knyghtes hospytallers of saynt Johan baptyst of Jerusalem*, trans. Robert Coplande [London, 1524], p. 6r).
20 Vatin, p. 347.
21 Vatin, p. 347.
22 Vatin, p. 347.
23 Vatin, p. 348, referencing Fontanus, p. 14r..
24 Bourbon, p. 121. In Bourbon's text the date is given as 28 July, but as he follows this with 19 July and it is before Suleyman has arrived at the siege, we feel that the print is mistaken here.
25 Bourbon, p. 121. See also Fontanus, p. 16v.
26 Bourbon, pp. 121–2. Fontanus also has a lengthy discussion of the Turkish artillery at Rhodes but his descriptions are difficult to understand because Latin has a limited technical vocabulary for gunpowder weapons (pp. 18v–19r).
27 This is calculated by using the formula $\frac{4}{3}\pi r^3$ for the volume of a sphere and assuming a specific gravity of stone of 2.6.
28 Dulle Griet, one of the largest surviving Western European guns, and now preserved in Ghent, has a bore of 64cm. On late medieval bombards, including Dulle Griet, see Robert D. Smith and Ruth Rhynas Brown, *Mons Meg and Her Sisters* (London: Trustees of the Royal Armouries, 1989). For the Turkish bombards see Appendix 1.
29 There is little published information about basilisks. For a short discussion of the term when applied to gunpowder weapons see Jan Piet Puype, 'The Basilisk *Stuerghewalt* of 1511 in Hertogenbosch, the Netherlands', in *ICOMAM 50: Papers on Arms and Military History, 1957–2007*, ed. Robert D. Smith (Leeds: Basiliscoe Press, 2007), pp. 360–87 and Gábor Ágoston, *Guns for the Sultan: Military Power and the Weapons Industry in the Ottoman Empire* (Cambridge: Cambridge University Press, 2005). On the Woolwich basilisk see J.P. Kaestlin, *Catalogue of the Museum of Artillery in the Rotunda at Woolwich, part 1: Ordnance*, 2nd ed. (London: Her Majesty's Stationery Office, 1970), no. II.191 (p. 28).
30 H.L. Blackmore, *The Armouries of the Tower of London. I: Ordnance* (London: Her Majesty's Stationery Office, 1976), pp. 173–4.
31 Fontanus, pp. 18r–v.
32 The inscription which contains the date of this gun is damaged – it is likely to be dated 1482 but it is not possible to be absolutely certain.
33 For a recent description of all the Rhodes guns in Paris see Sylvie Leluc, 'L'artillerie des chevaliers Hospitaliers de Saint-Jean de Jérusalem de Rhodes à Malte/The Artillery of the Knights of the Hospitaller Order of St John of Jerusalem from Rhodes to Malta', in *Entre glaive et la croix: Chefs-d'œuvre de l'armurerie de Malta/ Between the Battlesword and the Cross: Masterpieces from the Armoury of Malta* (Paris: Musée de l'Armée and Heritage Malta, 2008), pp. 80–99.
34 Another cannon, of which there is only a drawing made in the nineteenth century, is broken and must originally have been around 500cm. long, making it also a basilisk. See August von Essenwein *Quellen zur Geschichte der Feuerwaffen*, 2 vols (1877; rpt. Graz: Akademische Druck – u. Verlagsanstalt, 1969), pl. A. CVII–CVIII.

The Siege of 1522

35 Fontanus, p. 17r. Bourbon is better here, sometimes naming the areas of wall or the names of towers where the guns were, but he unfortunately never clarifies exactly where they were placed or how they were mounted.
36 Bourbon, p. 123. See also Fontanus, p. 14v.
37 Brockman, p. 126 and Vatin, p. 344.
38 In Rossi, II:30.
39 Bourbon, p. 123 and Brockman, p. 126.
40 Bourbon, p. 123.
41 In Rossi, II:29–30. Brockman (pp. 126–7) seems to have misread this document in placing the Ottoman army where he does.
42 Brockman, p. 127. Fontanus suggests that these ships also constantly fired their guns into the city (p. 17r).
43 Bourbon, p. 123.
44 Bourbon, p. 123. The intensity of the Hospitallers' gunfire against the Turks building the approaches is also recorded in Suleyman's official 'journal' of the siege. See Vatin, p. 354.
45 Bourbon, p. 123.
46 Bourbon, p. 123.
47 Bourbon, p. 123.
48 Bourbon, p. 124; Vatin, p. 354; Rossi, *Assedio*, p. 17; and 'Journal', p. 530.
49 'Journal', p. 531 and Lufti Pasha, p. 312, as quoted in Vatin, p. 354.
50 Bourbon, p. 124. Fontanus (f. 19r) comments on how limited the attack on St Nicholas was. He also states that no one was hurt during the bombardment of the tower.
51 Fontanus, f.17v and Setton, III: 206–7.
52 Brockman, pp. 130–1.
53 Bourbon, p. 124.
54 Bourbon, p. 124, and Brockman, p. 129.
55 Fontanus, pp. 14r–15v; Sanudo, 33:566; Bourbon, p. 122; and Setton, III:206.
56 Bourbon, p. 122.
57 Bourbon, p. 126.
58 Bourbon tallies 60 before 4 September; Piero da Campo 38–39 before 21 September; Hieronimo de la Torre 63 before 14 November; Albergo di Rouan 50 before 14 November; Domenego Trivixan more than 45 mines, with no date mentioned. See Vatin, p. 354.
59 Bourbon, p. 127.
60 Bourbon, p. 127.
61 Bourbon, pp. 127–8.
62 Bourbon, p. 128.
63 Bourbon, p. 128, and Fontanus, pp. 20r–v.
64 Bourbon, p. 129.
65 Because Bourbon uses the French *espirail* to describe the countermine, some modern commentators have interpreted these vents to be 'spiral,' when in fact the word derives from the same Old French root as *respirer*, *souffler* or *exspirer*. See, for example, Brockman, p. 134.
66 Bourbon, p. 129.
67 Bourbon, p. 129.
68 Bourbon, p. 129.
69 Bourbon, p. 129.
70 Bourbon, pp. 129–30.
71 This is Bourbon's account (p. 131) which is certainly accurate in the dismissal of Mustafa Pasha, but is less trustworthy without corroborating Ottoman sources about the reasons for the preservation of his life. Bourbon believes that it was also Mustafa's familial relation to the Sultan – he was married to his aunt – that saved him (Bourbon, p. 132). See also Fontanus, pp. 23r–24v.
72 Bourbon, p. 131.
73 Bourbon, p. 128. See also Brockman, p. 133.
74 Bourbon, p. 131.

75 Brockman, pp. 139–48, is totally against d'Amaral's guilt, and Vatin, pp. 356–7, agrees with him, while Setton, III:210, is much more circumspect about it.
76 Besides the secondary references cited in the note above, see Bourbon, pp. 111–2, 131, 135–6. L'Isle Adam's own feelings are expressed in a letter written on 13 November 1522 that he had not only to fight the Turks during the siege but also 'one of the greatest of our council, the which by envy and ambition had conspired to make an approach to the Turk and to surrender him the city' (Vatin, p. 357, citing Charrière, I:CXXXII).
77 Bourbon, pp. 131–2.
78 Bourbon, p. 132.
79 Bourbon, p. 132.
80 Bourbon, p. 133.
81 Bourbon, p. 133.
82 Bourbon claims that these were built in 'trois estages', but what he means by this is unclear. Were these three separate traverses, one built higher than that in front, or three storeys on the same traverse?
83 Bourbon, p. 133. See also Fontanus, pp. 25v–26r.
84 Bourbon's phrase is 'grosses cordes avec organes'; the use of the term 'organes' is confusing but seems to indicate something at the end of the rope which could grab hold of the wall. The 1524 English translator Robert Copelande translated it as 'anchor', although that would seem to be in error as Bourbon later uses the word 'ancre' for anchor.
85 Bourbon, p. 133.
86 Bourbon, p. 133.
87 Bourbon, p. 133.
88 Bourbon, p. 133.
89 Bourbon, p. 133 and Fontanus, p. 26v.
90 Bourbon, p. 137. Bourbon calls the remaining part of this 'terreplain' a 'canton' and specifies that it is only a third the size of the original fortification. There is a portion of the *tenaille* on this side of the walls of Rhodes still surviving, with a segment near the sea that juts out from the rest of the structure. Perhaps this is the 'canton' Bourbon is referring to. It is also important to note that the original size of this *tenaille* cannot be determined as it has been cut off to allow for a road to travel around the modern city.
91 Bourbon, p. 137.
92 Bourbon, p. 137.
93 Bourbon, p. 137.
94 Bourbon, p. 138.
95 Bourbon, p. 138.
96 Roberts, p. 712.
97 Bourbon, pp. 138–9.
98 Bourbon, p. 139.
99 Bourbon, p. 139 and Fontanus, pp. 29r–v.
100 This Council is reported by Bourbon (p. 140), but it seems he was not a part of it, that he only had heard what the reports said and the discussions were. On Tadini's return to action see Fontanus, pp. 30r–31r.
101 Bourbon, pp. 140–1.
102 Roberts, p. 712. As can be seen Roberts' text is damaged in places. Some of the gaps can easily guessed while others require more speculation. We have chosen to leave them as gaps in the text.
103 Bourbon, p. 142.
104 Bourbon, p. 143.
105 Bourbon, p. 143.
106 Bourbon, p. 143.
107 Bourbon, pp. 143–4 and Fontanus, pp. 27v–29v.
108 Bourbon, pp. 144–6.
109 Bourbon, pp. 146–8, and Fontanus, pp. 32r–v.
110 Nicholas means 'lowest' or 'most humble'.
111 Roberts, p. 713.

Part Two

A Story of Stone, Cannon and Men

Two sieges were laid against Rhodes, forty-two years apart, fought between soldiers from the same armies – the Ottoman Turks and the Knights Hospitaller. Few in either army fought in both sieges. Philippe Villiers de l'Isle Adam, Hospitaller Grand Master, and Andrea d'Amaral, Chancellor of the Order until executed for aiding the Ottoman Turks in 1522, did, but no other Hospitaller is recorded to have been there. Nor are any Turks reported to have been at both sieges; however, this may be more an indication of the lack of Ottoman records and the impreciseness of their narratives than anything else. As such it may have been only l'Isle Adam who witnessed the two completely different results of the sieges. At the first siege, fought in 1480, the Knights held out until the Turks retreated across the straits home; in the second, fought in 1522, the Hospitallers accepted a conditional surrender offered to them by the Ottoman Sultan, Suleyman, and left the island never to return. Technology certainly played a role, but was it decisive? Was the large gunpowder artillery train of Mehmed II effectively countered by the tall, relatively thin medieval walls of Rhodes? Did the improved gunpowder arsenal of Suleyman, larger, more powerful and more numerous, defeat the updated walls of the Knights, thickened, heightened, with new, 'state-of-the-art' towers, boulevards and *tenailles*?

Trying to understand the events of the siege of Rhodes in 1480 and to comprehend the motives and reasons behind the Turkish actions is very difficult. The eyewitness accounts are excellent but they are all from the Hospitaller side and thus only report a reaction to the Ottoman military decisions. We do not possess the necessary Turkish documents, official accounts or other narratives, to fully comprehend the motives behind Mesīh Pascha's tactical choices. Still, as historians we must try to make reasonable assumptions and theories as to what occurred. Fundamental to this analysis is the assumption that Mesīh Pascha made decisions informed by good intelligence, based on experience and excellent counsel, and that his commands were carried out with diligence — what he did was done for good tactical reasons even if sometimes what was done seems baffling.

It is in this light that we must look at the Ottoman decision to try to take the Tower of St Nicholas as a priority. Some commentators have either stated or implied that this was a mistake and determined the ultimate failure of the Turks in their 1480 siege of a city surrounded by walls that would still have to be penetrated even if the Tower of St Nicholas had fallen.[1] Yet, this was the Turks' first objective, so it was obviously seen by them as tactically important. That the Hospitallers responded with such a tenacious and ferocious resistance suggests that they, too, considered that the tower was integral to the defence of Rhodes.

So, why was the Tower of St Nicholas key to the capture of the city? Although Mehmed II was not at Rhodes, Mesīh Pascha was, and he used the same plan that Mehmed had used in 1453 to capture Constantinople. Initially, before attacking the walls at Constantinople, Mehmed had secured the waterways into and out of the city. This had not been easy to do, necessitating the construction of Rumeli Hisar castle on the European shore of the Bosphorus and the reconstruction of Andolu Hisar castle on the Asian shore, from where gunpowder weapons effectively kept ships from supplying the city from the Black Sea,[2] and the stationing of a large fleet in the Sea of Marmara to prevent resupply from the Mediterranean. Once the waterways were secured Mehmed was able to take his time in attacking the walls of the city.

The Tower of St Nicholas controlled all naval access to the city of Rhodes. By occupying it, and the mole leading to it, the Ottomans would have effectively blockaded the inner harbour, something that could not be done with ships alone. By placing large bombards and other gunpowder weapons in the tower and along the mole, the Turks would also have forced any relief or resupply ships to run the risk of being destroyed as they approached the harbour. When the Tower of St Nicholas was not captured, ships from Crete, Cos and Italy were able to sail to and from the besieged city. In 1480 Rhodes was never threatened by starvation or lack of supplies.

More importantly, had the Tower of St Nicholas fallen, Mesīh Pascha could have attacked the walls of Rhodes at his leisure, as Mehmed II had at Constantinople. In 1453 Mehmed could concentrate all his efforts, his guns and troops, in battering down and breaching the weakest part of the walls, which is how he eventually gained access to the city. At Rhodes, as the Tower of St Nicholas did not fall, Mesīh Pascha could not do the same. The weakest walls of Rhodes were those facing the harbours, which without control of the Tower of St Nicholas could not be attacked.

Once Mesīh Pascha had realised this he turned to a different strategy. He had to open a breach in the city wall to defeat the Hospitallers and take their city. He had powerful gunpowder weapons — at least as powerful as those at Constantinople in 1453 — and, as they had shown against the Tower of St Nicholas, they could cause a lot of destruction quite quickly.

Mesīh Pascha chose the Jewish Quarter as the point for his major assault on the city. Why this section of walls was chosen is not clear from the written sources. In

A Story of Stone, Cannon and Men

fact, it is not even clear from these sources exactly where the Jewish Quarter was in the city of 1480. This has given rise to most historians believing that the Turkish attack was levelled at the south-east corner of the walls, where the rounded Tower of Italy, built in 1515, and the Acandia Gate, a modern addition, now stand. This would have meant that Mesīh Pascha mounted his cannon on high ground across the moat and that in charging the walls his troops would pass through that same moat and then climb on to the rubble of the wall created by this gunfire to enter the city.[3]

It was here that the Turks were turned back after an incredible fight on the tops of the rubble and in the breach. But why did they not return? Rarely would a single assault on such a breach be the deciding factor in causing the retreat of an army which had devoted so much energy and so many resources and men to the capture of a city. Mesīh Pascha simply left once this attack failed, and the reasons why are, and will probably remain, a mystery. Had he run out of money? Had too many soldiers been killed? Had he been recalled by Mehmed? Was he worried about the approaching winter? Had his command structure broken down? Did he face a potential mutiny from his exhausted and continually defeated troops? One would think that none of these should have determined a retreat of an Ottoman Turkish army at this time in their history. But they did leave, and Rhodes still stood for Christendom.

The outcome of any siege was rarely, if ever, decided by simple expedients. The 1480 siege of Rhodes makes this point very clearly indeed. The Ottoman army was well prepared, well equipped and large; the defenders few and not all battle-hardened or professional troops. What appears, superficially at least, to have been a very unequal contest defies expectations. The resistance put up by the Knights in the defence of the Tower of St Nicholas was prodigious and their reactions swift and effective. Episodes such as the courageous removal of the fastening of the temporary bridge structure and the morale of the defenders were vital in the final outcome of that part of the siege. Later, when the Turks attacked the walls of the Jewish Quarter, the work of the city's inhabitants to repair and rebuild the walls were important factors.[4] The failure of the Turks to take St Nicholas meant that morale was high and the final, and most crucial, factor was the courageous leadership and example set by d'Aubusson himself. The final attack could, from the sources, have gone either way. But the appearance of the Grand Master and the unfurling of their banners were probably the events that tipped the balance in the Knights' favour.

So why did Mesīh Pascha not simply line his gunpowder weapons against the walls of Rhodes and batter the town into submission? Many historians hold that gunpowder weapons easily brought down medieval walls, as Maurice Keen has recently written: 'medieval walls were too high and too thin to resist prolonged bombardment.'[5] But examples of failed sieges from the same period show that gunpowder weapons did not always result in the easy capture of a city. High, thin medieval walls at Deventer in 1455, Belgrade in 1456, Beauvais in 1472 and Neuss in 1474–75 had all withstood the gunpowder weapons of the dukes of Burgundy, whose gunpowder train was equal to if not larger than that at Rhodes in 1480.[6]

Therefore, while the walls at Rhodes were also tall and thin in construction – built by grand masters Jean de Lastic and Jacques de Milly – they were not so vulnerable to bombardment by gunpowder weapons. Could the cannon that the Turks had brought with them smash down the walls of Rhodes in 1480? The answer is a very definite yes according to the narrative sources. But it is important to keep in mind just how the storming of a castle or fortification was achieved. Although a general might demolish a section of wall with his artillery, that in itself rarely brought the defeat of an enemy. What the sources at Rhodes report is that, although the Ottoman guns did considerable damage, this was easily repaired and made good during the night after the bombardment stopped. This is undoubtedly why from the time the Turks ended their attack on the Tower of St Nicholas and concentrated on the Jewish Quarter it took thirty-eight days to make a breach large enough to storm the city. Only then could the Turkish leader even think about capturing Rhodes. Yet, the final assault on this breach ended in victory not for the besiegers, but for the besieged. The Knights Hospitaller and the townspeople of Rhodes, with their determination not to be conquered by the Ottoman Turks, outfought them at the breach, chasing the Turks, who could not muster the same determination to conquer the Knights, back to their camp and then back to Turkey.

A lengthy period of peace followed the withdrawal of the Turks from Rhodes, lasting until 1522, although no one in 1480 believed it would last as long as it did. The reasons are numerous, ranging from the hosting of Cem, the exiled brother of Mehmed II's successor, Bāyezīd II,[7] to the Hospitallers' suspension of piracy against Ottoman and Muslim ships,[8] to Selim I's changing strategy, away from Christian Eastern Mediterranean and European targets to concentrate on the Mamluk-held Middle East and Egypt.[9] But, without any contemporary evidence as to why the Sultans did not attack Rhodes, the question will remain unanswered.

The grand masters during this period certainly expected that the peace would not last. And they took advantage of every second afforded them to repair and rebuild the city's fortifications. The most active of these, at least according to the number of his arms which appear around the walls, was Pierre d'Aubusson. The works that Grand Master d'Aubusson undertook were ambitious and were commented on by travellers visiting Rhodes following the siege of 1480. 'Monseigneur the Grand Master has had great repair work carried out, due to the Turks and the infidels who are near,' wrote Philippe de Voisins of his visit in 1490;[10] 'Rhodes is a highly fortified city and it is becoming even stronger, because it is fortified every day,' reported Dietrich von Schachten after his trip in 1491;[11] and, in 1494, Pietro Casola wrote: 'The city is highly fortified and is being constantly reinforced. There is continuous work on the walls, especially on the side of the sea, on a tower called St Nicholas.'[12] This work was made possible, von Schachten notes, because of the large number of Turkish and 'pagan' labourers forced to work for the Hospitallers.

But grand masters Emery d'Amboise and Fabrizio del Carretto also did their part. The former added the Battery of the Olives and the large fortified gate on the west, which still carries his name, while the latter added to the western defences – damaged by earthquake – including the *tenaille* and caponier, rebuilt the impressive Tower of Italy on the south-east and, perhaps most importantly for the siege that followed less than two years after his death, widened the walls. Even Philippe Villiers de l'Isle Adam, Grand Master for less than two years before the final siege, added to the fortifications, as recorded by his coats of arms on several places, most notably on St George's Tower.

All of these grand masters also acquired gunpowder weapons – almost all of the extant bronze ordnance was brought to Rhodes between the two sieges. One such gun (number 13 in the Cannon Catalogue below – N67 of the Musée de l'Armée in Paris), which carries the arms of Grand Master d'Amboise, was cast specifically to be mounted in the Tower of St Nicholas – as stated on the barrel. The Hospitallers were determined to be ready for the Ottomans, whenever they might return.

In June 1522 the Turks returned. Led by their new Sultan, Suleyman I, in only the second year of his reign, they returned to lay siege to Rhodes. As before, the determination of the Knights Hospitaller to hold on to their little bit of the Eastern Mediterranean faced the might of the Turkish army. Both had large numbers of gunpowder weapons, precipitating the largest and longest artillery duel fought to that date. The Knights had a significant advantage in their city's walls, largely rebuilt over the preceding forty years with all the most up-to-date defences. Suleyman had the might of the Ottoman Turkish Empire, the sheer weight of numbers – from experienced Janissaries to lowly pioneers and 'diggers' – the availability of almost unlimited supplies and the potential of reinforcements.

The course of the siege, though relatively well documented – although one always desires more – is at times quite easy to follow from textual evidence alone, while some of the events are difficult to analyse. Here an in-depth study of the walls and remaining guns provides an additional dimension of evidence. As the military theatres of Ottoman expansion moved much farther to the west following the conquest of Rhodes, the walls, once repaired, became frozen in history. That they were repaired immediately after the siege is attested to in a report written by the commander of the Turkish armies, Ahmed Pasha, only eleven days after the Knights left the island.[13] That they were never again attacked is witnessed to by the five centuries of subsequent history.[14]

Even before Suleyman himself arrived at Rhodes, gunpowder artillery batteries were being set up around the city. To reduce the range and therefore increase their effectiveness, the Turks placed their artillery at the very edge of the moat. They dug approaches towards the moat and constructed trenches and earthworks on the edge of the counterscarp, the latter being Bourbon's 'mountains'. Behind these Suleyman mounted his artillery, covered them with mantlets and began an intense bombardment which the sources suggest was quite damaging. These earthworks were taller than the walls opposite them, by 10 to 12ft (3–4m) according to Bourbon, and designed to give the Turks an advantage over the Hospitallers.

The Hospitallers had mounted large numbers of guns everywhere along their walls, in their boulevards and towers, and probably upon the *tenailles* that stood east of the walls of Italy, between the Tower of Spain and the boulevard of England and between the boulevard of England and the Tower of Provence. They could also move cannon around the walls on the enlarged wall walk, today called a *terreplein*, which had been constructed on the walls since the first siege. Though the evidence is somewhat contradictory, Bourbon makes it clear that at many points the Hospitallers were able to direct very accurate fire against the Turkish batteries and ensure that they were not always able to continue firing. Certainly at the post of Alamain and later, when they tried to attack the Tower of St Nicholas, Hospitaller gunnery was fully able to reduce the Turks to firing at night or to make them move their artillery further away. On the other hand, there are also reports of considerable damage to the walls and the need continually to make repairs.

But what is the definition of 'considerable damage'? Whether using stone or iron balls, even from bombards or basilisks, walls like those at Rhodes had to be hit many, many times in the same place to have any real effect. Parapets and thinner structures on the tops of the walls were easier to damage or destroy, as well as any soldier standing or gun placed behind them. To penetrate the wall and make a breach large enough for soldiers to enter the city would have taken concentrated fire for many days. Even after picking and hewing at the wall near the Tower of Spain, tunnelling beneath it, and exploding a mine – 'all the mine did was to leave the wall hanging over the enemies, which was more to their disadvantage than to our damage', Jacques de Bourbon writes during he siege – Turkish guns still had to bombard it for several days before it was destroyed.

It is clear that trying to create a breach in the walls of Rhodes by gunpowder weaponry alone was going to take a very long time due to the thickness of the walls and the ability of the Hospitallers to return effective gunfire. But gunpowder artillery was not the sole tactic in Suleyman's siege plans. Miners, pioneers and diggers in great numbers – 50,000 in Nicholas Roberts' tally – had accompanied the army to the island. Their role at the beginning of the siege had been the digging of the approaches and trenches and building earthworks, but their real function was to undermine the walls. By mid-August these men were at work. Hospitaller sources indicate that the Turks dug an incredible number of mines. In pre-gunpowder days siege mines would be supported by wooden struts that were then burned away to cause the collapse of the chamber and the ground above. Gunpowder enabled a quicker and more violent conclusion to the siege mine. At Rhodes mines were filled with gunpowder which, when set off, not only caused the chamber to collapse, but ensured a greater likelihood of the collapse of the wall above. With great skill and the engineering knowledge of Tadini, the Hospitallers managed to detect and countermine many of the Turkish mines so that some did not reach the walls or were countered and filled before they could be collapsed. Still some succeeded, although none caused the walls to collapse to any great extent, and even when the one noted above lifted the wall by its blast, the wall simply fell back into place.

So, Suleyman had to call on a third siege tactic, a human attack on the walls themselves. The bombardment and mining damage had succeeded in weakening the walls so that, starting on 24 September, the Ottomans began to make direct assaults on the walls and boulevards. But all were ineffective and resulted in large numbers of casualties. Even when they succeeded in climbing on to the walls of the boulevard of Spain, raising 'thirty or forty banners', they were beaten back when the Grand Master, l'Isle Adam, appeared with the banner of the Crucifix and rallied his Knights and soldiers.

Having failed in their assaults, the Turks still needed to create a significant breach in the walls in order to enter the city – whatever 'breaches' had been made so far were obviously insufficient. Aided by the clearing of the moat near the Tower of Spain by the Hospitallers – for reasons that are not made clear in the sources – the Turks dug trenches across the moat to the foot of the wall, where they proceeded to demolish it by hand. Apparently the pioneers working on the wall there were in a 'dead space', meaning they could not be effectively attacked from the walls. They hewed and hacked at the wall, obviously causing a great amount of damage, mined it, and then, finally, bombarded it with artillery until they had succeeded in making a breach large enough for men to pour into.

However, even when the Turks launched a full-scale assault through the breach, they were met and repulsed by a devastating crossfire from handguns and artillery mounted on the defences, the traverses built by Tadini inside the city. The very few who made it through still had to engage the Knights standing with l'Isle Adam.

Even with 'state-of-the-art' offensive and defensive military technologies, success or failure came down to men; from the leaders and elite soldiers to those who moved the artillery, carried the gunpowder and brought the food. Fatigue, demoralisation and despair were bearing down on both sides. Suleyman continued his assaults on the breach near the Tower of Spain and launched other assaults on the *tenaille* and walls of Italy and the *tenaille* between Spain and England. Ultimately both fell, and the walls of Italy were weakened, forcing l'Isle Adam to mass troops behind them as he had behind the breach near the Tower of Spain. Still, by the beginning of December the city had not fallen.

To this point the two leaders had by their very presence spurred on their respective armies. L'Isle Adam had been involved in the fighting for almost the entire siege. He had certainly led by example, both as a fighter and as a standard-bearer for the Hospitaller Order, and his personal bravery was unquestioned. However, his political acumen was possibly suspect, especially in dealing with the Amaral treason. Suleyman had not been personally involved in the combat, but unlike his predecessor, Mehmed II, he had at least been present at the siege. He also directed most of the Ottoman manoeuvres and pronounced punishments upon his generals when they failed, including the replacement of Mustafa Pasha by Ahmed Pasha after the September assaults had achieved nothing but a large number of casualties.

The Hospitaller Knights were, of course, all well trained in martial arts and, for the most part, experienced soldiers who were fighting for the very survival of their Order. If they were defeated at Rhodes there was nowhere to go and little purpose in their existence as a crusading order. What was important was that they were willing to die for their religion; in effect, death in battle against the infidel was expected as a sign of their faithfulness. They had no families to live for, only an Order to die for. Throughout the siege the bravery of their actions, although only recorded by members of the Order themselves, was clear. Their equivalents were the Janissaries. Although there is not as much information on them, as they had no eyewitness reporters among them, it is equally clear that they fought with a courage and determination that had by this time given them the reputation of skill, honour and loyalty that had spread throughout the Christian and Islamic world. There were also other soldiers: mercenaries and those who had chosen to stay and fight alongside the Knights so heralded by Bourbon in the beginning of his account, and the nameless thousands of Turks who participated and died in extremely large numbers.

Curiously, it is the common people, the ones who are almost never written about, who played extremely important roles in the siege. The miners, pioneers and diggers brought by Suleyman who shifted so much earth and rubble to provide protective earthworks for their own soldiers and to undermine the huge Rhodian fortifications in an effort to bring them down and allow access to the city. Labourers and slaves on the Hospitaller side were also extremely influential, although it is not until the end of the siege that their importance is recognised. When Tadini stands before the Council of the Order and reports 'that there were less labourers, that it was impossible to resist them any more', there is a finality in his words that convinces many that the siege was lost.

As at the siege of 1480, and really at almost all sieges, rumour and common talk were important factors, affecting the way people thought, the way they worked and fought and, crucially, their morale. Just as important were the threats from spies, suspected spies and, most especially, the way that traitors were dealt with. For example, it is very clear that the charge of treason against Amaral had a considerable impact, and the way it was dealt with at such length in Bourbon's account strongly suggests that it was very damaging to morale.

However, the citizens of Rhodes, so important to the victory in 1480, seem almost entirely absent from the accounts of the siege of 1522. Indeed, it is not until Suleyman had initiated talk of surrender that they appear on the scene, with one group trying to convince l'Isle Adam to accept surrender and another begging him to reject the terms and hold out against the Turkish besiegers. He gives in to both groups, although to the latter one only if they provide assistance in the defence of their own city. They agree, but it does not take long before they, too, decide that it is not worth it and agree to Suleyman's terms of surrender.

One question remains: why did Suleyman let the Knights leave and spare the lives and religion of the surviving townspeople? At Belgrade, only months before, the Sultan had razed the city after its surrender, massacred the garrison and killed or enslaved the populace. At Rhodes he did none of these things. In fact, he preserved and repaired the city, allowed the defending soldiers (and any who wished to go with them) to leave with their lives and possessions – even offering them cannon for the defence of their ships as they sailed away – and slew none of the citizens of Rhodes. He suspended their payment of taxes for five years, allowed them to practise Christianity or Judaism, and did not even recruit their sons for service in the army. The fears of the Rhodians, based on the precedent of Belgrade, proved to be unfounded. Perhaps Suleyman felt that the strategic and economic position of Rhodes was too important to destroy. Or, perhaps it shows that he so admired the bravery and honour of the Hospitallers that he could not destroy them. The answer cannot be found in the surviving sources. Trying to sum up the result of a siege, especially one of such complexity and length as that of Rhodes in 1522, is not easy. Modern accounts give the impression that the Knights were completely overrun by the Turks, that they could not prevent them from getting into the town and so were driven to surrender. Indeed, one suggests that the Turks were able to use ancient drains, conduits and cisterns to appear at will anywhere in the city.[15] Our reading of the sources – written documents, extant cannon and walls – however, is very different. Suleyman only managed to make one really significant breach through the walls of the city, and the assaults that were made through it were effectively turned back. And, although by early December the Knights were in a desperate plight, it appears that Suleyman must have thought that the city could hold out for much longer – if he had known it was so depleted of men and munitions would he not have continued fighting to take the town by storm? It seems that the walls of the city were easily able to withstand a considerable bombardment, and the combination of good leadership and a force of skilled, trained and determined men ensured that at the end they were actually able to negotiate from a position of considerable strength. The Knights Hospitaller left with all their possessions and honour intact – as Charles V is reported to have said, 'Nothing was so well lost'.[16]

After losing Rhodes, their home for over two centuries, the Knights spent the next seven years looking for a new base from which to continue their 'crusading'. Eventually, in 1530, they were given the islands of Malta and Gozo by Emperor Charles V, as King of Sicily. From Malta they continued their raids on Turkish shipping much as they had done from Rhodes. In 1565 the Turks tried once more to remove them from the Mediterranean. Suleyman, still the reigning Ottoman Sultan, sent a force to lay siege to the three cities the Knights had established on Malta. In what was almost a re-run of the 1480 siege of Rhodes, the Turks came within a hair's breadth of victory, but were repulsed by a similar combination of resourcefulness, tenacity and superb leadership, by Grand Master Jean de Valette. The Knights went on to establish the city of Valletta, remaining on Malta until they were ejected by the Emperor Napoleon in 1799.[17]

Notes

1. See Setton, II:354, for example.
2. Kritovolous, pp. 51–2. See also DeVries, 'Constantinople'.
3. Brockman, pp. 82–9.
4. See Kelly DeVries, 'Conquering the Conqueror at Belgrade (1456) and Rhodes (1480): Irregular Soldiers for an Uncommon Defense', in *A Guerra, Revista de História das Ideias* 30 (2009), pp. 227–32.
5. Maurice H. Keen, 'The Changing Scene: Guns, Gunpowder, and Permanent Armies', in *Medieval Warfare: A History*, ed. Maurice Keen (Oxford: Oxford University Press, 1999), p. 278 (but see the entire article, pp. 273–91). See also Clifford J. Rogers, 'The Age of the Hundred Years War', in *Medieval Warfare: A History*, ed. Maurice Keen (Oxford: Oxford University Press, 1999), pp. 136–60; Rogers, 'The Military Revolutions of the Hundred Years War', *Journal of Military History* 57 (1993), pp. 241–78 (also published in *The Military Revolution Debate: Readings on the Military Transformation of Early Modern Europe*, ed. Clifford J. Rogers [Boulder: Westport, 1995], pp. 55–94); Geoffrey Parker, *The Military Revolution: Military Innovation and the Rise of the West, 1500–1800* (Cambridge: Cambridge University Press, 1988); Thomas Arnold, *The Renaissance at War* (London: Cassell, 2001); David Eltis, *The Military Revolution in Sixteenth-Century Europe* (London: I.B. Tauris, 1995); and many others who have adopted this theory.
6. Kelly DeVries, '"The Walls Come Tumbling Down": The Myth of Fortification Vulnerability to Early Gunpowder Weapons', in *The Hundred Years War*, ed. L.J. Andrew Villalon and Donald Kagay (Leiden: Brill, 2005), pp. 429–46; Smith and DeVries, pp. 174–88; and DeVries, 'Conquering the Conqueror', pp. 221–6.
7. Vatin, *Sultan Djem*, and Freely.
8. Brummett, 'The Overrated Adversary'.
9. Hess, 'The Ottoman Conquest of Egypt'.
10. Quoted in Michel Balard, 'The Urban Landscape of Rhodes as Perceived by Fourteenth- and Fifteenth-Century Travellers', *Mediterranean Historical Review* 10 (1995), p. 26, from Philippe de Voisin, *Voyage à Jérusalem de Philippe de Voisin*, ed. Tamisey de Laroque, ed. (Paris: Société historique de Gascogne, 1883), p. 24.
11. In Balard, p. 26, from R. Röhricht and H. Meisner, ed., *Deutsche Pilgerreisen nach dem Heiligen Lande* (Berlin: Weidmann, 1880), p. 182.
12. In Balard, p. 26, from Pietro Casola, *Canon Pietro Casola's Pilgrimage in Jerusalem in the Year 1494*, ed. M. Newett (Manchester: Manchester University Press, 1907), p. 205.
13. In Vatin, annexe 26, pp. 503–15.
14. Destruction of the Second World War seems to have left the walls untouched, although parts of the city inside were damaged. Nor did the explosion of gunpowder in the crypt of the Church of St John in 1856 harm the walls, although it did destroy the Grand Master's Palace, leaving the Italian occupiers to rebuild it in a most inaccurate way. See Manoussou-Della, p. 75–6.
15. Quentin Hughes and Athanassios Migos, 'Rhodes: The Turkish Sieges', *Fort* 21 (1993), pp. 2–17. We do not find this argument convincing.
16. Brockman, p. 155.
17. For a history of the Knights Hospitaller in Malta see Ernle Bradford, *The Shield and the Sword: The Knights of St John* (London: Penguin, 2002) and H.J.A. Sire, *The Knights of Malta* (New Haven: Yale University Press, 1994). On the siege of Malta see Ernle Bradford, *The Great Siege: Malta, 1565* (London: The Reprint Society, 1961) and Roger Crowley, *Empires of the Sea: The Siege of Malta, the Battle of Lepanto, and the Contest for the Center of the World* (New York: Random House, 2008). As well, Francisco Balbi di Correggio's contemporary account of the siege, *The Siege of Malta, 1565*, trans. Ernle Bradford (London: Folio Society, 1965; rpt. Woodbridge: The Boydell Press, 2005), is easily accessible.

Appendix 1: The Artillery

Cannon Catalogue

Introduction

There exist today some twenty-two cannon which we know were used by the Knights Hospitaller at the sieges of Rhodes in 1480 and 1522, or were very likely to have been used by them. They date from 1478 to the very eve of the second siege – nine date to the two decades before 1500, seven from around 1500 to about 1515 and the remaining six from 1518 to 1521. They constitute an extremely important collection that allow us to chart the development of European artillery over a crucial stage in its development. Eight Turkish guns have also been identified which may have been at Rhodes, although their dating is less secure than the European pieces. These differ in size, form and – in two cases – in material from the extant Hospitaller guns.

The following list of guns is divided into three groups: Guns of the Knights Hospitaller Known or Likely to Have Been at the Sieges of Rhodes, catalogue numbers 1–22; European Guns Possibly at the Sieges of Rhodes, catalogue numbers 23–24; and Guns of the Ottoman Turks Made before 1522, catalogue numbers 25–32. In each the guns are listed in chronological order, with some closely dated by inscription and others dated to period by grand masters' arms and other marks. Each gun is described from the rear to the muzzle. Inscriptions, words and letters, and other marks are noted from the front of the barrel to the breech.

Catalogue number: 1
Collection/museum: Musée de l'Armée, Paris
Accession number: N58
Material: Copper alloy
Length Overall: 224
Bore barrel: 24
Inscriptions: AU COMMANDEMENT DE LOYS PAR LA GRACE DE DIEU ROI DE FRANCE ONZIEME DE CE NOM ME FIT FONDRE A CHATRES JAHAN CHOLLET CHEVALIER MAITRE DE L'ARTILLERIE DU DIT SEIGNEUR 1478 (around muzzle face)
Other marks: Shield with three *fleur de lys* surmounted by a crown, the arms of the King of France (front of barrel). Flower (possibly a rose) decoration around touch hole, consisting of a central flower with a branch on each side terminating in three leaves (rear of barrel).
Date: 1478
Dating evidence: Dated on gun
Description: This gun is an almost parallel-sided barrel divided into two sections. The barrel does not really have a cascable as such. Behind the very narrow raised ring that forms the base ring are a series of mouldings terminating in a slightly concave rear face. Two small square recessed features behind the base ring are probably the remains of an iron loop, now missing. The simple touch hole is formed in the centre of a decorative flower, possibly a rose, motif. The rear section is a roughly parallel-sided cylinder, relatively smooth and featureless. The trunnions are large parallel-sided cylinders set at 180 degrees from one another on the centre line of the barrel. The front section, marked by a moulding and a slight reduction in diameter, is divided into three fields by two complex mouldings. There is a band of zig-zag or diamond decorations at the rear of the front section. At the muzzle there is a shield under a crown, bearing the arms of the King of France, three *fleur de lys*. The muzzle is formed by a series of mouldings, and the muzzle face has the inscription noted above in relief and translated as:
At the command of Louis, by the grace of God king of France, eleventh of that name, was founded at Chartres by Jahan Chollet, Knight Master of Artillery of the said king, 1478.
Discussion: The surface of this piece is particularly rough, perhaps from weathering over the years or possibly showing that the surface was not cleaned up after casting and so still has the roughness typical of castings straight from the mould. The powder chamber has a smaller diameter than that of the barrel, like many of the guns cast at this period. It would have fired stone shot of approximately 15kg. This relatively simple gun was almost certainly cast muzzle down as the inscription around the muzzle face must have been cast in the mould at the lower end. The flat, slightly dished, face of the cascable also indicates that it was cast breech up. The flower motif around the touch hole is very unusual and is suggested to be an eglantine.[1] The identity of Jahan Chollet is unknown.
Provenance: In Rhodes until given by Ottoman Sultan Abdülaziz to Emperor Napoleon III in 1862 when it was transferred to Paris.
Notes: Inventory number N19 in the catalogue of the Musée d'Artillerie, 1862.

Catalogue number: 2
Collection/museum: Germanisches Nationalmuseum, Nuremberg
Accession number: W572
Material: Copper alloy
Length Overall: 328.5
Bore barrel: 27.5
Inscriptions: LA BUSSONA (around band on barrel); 1482 (on raised strip on barrel)
Other marks: Arms of Grand Master Pierre d'Aubusson with lion supporters – shield quartered, arms of the Knights Hospitaller and d'Aubusson (barrel).
Date: 1482
Dating evidence: Dated on gun
Description: This gun is a parallel-sided barrel in three sections. The rear of the barrel has no cascable but is flat behind the base ring which is wide and of much greater diameter than the rear section of the gun. The touch hole is very small and set within a small circular depression just forward of the semi-circular moulding which forms the front of the base ring. The cylindrical rear section is divided into two parts by a simple moulding. To each side of the rear part is a lion holding a shield with the cross of the Knights Hospitaller in high relief. The central section of the barrel, of greater diameter than either the rear or front sections, is divided from them by complex mouldings and split into two parts by a simple moulding. The rear part has a ribbon with the date 1482 in relief and the front part has the arms of Grand Master Pierre d'Aubusson with lion supporters. On either side of this section are two projections terminating in male, possible Turkish, heads. The front section, of similar diameter to the rear, is divided into four parts by mouldings. At the front is a band of decoration formed from stylised *fleurs de lys*. At the muzzle the barrel flares out and terminates in a wide muzzle band of similar form to the base ring.
Discussion: Where and by whom this piece was cast cannot be determined though it was made on the order of Grand Master d'Aubusson just after the first siege, presumably as part of his work on refortifying the city. The name *La Bussona* probably suggests a play on the Grand Master's name. This barrel has a very rough and coarse surface partly caused by corrosion and wear over the centuries, but also because it was a poor casting with many small casting pits and flaws, especially at the rear. The large number of these casting flaws, pits and irregularities at the rear would strongly indicate that the piece was cast muzzle down with the breech uppermost. Most intriguing is the base ring: an area of damage, from what appears to have been a direct hit from a bullet or a piece of shrapnel, has led to the supposition that this base ring and its associated moulding are a separate piece cast over the rear of the barrel as there appears to be a separate 'surface' underneath. Although this is possible, it is highly unlikely that a separate section could have been cast over the already finished barrel. The supporters of the arms of Pierre d'Aubusson are clearly two lions, but in other representations they are more commonly a griffin to the left and a lion to the right.[2] The lugs projecting from the central section are an early form of dolphins and may represent Turks' heads.[3] It would have fired a stone ball of about 24kg.
Provenance: Unknown

Catalogue number: 3
Collection/museum: Musée de l'Armée, Paris
Accession number: N500
Material: Copper alloy
Length Overall: 363.5
Bore barrel: 39
Inscriptions: DIE KATERI HUIS ICH VOR MEINEM GEHALT HUET DICH DAS UNRECHT STRAF ICH JORG ENDORFER GOS MICH (around muzzle face); SIGMUND ERTZ HERZOG ZE ÖSTERREICH FF MCCCC UND IM LXXXVII (front of barrel); JORG ENDORFER GOS MICH (rear of barrel).
Other marks: Two crowned shields side by side (front of barrel); double-headed eagle (on left); horizontal bar (on right).
Date: 1487
Dating evidence: Dated on gun
Description: This barrel has a very large bore and is a roughly parallel-sided barrel divided into three sections. It does not have a cascable, with the rear of the barrel flat behind the simple wide base ring. The touch hole is set in a rectangular raised moulding. To its left is a small lug and to the right two further lugs over which a hinged vent cover, now missing, would have fitted. The rear section of the barrel is divided into two fields by a simple moulding. The second of these has a rectangular area with the inscription 'Jorg Endorfer made me' and two horizontal, rectangular lugs on either side of the barrel. The middle section is of slightly larger diameter and is just a very plain cylinder, on top of which are two dolphins in the form of double-headed 'dragons'. The front section is roughly parallel-sided and divided into five fields by simple mouldings. On the second from the rear is the inscription 'Sigismund I, Duke of Austria, 1487'. On the third is a pair of horizontal lugs, like those at the rear of the gun. On the fourth are two coats of arms – one consists of a double-headed eagle beneath a crown and the other is divided into three horizontal fields, again beneath a crown. The muzzle consists of a simple wide band very similar to the rear of the barrel. The face of the muzzle has a long inscription in relief: 'I am named Catherine. Beware of what I hold. I punish injustice. Jorg Endorfer made me.'
Discussion: This large-calibre piece – it would have fired a stone shot of about 70kg – was made by one of the leading German gunfounders of the late fifteenth century, Jorg Endorfer, for Sigmund, Archduke of Austria. Sigmund was born in Innsbruck and was first Duke and then Archduke of Further Austria, and was the Habsburg Archduke of Austria and ruler of Tirol from 1446 to 1490. Jorg Endorfer worked at Hötting, just outside Innsbruck. He was in the service of Sigmund from 1479 to 1490, after Sigmund's death, when he entered the service of the Emperor. It is known that he cast many cannon but *Die Kateri* appears to be his only surviving piece. He died in 1509.[4] The inscription around the muzzle, the flat breech and the many casting flaws and imperfections at the rear of the barrel all indicate that this barrel was cast muzzle down. Internally, the powder chamber is of much smaller diameter than the barrel.
Provenance: In Rhodes until given by Ottoman Sultan Abdülaziz to Emperor Napoleon III in 1862 when it was transferred to Paris.
Notes: Inventory number N18 in the catalogue of the Musée d'Artillerie, 1862.

Catalogue number: 4
Collection/museum: Askeri Müzesi, Istanbul
Accession number: 387
Material: Copper alloy
Inscriptions: Turkish inscription (barrel)
Other marks: Arms of Pierre d'Aubusson – shield, quartered, arms of the Knights Hospitaller and of d'Aubusson (barrel)
Date: 1476–1503 (probably before 1489)
Dating evidence: Arms of d'Aubusson as Grand Master of the Knights Hospitaller, but not adorned with the cardinal's hat given to d'Aubusson when he was named cardinal of Asia in 1489
Description: A small, octagonal barrel. The cascable tapers down from the base ring to a simple roll moulding and terminates with a long tubular button. The base ring, like the rest of the barrel, is octagonal. The touch hole is set within a circular depression and appears to have been bushed with iron. The barrel tapers uniformly from the base ring to the muzzle and has no mouldings along its length. The trunnions are set low down on the barrel. The muzzle, which is also octagonal, is formed from two simple mouldings.
Discussion: This barrel is one of a group of faceted barrels that are known from around Europe and which have been studied by Renato G. Ridella.[5] Though their maker has not been identified as yet, it is likely that this form of cannon, the faceted barrel and very plain tubular cascable button, was largely made in France.
Provenance: When this cannon was sent from Rhodes to Istanbul is unknown, but it is probably the cannon with d'Aubusson's arms seen by Ettore Rossi at the Turkish Military Museum in 1925, then located in the church of St Irene next to the Topkapi Palace.[6]

Catalogue number: 5
Collection/museum: Musée de l'Armée, Paris
Accession number: N66
Material: Copper alloy
Length overall: 193
Bore barrel: 58
Internal length barrel: 97
Bore chamber: 23
Internal length chamber: 77
Inscriptions: F PETRVS DAUBUSSON M HOSPITALI IHER (Fra Pierre d'Aubusson magister [Master] of the Hospital of Jerusalem) (around muzzle band). Turkish Inscription (barrel)
Other marks: Arms of d'Aubusson – shield, quartered, arms of the Knights Hospitaller and of d'Aubusson (barrel). Floral decoration (trunnion ends) 
Date: 1476–1503 (probably before 1489)
Dating evidence: Arms of Pierre d'Aubusson as Grand Master of the Knights Hospitaller, but not adorned with cardinal hat given to d'Aubusson when he was named cardinal of Asia in 1489.
Description: A short, mortar-like piece, the bore of the barrel, 58cm, slightly more than half the internal length of the barrel, 97cm. The powder chamber is, externally, roughly parallel-sided and divided into two by a complex moulding. The rear face is slightly convex. A broad band at the rear is pierced with rectangular slots. The barrel is of much greater diameter and is again parallel-sided, the transition between it and the powder chamber marked by a series of mouldings. The trunnions are cylindrical and their ends decorated with a foliate device. The muzzle is very similar to the rear with a large diameter, broad band with rectangular slots. The muzzle face is decorated with a series of concentric circles. On the top surface is a large shield with the arms of the Knights and of d'Aubusson. Beneath this is an inscription in Turkish within a roughened, irregular area which may have been where an earlier inscription or device was chiselled off.
Discussion: This very short piece is probably a mortar, intended to fire large projectiles, stone balls in the region of 225kg weight, at high trajectory, although it may also have been used at a short distance to fire at a low trajectory. Mortars are not unknown at this period but are not common. Like many late fifteenth-century pieces, the powder chamber is of smaller internal diameter than the barrel – see for example Mons Meg in Edinburgh or Dulle Griet in Ghent.[7] The rectangular slots at the front and rear are also not uncommon and may have been where long bars – of wood or possibly iron – could be inserted, providing a lever with which to move the gun more easily. The most famous example is the great Turkish piece now belonging to the Royal Armouries, England (no. 25), and dated to 1464. That cannon was made in two parts and the slots used to turn the separate barrel and powder chamber. The same form of construction is also depicted in a drawing by Leonardo da Vinci.[8] It was obviously made at the command of the Grand Master d'Aubusson, but where and by whom are unknown.
Provenance: In Rhodes until given by Ottoman Sultan Abdülaziz to Emperor Napoleon III in 1862 when it was transferred to Paris. It is probably that pictured in Johannes Hedenborg's manuscript, Plate 33.[9] Alexandra Stefanidou reports Hedenborg's claim that it was still on the walls in 1849, in the first gun emplacement of the wall of the Tongue of Germany 'near a gate, which was still there in 1848'.[10]
Notes: Inventory number N21 in the catalogue of the Musée d'Artillerie, 1862.

Catalogue number: 6
Collection/museum: Musée de l'Armée, Paris
Accession number: N59
Material: Copper alloy
Length overall: 256
Bore barrel: 18
Inscriptions: Turkish inscription (barrel)
Other marks: *Fleur de lys* (central section)
Date: 1470–97 (?)
Dating evidence: It has been suggested that the *fleur de lys* date it to the reign of Louis XI,[11] but there is no corroborative evidence.
Description: This gun is a tapering barrel divided into three sections. The cascable is very flat but unfortunately obscured by the floor on which it is set. On the base ring are two small square depressions filled with iron, probably the remains of an iron loop. The vent is a simple hole set in a small tulip-shaped depression. The rear section – not really a reinforce as in later pieces – is divided into three wide and three narrow sections, very much in imitation of the construction of wrought-iron artillery. The middle section, of slightly greater diameter, is smooth and decorated with *fleurs de lys*, in relief, set in alternating lines. The trunnions are very large, essentially parallel-sided cylinders, and set at roughly 180 degrees to one another. The front section is divided into six fields by simple mouldings with a band of simple stylised floral design at its front. The muzzle is marked by a very simple moulding.
Discussion: This piece, which would have fired a stone ball of approximately 6kg, has a smaller diameter powder chamber than the barrel. Like many early pieces of copper-alloy artillery, the outer appearance imitates the characteristic hoop and band construction of wrought-iron artillery. There are two very similar Hospitaller guns in Istanbul (nos 7 and 8).
Provenance: In Rhodes until given by the Ottoman Sultan, Abdülaziz, to Emperor Napoleon III in 1862 when it was transferred to Paris.
Notes: Inventory number N20 in the catalogue of the Musée d'Artillerie, 1862.

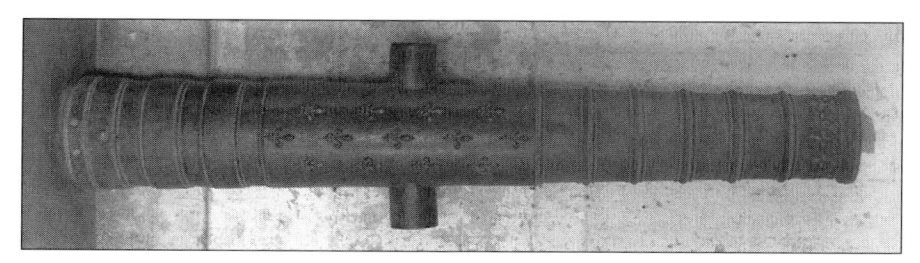

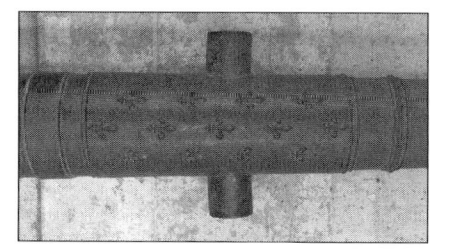

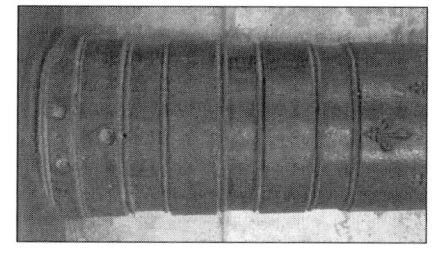

Catalogue number: 7
Collection/museum: Askeri Müzesi, Istanbul
Accession number: 342
Material: Copper alloy
Inscriptions: Turkish inscription on barrel behind trunnions
Other marks: Shield with three *fleur de lys* (chase); *Fleur de lys* in relief (centre section)
Date: 1470–97 (?)
Dating evidence: It has been suggested that the *fleur de lys* date it to the reign of Louis XI, but there is no corroborative evidence.
Description: This cannon is a parallel-sided barrel divided into three sections. The cascable is a series of very low mouldings without a protruding button. At the rear is a short section which has the appearance of a series of narrow bands – possibly in imitation of the bands of a wrought-iron cannon. The middle section, of slightly greater diameter, is decorated with raised *fleur de lys* set in alternating lines. The trunnions are very large and set at roughly 180 degrees to one another. The front section is divided into four fields by simple mouldings, a raised shield with three *fleur de lys* on the front field. The muzzle is marked by a very simple moulding.
Discussion: This gun has a smaller diameter powder chamber than barrel. Like many early pieces of copper-alloy artillery, its outer appearance imitates the characteristic hoop and band construction of wrought-iron artillery. There are two very similar guns (nos 6 and 8).
Provenance: As this does not contain the arms of a Hospitaller Grand Master, Rossi does not include it in his list of cannon seen at the Istanbul Military Museum in 1925.

Catalogue number: 8
Collection/museum: Askeri Müzesi, Istanbul
Accession number: 226
Material: Copper alloy
Length Overall: 272.5
Length to base ring: 265
Bore barrel: 25
Date: 1470–97 (?)
Dating evidence: Similarity to no. 6
Description: This cannon is a parallel-sided barrel divided into three sections. The cascable is a series of very low mouldings without a protruding button. At the rear is a short section which has the appearance of a series of narrow bands – possibly in imitation of the bands of a wrought-iron cannon. The middle section, of slightly greater diameter, is undecorated. The trunnions are very large and set at roughly 180 degrees to one another. The front section is divided into four fields by simple mouldings. The muzzle is marked by a very simple moulding.
Discussion: This piece, which would have fired a stone ball of approximately 17kg, has a smaller diameter powder chamber than barrel. Like many early pieces of copper-alloy artillery, its outer appearance imitates the characteristic hoop and band construction of wrought-iron artillery. There are two very similar guns (nos 6 and 7 above).
Provenance: As this does not contain the arms of a Hospitaller Grand Master, Rossi does not include it in his list of cannon seen at the Istanbul Military Museum in 1925.

Catalogue number: 9
Collection/museum: Askeri Müzesi, Istanbul
Accession number: 388
Material: Copper alloy
Bore barrel: 7.7
Other marks: Arms of Grand Master d'Aubusson surmounted by cardinal's hat and eagle
Date: 1489–1503
Dating evidence: Date of Grand Master d'Aubusson being appointed a cardinal to his death
Description: A long thin barrel with a single reinforce. Behind the base ring the cascable tapers sharply in a series of mouldings to a long tubular button. Evidence of the chaplets, which held the mould that formed the bore of the cannon whilst it was being cast, is clear from the four iron corrosion stains on the rear side of the base ring. The touch hole is large, the area around it damaged and pitted. The trunnions are set at approximately at the centre line of the barrel just behind the small step reduction in diameter that marks the end of the reinforce. The chase is long and tapers to the muzzle which flares out in a series of mouldings. There is a wide band of decorative leaf scrolling just behind the taper of the muzzle. The top of the chase has the arms of Grand Master d'Aubusson with the cardinal's hat which he received in 1489 surmounted by an eagle. The arms have been defaced, probably intentionally, by five semi-circular depressions.
Discussion: This piece is the only surviving cannon with the arms of Grand Master d'Aubusson after he was made a cardinal in 1489.
Provenance: The provenance of this piece is unknown but it is very likely to have been in Rhodes at the time of the second siege.

Catalogue number: 10
Collection/museum: Musée de l'Armée, Paris
Accession number: N71
Material: Copper alloy
Length overall: 300
Bore barrel: 23
Length to base ring: 283.5
Inscriptions: Turkish inscription (barrel); FAIT A LYON (barrel); 1507 (barrel); L (barrel); SAINT GILLES (on raised ribbon on barrel).
Other marks: Alternating *fleurs de lys* and lions *en passant* in relief (on chase); *fleurs de lys* in relief (on first reinforce); two coats of arms: (on left) raised shield with Cross of the Knights Hospitaller; (on right) raised shield with arms of House of Bourbon (barrel).
Date: 1507
Dating evidence: Dated by inscription
Description: This gun is a parallel-sided barrel divided into two sections. The cascable is in the form of a lion's head with its mane spreading out around it. A horizontal hole through the mouth of the lion was probably for an iron ring, which is now missing. On the wide, flat base ring are the remains of two square iron lugs which were probably part of an iron loop. The vent is a simple round touch hole set in a crescent-moon-shaped feature, in relief, probably for priming powder. The rear is a smooth cylinder with a number of inscriptions. The front one of these is an incised Turkish inscription followed by a *fleur de lys* in relief. Below this are the inscriptions *fait + a + lion*, the date *1507* and the letter *L*, all in relief. Two shields in relief are next, on the left the arms of the Knights Hospitaller and on the right the arms of the House of Bourbon. Finally, within a broad, raised band is the inscription *Saint Gilles*. The trunnions are short parallel-sided cylinders set at 180 degrees on either side of the barrel. The chase, marked by a moulding and a reduction in diameter, is dodecagonal and divided into four sections by simple mouldings. Each facet is decorated with alternating *fleurs de lys* and crowned lions *en passant* all in relief. The muzzle has a moulding and ends with a simple flat band.
Discussion: The internal diameter of the powder chamber of this very fine barrel has a smaller diameter than that of the barrel. It fired a stone shot of approximately 14kg. The three cannon, catalogue numbers 9, 10 and 11, were all made in Lyon in 1507 and show both remarkable similarities and differences. They were all probably made by the founder Jean Barbet who was appointed *Cannonnier du Roi* at Lyon in 1491. Subsequent documents refer to him as being responsible for supervising the city's artillery and for casting cannon and cannonballs. He is first noted in 1475 when he signed a bronze angel, now in the Frick Collection in New York City: *le xxviii jour de mars / lan mil cccc lx+xv jehan barbet dit de lion fist cest angelot*. He died in 1514.[12] All three have the inscription *fait a lyon*, the date 1507, and the letter L. However, cannon 10 and 11 have names, *Le furieux* and *horrible*, while number 9 has the name Saint Gilles, the noted priory of the Hospitallers. Similarly 10 and 11 have the arms of Grand Master Emery d'Amboise quartered with those of the Hospitallers, while number 9 has two shields of different form, one with the arms of the Bourbon family, although why is unclear. The Bourbons were not, as far as we know, associated with the priory of St Gilles and did not, at this period, have close associations with the Hospitallers.[13] While all three guns have the letter L it is unclear what this stands for. The use of a lion's head as a cascable appears to have been a speciality of the foundry, the cascable of numbers 9 and 10 being remarkably similar, though they are also found on Spanish pieces dating from around 1505 to 1530.[14] The third gun, no. 11, is very unlike the other two pieces although it does have a very similar calibre, 21cm, as the other two, 23 and 26cm. Its cascable, rather than a lion's head, is of similar form to that adopted around the turn

of the sixteenth century and which went on to be used for the next three centuries; the lion's head was to become obsolete in the 1520s. Guns number 9 and 10 are based on the forms that developed in the later fifteenth century, while number 11 tapers from the breech to the muzzle, as do all later barrels, although it does not have the reinforces that were to become a standard feature of later guns. It seems remarkable that while these three pieces were made in the same year, that they have both older and more modern features. What they possibly illustrate is an industry in transition – mixing older and newer forms.

Provenance: In Rhodes until given by the Ottoman Sultan, Abdülaziz, to Emperor Napoleon III in 1862 when it was transferred to Paris.

Notes: Inventory number N30 in the catalogue of the Musée d'Artillerie, 1862.

Catalogue number: 11
Collection/museum: Musée de l'Armée, Paris
Accession number: N69
Material: Copper alloy
Length overall: 290
Length to base ring: 266
Bore barrel: 26
Inscriptions: FAIT A LION (first reinforce); 1507 (first reinforce); LE FURIEUX (first reinforce); L (first reinforce); Turkish inscription (first reinforce).
Other marks: Coat of arms of the Knights Hospitaller quartered with those of Grand Master Emery d'Amboise (first reinforce).
Date: 1507
Dating evidence: Dated by inscription
Description: This gun is a large calibre piece with a single reinforce. The cascable is in the form of a lion's head with its mane spreading out around it. A horizontal hole through the mouth of the lion was probably for an iron ring – now missing. The wide base ring has the remains of two square iron lugs which are probably the remains of an iron loop. The small touch hole is set within a crescent-moon-shaped raised feature probably for containing priming powder. A moulding separates the base ring from the first reinforce which is a slightly tapering cylinder with a number of marks and inscriptions. At the front is a raised shield with the arms of the Hospitaller Order quartered with those of Grand Master d'Amboise. Below this is the inscription *fait a lion*, the date 1507, the name *le furieux* and a letter L, all in relief. The trunnions are short, large-diameter cylinders set at 180 degrees on either side of the barrel. The cylindrical chase, marked by a small reduction in diameter and a moulding, is divided into three fields by simple mouldings. The muzzle is very complex and decorated. At its rear is a wide band decorated with stylised leaves and *fleur de lys*. The forward part is dodecahedral and decorated with a raised twisted ring.
Discussion: This piece, in its outward form, is similar to no. 9, although it does not have the decorated chase. For a detailed discussion see no. 9.
Provenance: In Rhodes until given by the Ottoman Sultan, Abdülaziz, to Emperor Napoleon III in 1862 when it was transferred to Paris.
Notes: Inventory number N27 in the catalogue of the Musée d'Artillerie, 1862.

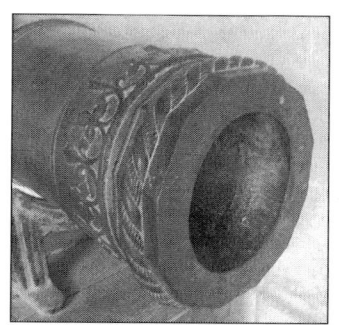

Catalogue number: 12
Collection/museum: Germanisches Nationalmuseum, Nuremberg
Accession number: W578
Material: Copper alloy
Length to base ring: 351
Bore barrel: 21
Inscriptions: Turkish inscription (barrel); FAIT A LION (barrel); 1507 (barrel); L'HORRIBLE SUIS (barrel); L (barrel).
Other marks: Shield with arms of the Order of Knights Hospitaller quartered with those of Grand Master Emery d'Amboise (barrel).
Date: 1507
Dating evidence: Dated by inscription
Description: This cannon, which has a large bore in relation to its overall diameter, is tapered from rear to front. The cascable consists of a series of concentric mouldings terminating in a long tubular button with a semi-circular end. Just in front of the very narrow base ring are two rectangular iron lugs, possibly the remains of an iron loop which has been removed. Just in front of the touch hole, which is small and within a circular raised feature, is the first of a series of mouldings which divide the whole length of the barrel into short sections – giving the piece the appearance of a wrought-iron cannon. On the first wide section are the arms of Grand Master d'Amboise quartered with those of the Knights Hospitaller in relief. In front of this are the inscription *fait a lion*, the date 1507 and the letter L, possibly the initial of the founder. The trunnions, which are short and positioned at the centreline of the barrel, are not at right angles to the barrel but point slightly downwards. The barrel tapers from the rear to the front where there is a band of *fleurs de lys* decoration. The muzzle is made up of a series of narrow bands.
Discussion: See discussion of no. 9.

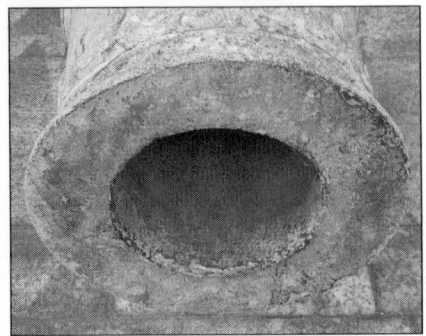

Catalogue number: 13
Collection/museum: Musee de l'Armée, Paris
Accession number: N67
Material: Copper alloy
Length overall: 260
Length to base ring: 255
Bore barrel: 23
Inscriptions: TVRIS + S + NICOLAI + PRO + DEFĒSOR (chase); Turkish inscription (first reinforce).
Other marks: Three shields in relief (chase): arms of the Hospitallers (on left); arms of Grand Master Emery d'Amboise; unidentified arms.
Date: 1503–12
Dating evidence: Dated to the rule of Grand Master d'Amboise.
Description: This is a relatively short, large-calibre piece. The cascable is extremely short, consisting of just a simple curving reduction in diameter terminating in a flat end. The base ring is very wide and has the remains of two iron lugs. The base ring tapers and is delineated from the first reinforce by a moulding. The small touch hole is set within a crescent-moon-shaped feature, in relief, probably a small pan for the priming powder. A Turkish inscription appears at the rear of the first reinforce. The trunnions are plain parallel-sided cylinders set midway on the diameter of the barrel. The chase, separated from the first reinforce by a moulding and a reduction in diameter, is divided into four sections by simple mouldings. The inscription TVRIS + S + NICOLAI + PRO + DEFĒSOR (the line over the second E in DEFĒSOR indicating that the word should be read DEFENSOR), 'For the Defence of the Tower of St Nicholas', in relief runs parallel to the barrel and is slightly off centre. On the forward section of the chase are three shields in relief – the arms of the Knights Hospitaller, those of Grand Master d'Amboise and an unidentified shield. A moulding at the front marks the muzzle which is a simple wide band.
Discussion: This gun, dating to the first decade of the sixteenth century, shares many characteristics of other cannon cast at the same time (see, for example, nos 9 and 10). It has the long single reinforce and the chase has been divided into fields by simple mouldings in imitation of wrought-iron guns. Uniquely among this assemblage, and almost unknown anywhere else, this piece has the name of where it was to be mounted cast into it. Of note, this means that it was designated to be a gun to defend the Tower of St Nicholas in Rhodes before it was actually cast.
Provenance: In Rhodes until given by the Ottoman Sultan, Abdülaziz, to Emperor Napoleon III in 1862 when it was transferred to Paris.
Notes: Inventory number N28 in the catalogue of the Musée d'Artillerie, 1862.

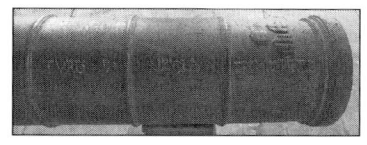

Catalogue number: 14
Collection/museum: Musée de l'Armée, Paris
Accession number: N68
Material: Copper alloy
Length overall: 540
Length to base ring: 511
Bore barrel: 16.5
Inscriptions: Turkish inscription (first reinforce).
Other marks: Arms quartered of Grand Master Emery d'Amboise and the Knights Hospitaller (first reinforce).
Date: 1503–12
Dating evidence: Dated to the rule of Grand Master d'Amboise.
Description: This extraordinarily long piece has two reinforces and a chase, though there is little, if any, reduction in diameter from one to another and it tapers uniformly from rear to muzzle. The cascable is extremely short and composed of two mouldings terminating in a flat plate with a rectangular extension which projects backwards (see also N74). The base ring is facetted, sixteen-sided like the rest of the barrel, with a simple wide band. At the rear of the first reinforce is a band of stylised *fleur de lys* decoration. The touch hole is a simple hole. Incised into the first reinforce is a Turkish inscription and the arms of Grand Master d'Amboise quartered with those of the Knights Hospitaller are in relief. The second reinforce is simply marked by the offsetting of the faceting of the barrel by half of one facet. The trunnions are parallel-sided cylinders. Their ends are decorated with concentric circles. The chase is marked by the same offsetting of the faceting and has a band of decoration, similar to that on the first reinforce. The muzzle flares slightly and ends in a simple flat band.
Discussion: This cannon, extraordinary for its length and its small calibre, is probably a basilisk and is similar to an illustration of one so identified in the artillery book of the Emperor Maximilian.[15] The bore is uniform throughout its length, as in later cannon, and it would probably have fired an iron shot weighing in the region of 13kg. Where and by whom it was made is unknown, but it must have been an extremely experienced and competent founder to make something as long as this. The rectangular extension at the rear is common for barrels of this period but was to be superseded by the normal cascable extending backwards from the centre of the cannon.
Provenance: In Rhodes until given by the Ottoman Sultan, Abdülaziz, to Emperor Napoleon III in 1862 when it was transferred to Paris.
Notes: Inventory number N26 in the catalogue of the Musée d'Artillerie, 1862.

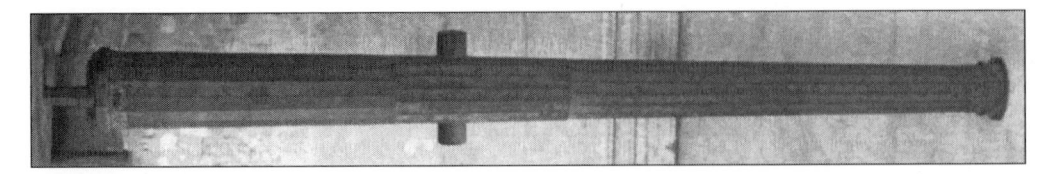

Catalogue number: 15
Collection/museum: Musée de l'Armée, Paris
Accession number: N70
Material: Copper alloy
Length to base ring: 405
Bore barrel: 17.5
Inscriptions: Turkish inscription (first reinforce).
Other marks: A porcupine under a crown in a rectangular frame all in relief with radiating lines in relief around (first reinforce).
Date: 1498–1515
Dating evidence: Dated to reign of Louis XII.
Description: This gun is a long, thin tapered barrel with two reinforces. The very short cascable is composed of two concentric mouldings and a flat face. The base ring is wide and divided into three narrow sections and has the remains of two iron lugs. The touch hole, just in front of the base ring, appears to have had an iron insert. The rear of the first reinforce is decorated by a band composed of linked *fleurs de lys*. The first reinforce tapers slightly and has a Turkish inscription and the emblem of Louis XII, a porcupine surrounded by radiating quills.[16] The second reinforce is marked by a moulding and a very slight reduction in diameter. At its rear is a band of decoration, similar to that at the rear of the first reinforce. The trunnions are cylindrical and parallel-sided. The chase, marked by a moulding and a band of *fleurs de lys* like that on the first and second reinforces, is decorated with *fleurs de lys* in relief. At the muzzle the barrel flares out and terminates in a simple flat band.
Discussion: This long, thin cannon would have fired an iron shot of approximately 15kg. Like many early guns, but unlike later pieces, the cascable is very short – just a simple moulding behind the base ring. Where and by whom this piece was made is unknown, although it is almost identical to no. 15, and must have been made by the same founder.
Provenance: In Rhodes until given by the Ottoman Sultan, Abdülaziz, to Emperor Napoleon III in 1862 when it was transferred to Paris.
Notes: Inventory number N29 in the catalogue of the Musée d'Artillerie, 1862.

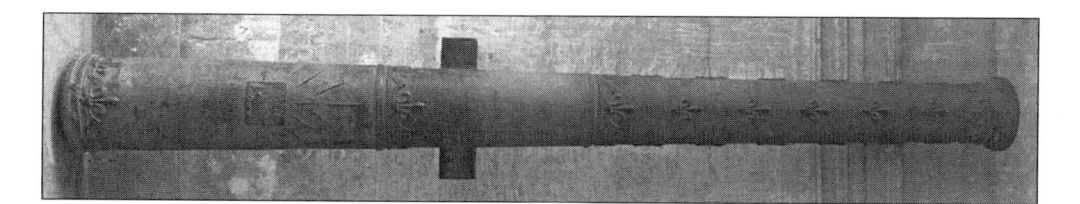

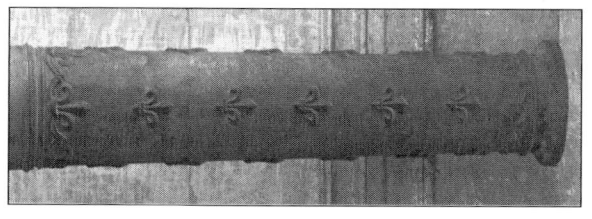

Catalogue number: 16
Collection/museum: Germanisches Nationalmuseum, Nuremberg
Accession number: W574
Material: Copper alloy
Length to base ring: 402.5
Bore barrel: 17
Inscriptions: Turkish inscription (first reinforce).
Other marks: Porcupine emblem within raised rectangular field with radiating rays in relief (first reinforce); *fleurs de lys in relief* (chase).
Date: 1498–1515
Dating evidence: Dated to reign of Louis XII (the porcupine was his emblem).
Description: This gun is a long, thin tapered barrel with two reinforces. The very short cascable is composed of two concentric mouldings and a flat face. The base ring is wide and divided into three narrow sections and has the remains of two iron lugs. The touch hole, just in front of the base ring, appears to have had an iron insert. The rear of the first reinforce is decorated by a band composed of linked *fleurs de lys*. The first reinforce tapers slightly and has a Turkish inscription and the emblem of Louis XII, a porcupine surrounded by radiating lines in relief. The second reinforce is marked by a moulding and a very slight reduction in diameter. At its rear is a band of decoration, similar to that at the rear of the first reinforce. The trunnions are cylindrical and parallel-sided. The chase, marked by a moulding and a band of *fleurs de lys* like that on the first and second reinforces, is decorated with *fleurs de lys* in relief. At the muzzle the barrel flares out and terminates in a simple flat band.
Discussion: A long, thin piece which fired an iron shot of approximately 14kg, it is almost identical to no. 14 in the Musee de l'Armee, Paris, and must have been made by the same founder. See discussion for no. 14.

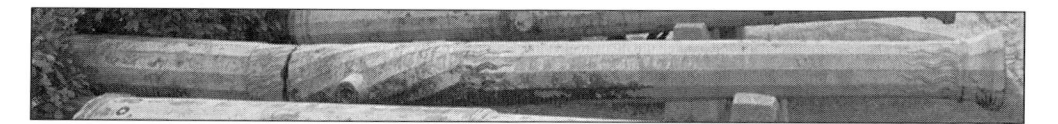

Catalogue number: 17
Collection/museum: Askeri Müzesi, Istanbul
Accession number: 401
Material: Copper alloy
Inscriptions: AVE + ⌧M + G + P + D + T (chase); F F D C (either side of shield); MANOLI LAMBADIS (first reinforce); 1518 (base ring).
Other marks: Shield, held up by an eagle, with arms of the Knights Hospitaller quartered with those of Grand Master Fabrizio del Carretto (first reinforce).
Date: 1518
Dating evidence: Dated on gun.
Description: This is a long facetted gun broken into two parts. The cascable is a single decorated moulding terminating in a tapered cylindrical button. The base ring is inscribed with the date 1518. There are three lugs, which held a vent cover, now missing, on either side of the very small touch hole just forward of the base ring. The first section of the barrel is twelve-sided with a flame running forwards on each facet. The arms of Grand Master Carretto are quartered with those of the Knights Hospitaller in a shield held up by an eagle. On either side of the shield are the letters F F D C (probably for Fra Fabrizio del Carretto). To the right the name MANOLI LAMBADIS is inscribed in a ribbon running along a facet. In the middle section the facets make a half twist round the barrel, with no change in diameter from the rear section. The barrel is broken in two just behind the cylindrical trunnions which are relatively large and set at the mid-point of the circumference of the barrel. The front section reverts to the same straight faceting as at the rear and has the letters AVE + ⌧M + G + P + D + T (*Ave Maria Gratia Plena, Dominus Tecum* – 'Hail Mary full of grace, God is with you') in relief running along the top facet. The muzzle flares out to end in a wide muzzle band which is again twelve-sided.
Discussion: This relatively small, highly decorated piece was made by Manoli Lambadis. Almost nothing is known about Lambadis, but it is possible that he worked on Rhodes itself, as he was likely related to Georgios Lambadis who cast no. 17 in Rhodes.
Provenance: Currently in the courtyard of the Askeri Müzesi (Military Museum) in Istanbul; in 1925 Ettore Rossi reports that it was in the Byzantine church of Saint Irene, next to the Topkapi Palace, where the Military Museum was then located.[17] Guido Sommi Picenardi saw this gun on Naillac Tower when he visited Rhodes at the end of the nineteenth century,[18] but Johannes Hedenborg illustrates it with two other bronze cannon on the Tower of St Nicholas in 1880.[19]

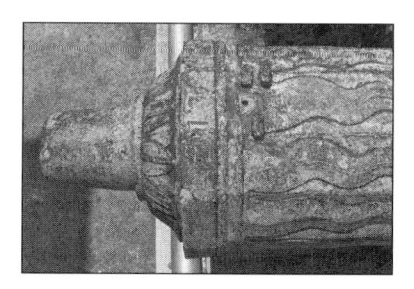

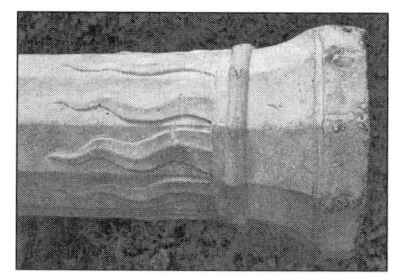

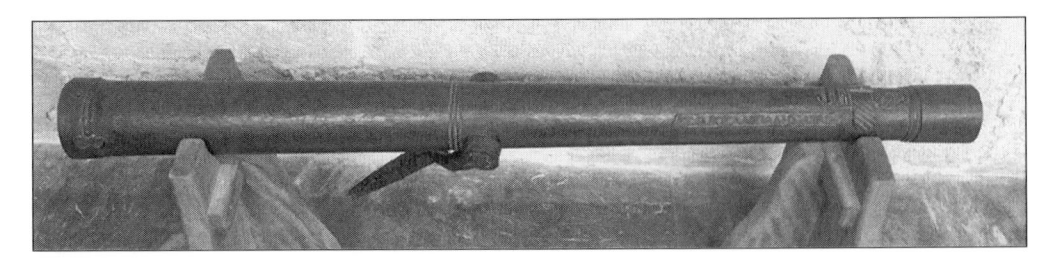

Catalogue number: 18
Collection/museum: Grand Master's Palace, Rhodes
Material: Copper alloy with wrought-iron swivel
Length Overall: 134.5
Bore barrel: 2.5
Inscriptions: ΓΕΩΡΓΙΟΣΛΑΜΙΑΔΗΣΔΕΡΟΔΩ (near muzzle).
Other marks: Relief of Virgin and child (near muzzle); shield with unknown arms (near muzzle); shield with arms of the Knights Hospitaller (near muzzle); shield with arms of Grand Master Fabrizio del Carretto (near muzzle).
Date: 1513–21
Dating evidence: Dated to the rule of the Grand Master Carretto.
Description: A small swivel gun with an iron swivel. The end of the barrel is flat. The rear of the barrel consists of a tapering band, with the remains of a small sight on top, followed by a moulding. On the right side is a horizontal projection with a depression forming the pan for powder next to the touch hole. In front of a moulding are trunnions over which an iron swivel is fitted. At the front is a long inscription in Greek, translated as 'Georgios Lambadis de Rodo', and three small shields. At the rear is a shield with unidentifiable arms while the other two have the arms of the Hospitallers and those of Grand Master Carretto. Just forward of the shields is a relief of the Virgin and child. There is a small moulding behind the long tubular muzzle.
Discussion: This is the only surviving piece of small artillery from the siege of Rhodes in 1522. Apart from his name on this gun, no other pieces by Georgios Lambadis are known. His relationship with Manoli Lambadis (see no. 17) is unknown but it is possible, as the inscription on this piece suggests, that both worked on Rhodes. This type of small gun, with a swivel mount, was used primarily as a close-range anti-personnel weapon. They would have fired either a small, solid shot of lead, iron or stone, or would have been loaded with small fragments of stone or lead balls, usually held in some form of bag or container. In one of the small towers between the Virgin's Tower and the Tower of Spain there is a gun loop with a socket in the stone sill into which the peg of a swivel would have fitted (see Appendix 2).
Provenance: Said to have been found while dredging the harbour of Rhodes.

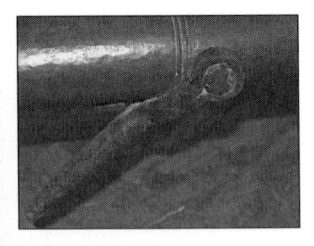

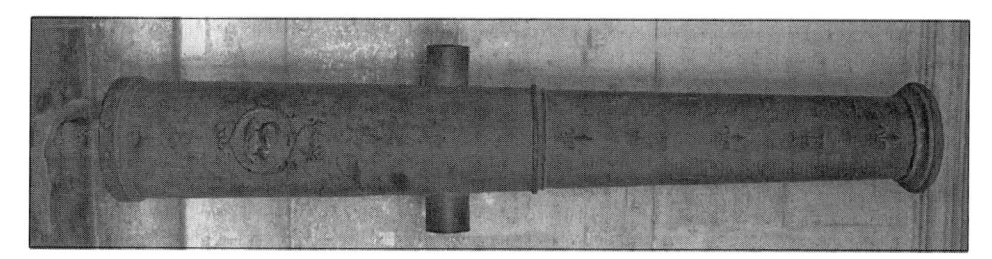

Catalogue number: 19
Collection/museum: Musée de l'Armée, Paris
Accession number: N75
Material: Copper alloy
Length overall: 315
Length to base ring: 283
Bore barrel: 17.5
Inscriptions: Turkish inscription (first reinforce).
Other marks: Alternating *fleur de lys* and the letter *F* in relief (chase); salamander beneath a crown, within a frame of two entwined foliated torches (first reinforce).
Date: 1515–22
Dating evidence: Dated to the reign of Francis I (the salamander was his emblem) and to the first siege.
Description: This is a long tapered gun with a single reinforce. The cascable is initially very flat and terminates in a cylindrical, waisted button decorated with stylised leaves and pierced with a hole. The base ring is a flat band with the fragmentary remains of two iron fittings – probably the ends of an iron loop – and inscribed with the weight, 4225. The touch hole is set in a slight recess and there is evidence that it had had an iron bush. The first reinforce is a simple tapered cylinder, undecorated except for the emblem of Francis I, the salamander beneath a crown, within a frame of two entwined foliated torches, all in relief. The trunnions are parallel-sided cylinders set midway to the centreline of the barrel. The chase, marked by a simple moulding and a very small reduction in diameter, is also a tapering cylinder decorated with a pattern of alternating *fleur de lys* and the letter *F* in relief. The muzzle is very simple consisting of an ogee moulding and a narrow band.
Discussion: This relatively large bore gun, with a single reinforce, illustrates important changes in barrel design in that it is tapered from rear to muzzle and has the definite reduction in diameter between the reinforce and the chase. These important changes, linked to the change in casting from breech up to muzzle up, paved the way for the development of the modern cannon which exploited the full power of blackpowder while keeping the weight of the barrel to a minimum. Unfortunately, by whom and where it was cast are unknown, although it is likely that it was made in France. It would have fired iron shot of approximately 15kg.
Provenance: In Rhodes until given by the Ottoman Sultan, Abdülaziz, to Emperor Napoleon III in 1862 when it was transferred to Paris.
Notes: Inventory number N33 in the catalogue of the Musée d'Artillerie, 1862.

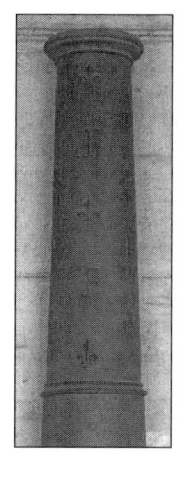

Catalogue number: 20
Collection/museum: Musée de l'Armée, Paris
Accession number: N78
Material: Copper alloy
Length to base ring: 307
Bore barrel: 18
Other marks: Salamander emblem of Francis I with the motto NUTRISCO ET EXTINGO beneath a crown in relief (first reinforce).
Date: 1515–47
Dating evidence: Reign of Francis I.
Description: This gun is a long tapered piece with a single reinforce. The cascable consists of three simple mouldings and terminating in a circular button, the whole very small and delicate for so large a barrel. The base ring is a flat band with the fragmentary remains of two iron fittings – probably the ends of an iron loop. The first reinforce is a simple tapered cylinder, undecorated except for the emblem of Francis I, the salamander with the motto NUTRISCO ET EXTINGO ('I nourish and I extinguish') beneath a crown, all in relief. The trunnions are parallel-sided cylinders set at midway to the barrel. The chase, marked by a simple moulding and a very small reduction in diameter, is again a tapering cylinder though now decorated with a pattern of *fleurs de lys* in relief. The muzzle is very simple consisting of an ogee moulding and a narrow band.
Discussion: This piece is very similar to catalogue no. 18 above.
Provenance: In Rhodes until given by the Ottoman Sultan, Abdülaziz, to Emperor Napoleon III in 1862 when it was transferred to Paris.
Notes: Inventory number N34 in the catalogue of the Musée d'Artillerie, 1862.

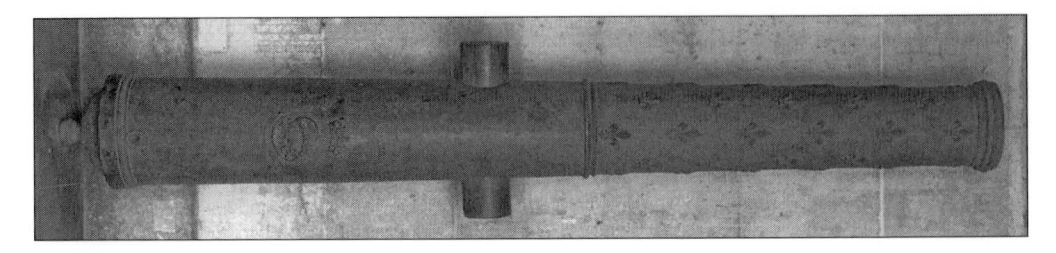

Catalogue number: 21
Collection/museum: Musée de l'Armée, Paris
Accession number: N74
Material: Copper alloy
Length overall: 367
Length to base ring: 338
Bore barrel: 14.5
Inscriptions: Turkish inscription (first reinforce).
Other marks: Arms of Grand Master Philippe Villiers l'Isle Adam quartered with the arms of the Hospitallers (first reinforce).
Date: 1521–22
Dating evidence: Dated to the rule of Grand Master l'Isle Adam and to the second siege.
Description: This unusual piece has two reinforces and is sixteen-sided throughout its length. The cascable consists of a series of simple mouldings ending in a flat disc decorated with the rays of the sun in relief. A short rectangular shaped extension projects backwards from the base ring probably to engage in the carriage (see also N68). The base ring is a flat, slightly tapered band. The touch hole is enclosed within a circular, crescent-moon-shaped feature in relief. On the first reinforce is an incised Turkish inscription and, in front of it, the arms of Grand Master l'Isle Adam in relief, consisting of a shield with the arms of the Knights Hospitaller quartered with those of l'Isle Adam. The shield is enclosed within a border composed of two stylised fishes secured to a central flag pole from which a pennant flies. The facets of the second reinforce are offset by half of one facet and marked by a moulding and a slight reduction in diameter. The trunnions, set slightly below the mid-point of the diameter of the barrel, are parallel-sided cylinders. The chase is marked by offsetting the facets, a moulding and a slight reduction in diameter, and is divided into four sections, each marked by a moulding and an offset of half a facet. The muzzle flares out slightly, ending in a wide flat muzzle ring.
Discussion: Bearing the arms of Grand Master l'Isle Adam means that this gun can be dated to between the date of his election as Grand Master in January 1521 and the beginning of the siege in 1522. It is most likely that he commissioned it soon after his election and took it with him to Rhodes, where he arrived at the end of October, dating its manufacture to 1521. Who made this piece and where are unknown, but it must have been made by a very experienced and competent founder. Although the barrel tapers from breech to muzzle, it is unusual in having facets along its entire length, from the base ring to muzzle, as well as the way that the faceting changes by half a facet at each change in the barrel, a feature of two cannon now in Neuchatel in Switzerland and dated to 1488. Making barrels with facets continued well into the sixteenth century, but it was increasingly rare and only used where extravagance was an issue – for displays of wealth or expertise. This piece is also very unusual in having the sunburst decoration and a rectangular extension at the rear instead of the, by 1520, more common cascable centred on the rear of the barrel (see no. 21 for a piece of similar date). It would have fired iron shot of about 8kg.
Provenance: In Rhodes until given by the Ottoman Sultan, Abdülaziz, to Emperor Napoleon III in 1862 when it was transferred to Paris.
Notes: Inventory number N32 in the catalogue of the Musée d'Artillerie, 1862.

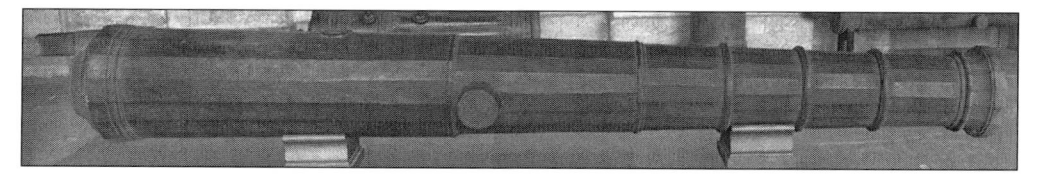

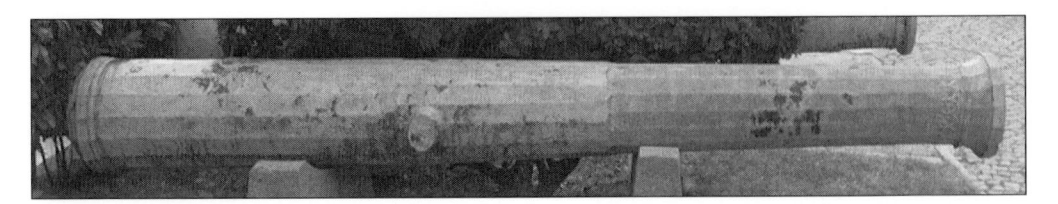

Catalogue number: 22
Collection/museum: Askeri Müzesi, Istanbul
Accession number: 409
Material: Copper alloy
Length to base ring: 385
Bore barrel: 13.5
Other marks: Arms of the Knights Hospitaller quartered with those of Grand Master Philippe Villiers de l'Isle Adam (first reinforce).
Date: 1521–22
Dating evidence: Dated by rule of Grand Master l'Isle Adam and the second siege.
Description: This unusual piece has two reinforces and is sixteen-sided throughout its length. The cascable, which consists of a series of mouldings terminating in a tubular button, is faceted like the rest of the barrel. The base ring is a flat, slightly tapered band. The touch hole is enclosed within a circular, crescent-moon-shaped feature in relief. On the first reinforce are the arms of Grand Master l'Isle Adam in relief, consisting of a shield with the arms of the Knights Hospitaller quartered with those of l'Isle Adam. The shield is enclosed within a border composed of two stylised fish secured to a central flag pole from which a pennant flies above the whole. The facets of the second reinforce are offset by half of one facet and marked by a moulding and a slight reduction in diameter. The trunnions, set slightly below the mid-point of the diameter of the barrel, are parallel-sided cylinders, their ends slightly depressed within an outer ring. The chase is again marked by offsetting the facets, a moulding and a slight reduction in diameter. At the front is a band of stylised *fleur de lys* decoration. The muzzle flares out slightly ending in a wide flat muzzle ring.
Discussion: Bearing the arms of Grand Master l'Isle Adam means that this gun can probably be dated to between the date of his election as Grand Master in January 1521 and the beginning of the siege in 1522. It is most likely that he commissioned it soon after his election and took it with him to Rhodes where he arrived at the end of October – dating its manufacture to 1521. It is unusual in having facets along its entire length, from the base ring to muzzle, as well as the way that the faceting changes by half a facet at each change in the barrel, a feature of two cannon now in Neuchatel in Switzerland and dated 1488. This piece is very similar to no. 20, but has the more normal form of cascable.
Provenance: This cannon, with the distinctive arms of l'Isle Adam, was not listed by Rossi in his list of Hospitallers' guns at St Irene in 1925. He does, however, mention two d'Amboise guns which can no longer be found.[20]

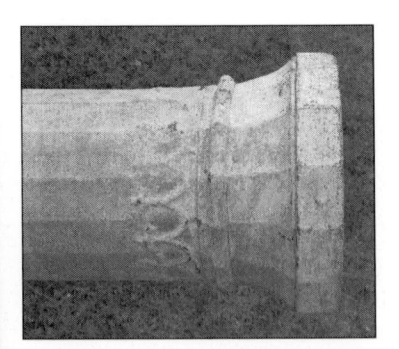

Catalogue number: 23
Collection/museum: Germanisches Nationalmuseum, Nuremberg
Accession number: W579
Material: Copper alloy
Length to base ring: 482
Bore barrel: 22
Inscriptions: Turkish inscription; M (around touch hole).
Other marks: Three rows of three heads in relief in alternating lines (chase); figure of St John in relief in a raised rectangular field (between trunnions); shield with helmet crest (first reinforce); figure of St John in relief (cascable).
Date: Unknown
Description: This is a long gun with an unusual cascable and two reinforces. The cascable consists of a single moulding terminating in a flat face on which is the figure of St John in relief. The base ring is wide and has the remains of two iron lugs. The touch hole, situated just in front of the base ring, has a lip around it with the letter M in relief. At the front of the first reinforce there is a coat of arms consisting of a shield with a helmet and decorative ribbons. The second reinforce, marked by a small reduction in diameter and a simple moulding, has an image of St John in a rectangular frame in relief. The trunnions are cylindrical and have concentric rings in their ends. The chase, marked by a small reduction in diameter and a complex moulding, is decorated with alternating heads in rectangular frames in relief. These heads are of three types. The first, a full face, wearing a helmet and dressed in a coat with a wide collar, has very full lips. The second and third are in profile, facing left and right; both wear a helmet with flowing scarf and very full lips. The muzzle flares slightly and terminates in a wide flat band.
Discussion: Unfortunately it is not possible, at the present time, to date this piece, although it is very likely that it belonged to the Hospitallers as it has the figure of St John, the patron saint of the Order. Overall, it has a very 'modern' form, the taper from back to front and the two reinforces, and may date from after the second siege but well illustrates the form of cannon that was to dominate across Europe until the middle of the nineteenth century. The cascable is unusual in its ornamentation, but it was not uncommon for cannon to be subject to particular decoration treatments for specific reasons – as here to mark that the piece belonged to the Hospitallers. The M at the touch hole is probably the mark of the, unidentified, gunfounder. This very long, heavy piece would have fired iron shot of about 30kg though it may have been intended to fire stone shot, as the drawing of a similar gun in Essenwein (no. 23) shows that is has a smaller diameter of powder chamber.[21]
Provenance: Possibly in Rhodes (by Turkish inscription) and associated with the Knights Hospitaller because of the religious figures on the barrel and cascable.

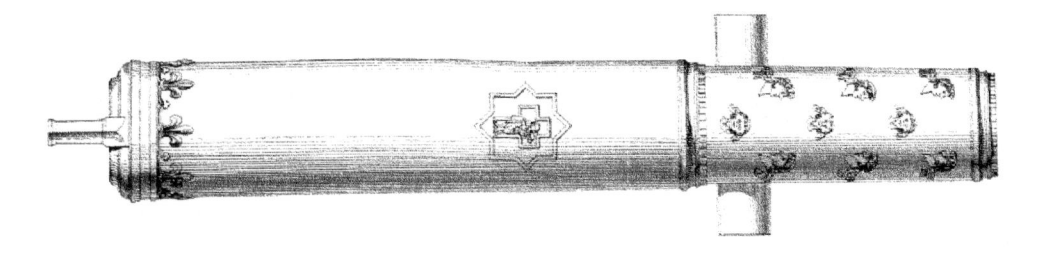

Catalogue number: 24
Material: Copper alloy
Length to base ring: 340 to front of second reinforce where it is broken
Other marks: Three rows of three heads in relief in alternating lines (second reinforce); figure of St John in relief in a raised cross in eight-pointed star (first reinforce); *fleurs de lys* (around rear of first reinforce).
Date: Unknown
Description: This picture portrays a fragment of a very long gun broken off at the end of the second reinforce. The cascable consists of a two simple mouldings, the rear being a flat disc. On top of the cascable a short rectangular-shaped extension projects backwards, probably to engage in the carriage. The base ring is divided into three narrow bands. The rear of the first reinforce is decorated with a band of *fleur de lys* decoration and incorporates the touch hole. To the front of the first reinforce is an eight-sided star within which is a relief of St John enclosed in a cross. The second reinforce is of smaller diameter than the first, the division marked by a series of narrow mouldings. The trunnions are large and tubular and are positioned below the centre line of the barrel. The second reinforce is also decorated with alternating heads in rectangular frames in relief. These heads are of three types. The first, a full face, wearing a helmet and dressed in a coat with a wide collar, has very full lips. The second and third are in profile, facing left and right; both wear a helmet with flowing scarf and have very full lips. The barrel is broken off just in front of the mouldings that mark the division between the second reinforce and the chase.
Discussion: This piece is of very similar form to no. 22, especially in the use of the human heads as decoration and the figure of St John. (See no. 22 for further discussion.)
Provenance: This gun was in Istanbul at the time August von Essenwein depicted it in the illustrations reproduced here (1877). It is unclear whether this was taken from Rhodes, but the use of the figure of St John indicates strongly that it was made for the Knights Hospitaller, who were also known as the Order of St John. It has not been located in Istanbul today.

Catalogue number: 25
Collection/museum: Royal Armouries, Fort Nelson
Accession number: XIX.164
Material: Copper alloy
Length Overall: 518
Bore barrel: 63.5
Bore chamber: 23

Inscriptions: Turkish inscription (muzzle face) which translate as: Help O God. The Sultan Mohammed Khan son of Murad; The work of Munir Ali in the month of Rejeh; In the year 868; Turkish inscription (near touch hole) which translate as: diameter, chamber, 7 parmak, 80 notka (24cm); muzzle, 20 parmak (68cm); shot, 19 parmak, 25 notka (60.5cm). Weight of shot, 240 okes (306kg). Charge, 17.5 okes (22.5kg) (near the touch hole).

Date: 1464

Dating evidence: Dated on gun.

Description: This is a unique large-calibre bombard made in two separate sections. The rear section, the powder chamber, has a flat breech. The broad band at the rear, like that at the front, is pierced with regular slots into which, it is assumed, levers were placed to enable it to be turned. The body of the rear section is divided into four sections by mouldings, the first and last decorated with stylised leaf motif. The front has the male thread to which would be screwed the barrel section. This has the matching female thread cut into its rear. Like the powder chamber section, the barrel is divided into sections by simple mouldings, six in this case, and the front and back have the same pierced bands. The first and sixth sections are similarly decorated as the powder chamber. The face of the muzzle has six inscriptions, in Turkish, around it in relief.

Discussion: The inscriptions on the face of the muzzle indicate that this gun was made for Sultan Mehmed II by Munir Ali in 1464. The screw thread is a work of great skill proving that Munir Ali and his workshop were obviously founders of considerable skill and expertise. The powder chamber section was probably cast vertically with the back uppermost, as shown by the casting flaws at that end. The barrel was also cast vertically with its muzzle down. This unique piece, which would have fired a stone shot of about 300kg, was made in two parts for ease of transport and not, as is sometimes said, for loading. The internal diameter of the powder chamber is very much less than the barrel, as was common at this time.

Provenance: The gun was acquired from the Ottoman Turkish government in 1868 by Major General J.H. Lefroy and transferred in 1929 from the Rotunda Museum, Woolwich, to the Royal Armouries.[22]

Catalogue number: 26
Collection/museum: Askeri Müzesi, Istanbul
Material: Copper alloy
Length Overall: 424
Bore barrel: 63
Internal length barrel: 186
Bore chamber: 23
Internal length chamber: 167
Date: Unknown

Description: This is a very large-calibre bronze barrel. The back of the barrel of this gun is flat. The rear part, the powder chamber, is divided into short sections by broad mouldings and tapers from the rear to the barrel. The touch hole is set within a rectangular recess. On each side, at the rear, are two small downward-turned lugs. The surface at the rear is very badly pock-marked, full of holes and casting flaws. The front section is of larger diameter than the rear and is again divided into short sections by broad, raised bands. At the front are two semi-circular loops through which iron rings are fitted. The muzzle is simple and consists of two bands of increasing diameter.

Discussion: This large bombard, and the following group, nos 26, 27 and 28, are of very similar dimensions as no. 24, although made in a single piece. Just where and when they were cast are not known. A similar gun, now destroyed but which survived in Brunswick in Germany until the eighteenth century when it was drawn, had the date 1411. Whether these four pieces date form the same time is unlikely, though, and a date of around 1450 seems more probable.[23] The bombard was a common type of gun from the very end of the fourteenth until the later fifteenth century. Yet, it is important to note that there was never any set or standardised size, either in length or bore, although they were usually of very large size, as here.[24] All four of these barrels have a remarkable number of casting flaws, pits and cavities around the breech area and this, linked to the fact that the breeches are flat, indicates that they were all cast muzzle down and breech up. Interestingly, three of these pieces have very strong Ottoman Turkish provenances, while the image of the gun in Brunswick has inscriptions in German. These large artillery pieces fired stone shot in the region of 300kg weight.

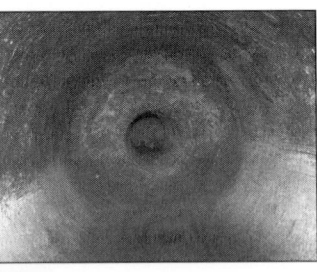

Catalogue number: 27
Collection/museum: Rumeli Hisar, Istanbul
Accession number: 19
Material: Copper alloy
Length Overall: 427
Bore barrel: 68
Internal length barrel: 184
Internal length chamber: 185
Date: Unknown
Description: This is a very large-calibre bronze barrel. The back of the barrel of this gun is flat. The rear part, the powder chamber, is divided into short sections by broad mouldings and tapers from the rear to the barrel. The touch hole is set within a rectangular recess. On each side, at the rear, are two small downward-turned lugs. The surface at the rear is very badly pock-marked, full of holes and casting flaws. The front section is of larger diameter than the rear and is again divided into short sections by broad, raised bands. At the front are two semi-circular loops through which iron rings are fitted. The muzzle is simple and consists of two bands of increasing diameter.
Discussion: See the discussion of no. 25. Note that the line down the side of the barrel is not a casting line but a change in colour in the metal, possibly due to a long-term burial of the barrel up to this mark.

Catalogue number: 28
Collection/museum: Rumeli Hisar, Istanbul
Accession number: 20
Material: Copper alloy
Length Overall: 423
Bore barrel: 64
Internal length barrel: 182
Internal length chamber: 193
Date: Unknown
Description: This is a very large-calibre bronze barrel. The back of the barrel of this gun is flat and has evidence of small plugs. The rear part, the powder chamber, is divided into short sections by broad mouldings and tapers from the rear to the barrel. The touch hole is set within a rectangular recess. On each side, at the rear, are two small downward turned lugs. The surface at the rear is very badly pock-marked, full of holes and casting flaws. The front section is of larger diameter than the rear and is again divided into short sections by broad, raised bands. At the front are two semi-circular loops through which iron rings are fitted. The muzzle is simple and consists of two bands of increasing diameter.
Discussion: See the discussion of no. 25.

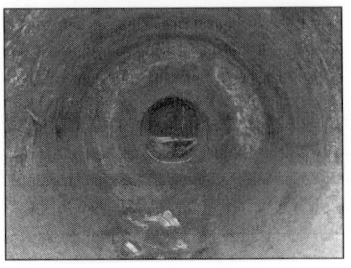

Catalogue number: 29
Collection/museum: Museo Storico Nazionale di Artiglieria (Artillery Museum), Turin
Material: Copper alloy
Length Overall: 319
Bore barrel: 69
Internal length barrel: 181.5
Date: Unknown
Description: This is a very large-calibre bronze barrel. The back of the barrel of this gun is flat. The rear part, the powder chamber, is divided into short sections by broad mouldings and tapers from the rear to the barrel. The touch hole is set within a rectangular recess. On each side, at the rear, are two small downward turned lugs. The surface at the rear is very badly pock-marked, full of holes and casting flaws. The front section is of larger diameter than the rear and is again divided into short sections by broad, raised bands. At the front are two semi-circular loops through which iron rings are fitted. The muzzle is simple and consists of two bands of increasing diameter.
Discussion: See the discussion of no. 25.

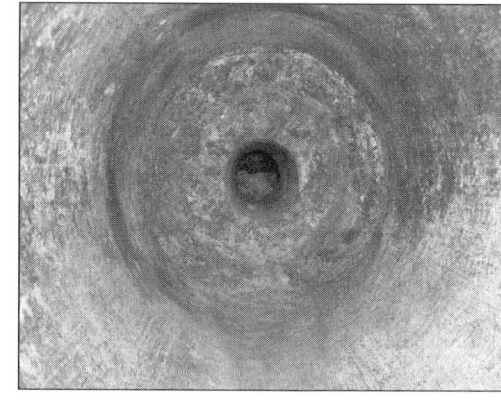

Catalogue number: 30
Collection/museum: Germanisches Nationalmuseum, Nuremberg
Accession number: W571
Material: Copper alloy
Length Overall: 322
Bore barrel: 29
Bore chamber: 15
Date: Unknown

Description: This is a long, thin gun with almost parallel sides. The rear is flat behind a slightly raised breech band. The touch hole is set within a larger rectangular recess. The rear section, the powder chamber, is divided into three parts by broad mouldings. Two rectangular lugs protrude from the rear section – that on the right has a flat top and curved bottom, while the one on the left has a curved top and a flat bottom. Where the powder chamber meets the main barrel is marked by a complex series of mouldings. The barrel section is very similar in diameter to the powder chamber and is also divided into four parts by mouldings of the same form as those at the rear. The muzzle is a wide, flat band. Two transverse lugs on the forward part are pierced and have rings.

Discussion: Although this cannon has no date or any identifying markings, it is extremely close in form to the bombards in Istanbul, Rumeli Hisar and Turin. It has many of the same features, the form of the mouldings, the lugs at the rear and the iron rings secured through transverse loops. It is highly probable that this group of guns were made in the same workshop or at least in the same geographical area. See the discussion of no. 25.

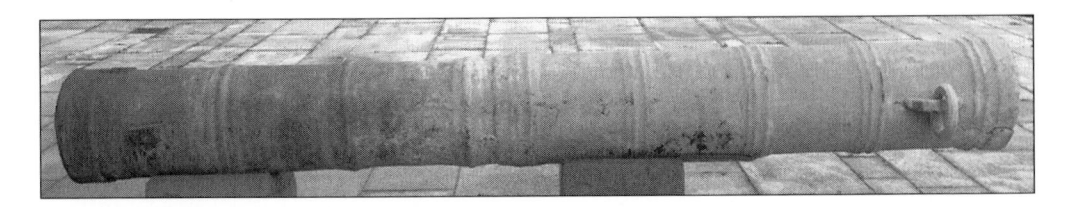

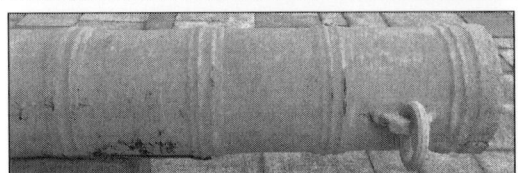

Catalogue number: 31
Collection/museum: Deniz Müzesi Komutanl (Naval Museum), Istanbul
Accession number: 2504
Material: Wrought iron
Length Overall: 700
Bore barrel: 24.5
Inscriptions: Turkish inscription (front of chase).
Date: c.1517
Dating evidence: By reference to its use in the conquest of Egypt.
Description: A very long wrought-iron barrel with a relatively small calibre. It has no cascable, the rear having a slightly convex central part. There are two narrow triangular mouldings just in front of the base ring. At the rear are two transverse lugs. The surface of the barrel is essentially smooth and tapers from rear to front, but at about one-third of its length there is a single small moulding and a marked small reduction in diameter. Clearly discernible along the entre barrel's length are concentric lines. At the muzzle is a Turkish inscription in a rectangular cartouche. The barrel swells out at the muzzle and the end is marked by a wide muzzle band.
Discussion: The concentric lines along the barrel clearly indicate that it was made from wrought iron in the traditional way from long staves bound with hoops, the lines being where the hoops meet together.[25] The convex rear is evidence that this cannon was originally made as an open tube and the rear sealed with a plug. This enormously long barrel would have been called a basilisk (see no. 13). This massively long gun fired an iron shot of about 42kg.

Catalogue number: 32
Collection/museum: Deniz Müzesi Komutanl, Istanbul
Material: Wrought iron
Length Overall: 747
Bore barrel: 25
Date: *c.*1517
Dating evidence: By reference to its use in the conquest of Egypt.
Description: A very long wrought-iron barrel with a relatively small calibre. It has no cascable but is essentially flat behind the base ring. The touch hole is set within a trapezoidal recess. There are three pairs of loops, through which iron rings are secured, along the entire length of the barrel. The surface of the barrel is essentially smooth and tapers from rear to front, but at just under halfway along there is a small reduction in diameter. Clearly discernible along the entre barrel's length are concentric lines, and at the muzzle there is a small moulding decorated with knurling. The barrel swells out at the muzzle and the end is marked by a wider band of knurled decoration and a wide muzzle band.
Discussion: For discussion see no. 30.
Notes: Despite being identical in form to no. 30, it should be noted that this gun is 47cm longer.

Notes

1. Sylvie Leluc personal communication.
2. See, for example, the arms of d'Aubusson on the Virgin's Gate and on the harbour walls of the city of Rhodes.
3. Lugs of various forms on the sides of barrels seem to have used before the system of casting handles, called dolphins, at the centre of gravity of the barrel became common around 1500.
4. A.N. Kennard, *Gunfounding and Gunfounders: A Dictionary of Cannon Founders from Earliest Times to 1850* (London: Arms and Armour Press, 1986), p.71. See also Erich Egg, *Der Tiroler Geschutzguss 1400–1600* (Innsbruk: Universitatsverlaf Wagner, 1961), pp. 39–48.
5. Renato G. Ridella, 'Two 16th century Papal Esmerils in the Cleveland Museum of Art, Ohio, and Some Notes on Bronze Pieces of Ordnance with a Polygonal Section', *Journal of the Ordnance Society 19* (2007), pp. 5–38.
6. Ettore Rossi, 'Memorie dei cavalieri di Rodi a Costantinopoli', *Annuario della Scula archeologica di Atene e delle missioni italiane in Oriente* 8–9 (1920), 340.
7. Smith and Brown, pp. 1–38.
8. Plate 25 in Marco Cianchi, *Leonardo's Machines*, trans. Lisa Goldenberg Stoppato (Florence: Becocci editore, 1984).
9. Johannes Hedenborg, *Geschichte der Insel Rhodes, von der Urzeit bis auf die heutigen Tage nebst einer historischen Übersicht der Völker, Griechen, Römer, Araber, Franken und Türken, welche die Insel beherrscht haben, mit einer Sammlung vieler Inscriptionem so wie vieler Abbildungen von Monumenten besonders aus dem Mittelalter*, vol. 2, 3 (Rhodes: Historical and Archaeological Institute of Rhodes Library, Manuscript), pl. 33.
10. Alexandra Stefanidou, 'The Cannon of the Medieval City of Rhodes, based on the Manuscript and Illustrations of Johannes Hedenborg (1854)', in *Greek Research in Australia: Proceedings of the Sixth Biennial International Conference of Greek Studies, Flinders University June 2005*, ed. E. Close, M. Tsianikas and G. Couvalis (Adelaide: Flinders University Department of Languages - Modern Greek, 2005), p. 299.
11. As far as we can tell this originates with Tabersac, p.419, but can also be found in the *Catalogue des collections composant le Musée d'Artillerie*, p. 884, and Leluc, pp. 84–5.
12. Franklin M. Biebel, 'The 'Angelot' of Jean Barbet', *The Art Bulletin 32* (1950), pp. 336–44.
13. Jacques de Bourbon, the chronicler of the 1522 siege, was a members of the Hospitallers. St Gilles was a priory of the *Langue* of Provence.
14. Javier Lopez-Martin, *Historical and Technological Evolution of Artillery from its Earliest Widespread Use until the Predominance of Mass-Production Techniques* (PhD dissertation, London Metropolitan University, 2007), pp. 342–3.
15. Essenwein, pl. ALXXX–ALXXXI.
16. At this period it was believed that the porcupine could shoot its quills outwards to defend itself – it had the ability to wound near and far, *cominus et eminus*. For a discussion of the porcupine emblem of Louis XII see Nicole Hichner, 'Louis XII and the Porcupine: Transformatuions of a Royal Emblem', *Renaissance Studies 15* (2001), pp. 17–36.
17. Rossi, 'Memorie dei cavalieri', p. 340.
18. Guido Sommi Picenardi, *Itinéraire d'un chevalier de Saint Jean de Jérusalem dans l'île de Rhodes* (Lille: Société de Saint Augustin, Desclée, de Brouwer et cie, 1900), p.147.
19. Hedenborg, V, pl. 33. See also Stefanidou, p.292.
20. Rossi, 'Memorie dei cavalieri', p. 340.
21. Essenwein II:pl. ACIX–ACX.
22. Blackmore, p.172. For an account of the acquisition of the piece and its examination immediately after see J.H. SEQ CHAPTER \h \r 1Lefroy, 'An Account of the Great Cannon of Muhammad II. Recently Presented to the British Government by the Sultan, With Notices of Other Great Oriental Cannon', *Minutes of Proceedings of the Royal Artillery Institution* (1870); rpt. (Cambridge: Ken Trotman, 2005).
23. It is possible, though not altogether certain, that they were made for the siege of Constantinople in 1453, as there is some evidence that large guns were made for the siege. See DeVries, 'Constantinople'.
24. See Smith and DeVries, pp. 204–11, and Smith and Brown.
25. For a description of how wrought-iron guns were made see Robert Douglas Smith, 'The Technology of Wrought-Iron Artillery', *Royal Armouries Yearbook 5* (2000), pp. 68–79.

Appendix 2: The Walls

An Exploration of the Walls Surrounding Rhodes during the Sieges of 1480 and 1522

Introduction

Whoever has not seen Rhodes… has never seen a fortress.[1]

This comment on the walls of Rhodes was written by a Jewish traveller, Obadiah of Bertinoro, on a visit to the city in 1495. It is still true today. The walls of the city of Rhodes are among the finest surviving defences from the late fifteenth and early sixteenth centuries in Europe, and, even without the modification and changes undertaken in the decades between 1480 and 1522, warrant study in detail. However, it is those changes that make them so valuable to an understanding of how walled defences developed in this crucial period. After the siege of 1522 the walls were repaired but little further work was carried out, so that what we see today is largely the work of the Knights Hospitaller.

It is thus possible to see how those responsible for fortification construction reacted to the developments in artillery and gunpowder and what they did to counter them. The final development of fortresses and city walls, the bastion defence and all its supporting structures – ravelins, hornworks, *terrepleins*, etc. – was not arrived at without intermediary steps. Rhodes shows several of these steps, as the city fortifications developed from medieval thin, tall defensive walls to early modern thick, low offensive structures.

Many of these developments are covered in the main text of the book. This appendix, a photographic survey of the surviving walls together with selected modern and contemporary images, provides a fuller account. Here the fortifications of the city of Rhodes are described beginning with the harbour walls and going clockwise around the city, ending with the defences just to the west of the harbour. Crucial to this survey is the work conducted by Albert Gabriel in the first two decades of the twentieth century and published between 1921 and 1923; we have used his wonderful drawings and illustrations widely.[2] Also important have been the detailed drawings of Stephen Spiteri (often based on originals by Gabriel) which have been a further useful source of illustrations.[3]

The initial medieval walls and the subsequent changes may be dated by the arms of the various grand masters, although there are certainly parts of the defences which have no means to date them accurately. Unfortunately, it was not always possible to see the internal structures of many of the towers and gates.

Rhodes Besieged

The Harbour Walls from the Gate of the Arsenal to St Catherine's Gate

The wall follows the sea shore around the south of the commercial harbour from St Paul's Tower, in the west, to the north-eastern corner of the city wall at St Catherine's Gate. Throughout its length it is essentially a tall, thin wall topped with characteristic triangular crenels and simple rectangular merlons. For much of its length it is relatively featureless and is pierced by a number of openings – some of them modern. Of these openings the most important is the Marine Gate – for centuries the main entry to the city from the sea. It consists of two drum towers separated by a simple semi-circular arched doorway (right).

Over this gate is a carved relief with three figures atop three armorial shields beneath, all under a canopy. The three figures are St Peter, the Virgin and child and St John the Baptist, though all are disfigured and unclear. The three shields are also mutilated. The shield on the left has the arms of the Knights Hospitaller; the middle shield, surmounted with a crown, is either the arms of France, the three *fleurs de lys* or the arms of the dukes of Burgundy; and on the right are what appears to be the arms of Grand Master Pierre d'Aubusson (left).

On the inner face of the Marine Gate is a carved relief which has the figure of an angel with the shields of the Knights Hospitaller and of Pierre d'Aubusson (right). Beneath is a stone slab with the inscription, given by Baron de Belarbe, D F PETRUS DAUBUSSO RHODI MAGR HAS TURRES EREXIT MCCCCLVIII (Lord Brother Pierre d'Aubusson, Master of Rhodes, built these towers, 1478).[4]

Although the harbour walls are largely plain and featureless, there is a small projecting square tower to the west of the Marine Gate (left).

On this tower on the harbour walls are three coats of arms. On the left are the arms of Philibert de Naillac, Grand Master of the Hospitallers from 1396 to 1421; in the middle the arms of the Knights Hospitaller; and on the right the arms of Giovanni Battista Orsini, Grand Master from 1467 to 1476 (below, right). This probably indicates that the walls were built by Naillac at the beginning of the fifteenth century and later repaired or rebuilt during the time of Orsini.

At the far east of the harbour walls is a small gateway, more like a postern, called St Catherine's Gate. Above the outer gateway are two shields: that on the left has the arms of the Knights Hospitaller, but the other is too damaged to be certain whose it is, although it is thought to be those of d'Aubusson.[5] The opening is guarded by a gunport on the left side (overleaf).

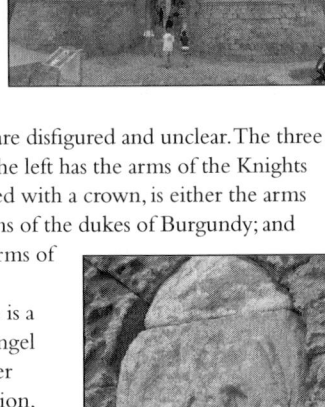

The Walls

The eastern section of the harbour walls. The square tower is on the right.

The Tower of St Nicholas

The Tower of St Nicholas stands at the end of a promontory due north of the city and commands the entry into the military harbour to the west as well as the outer approaches to the commercial harbour to the east (right). Originally a relatively simple drum-like tower with a circular curtain and an external staircase, it was substantially rebuilt after being badly damaged during the siege of 1480. The photograph (below, left) shows

St Catherine's Gate.

the mole from the Tower of St Nicholas with the city in the background.

This conjectural plan (below, right) shows the tower as it was in 1480.[6] The central circular drum tower was surrounded by a curtain wall pierced with loops for both artillery and handguns. The upper floors were reached by a stair in a separate tower.

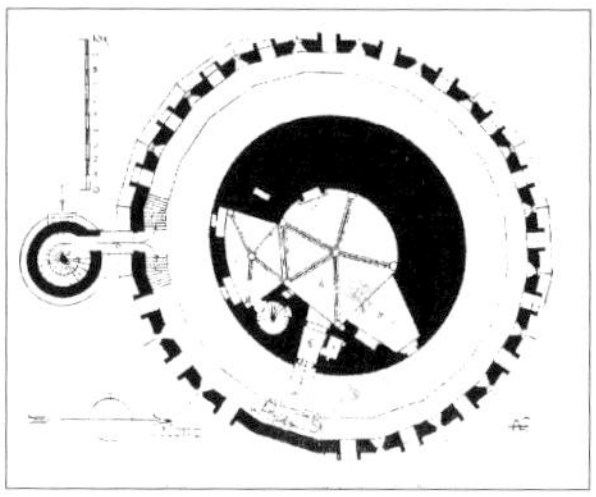

The central tower is protected by a curtain and with a separate staircase tower (this is clearly shown in the Colour Plates). The tower was badly damaged during the siege of 1480 and much of its west side was demolished by artillery fire from the Turks.

The original tower was built by Grand Master Piero Raimondo Zacosta starting in 1464. In 1465 the Hospitallers received a donation of 10,000 gold *soldi* from Philip the Good, Duke of Burgundy, specifically to help pay for the construction of the tower. It was largely completed by 1467. A condition of the donation was that it carried the coat of arms of the duke, which are on the east side of the central tower next to the arms of the Knights Hospitaller, Grand Master Zacosta and a shield with a lion. Above them stands a relief of St Nicholas (below).

After the siege of 1480 the tower was substantially rebuilt to withstand artillery bombardment, especially from the west – the land side where the Turks had attacked it. Around the original tower and curtain a polygonal bulwark was constructed. On the west side this was extremely thick and furnished with embrasures for heavy artillery. On the east, facing the sea, the wall is much thinner.[7]

Overleaf are images of the gunports on the east side of the Tower of St Nicholas, and the view from the top of the tower looking west to the site of the chapel of St Anthony, now rebuilt, where the Turks sited their main battery. The quays are modern. Also, a reconstruction of the Tower of St Nicholas as it might have appeared in 1522.[8]

171

Rhodes Besieged

Gunports on the east side of the Tower of St Nicholas.

View from the top of the Tower of St Nicholas.

Reconstruction of the Tower of St Nicholas in 1522.

Naillac Tower and Mole[9]

The Naillac Tower stood on the end of a mole which runs eastwards from the city. It was destroyed by an earthquake in 1863 but is well known from illustrations and its base, which still exists. It controlled access into the commercial harbour and, in times of war, was where one end of a chain across the harbour was secured to the Tower of the Windmills. The tower was probably built by Grand Master Naillac, as it carries his name, while the wall along the mole was built by Grand Master Fluvian and repaired by d'Aubusson. The reconstruction drawing by Gabriel (right) shows how it must have appeared in 1480.[10]

The Naillac Tower was rectangular with four corner towers at parapet level and an octagonal turret. The entry was at first-floor level and reached by a detached staircase tower or a bridge from the mole – both survive. The tower was very tall – Gabriel estimates that it was 46m from sea level to the top of the turret.[11] The image to the left shows the end of the mole from the south, the plinth, the base of the tower, the bridge and the staircase tower. Right is a detail image of the walkway connecting the tower to the mole. The staircase that served the tower survives, although it has been much reconstructed (below, left).

The base of the tower is now just a low rectangular wall. On the east side is the fitting for the end of the chain across the harbour to the Tower of the Windmills. The chain passed through the wall secured around the post. Outside the tower the chain ran through a channel from the sea (below, right).

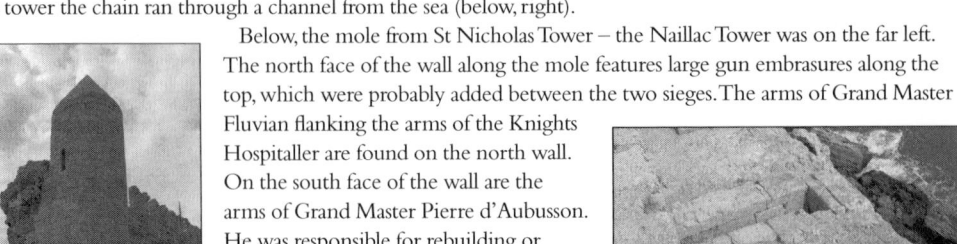

Below, the mole from St Nicholas Tower – the Naillac Tower was on the far left. The north face of the wall along the mole features large gun embrasures along the top, which were probably added between the two sieges. The arms of Grand Master Fluvian flanking the arms of the Knights Hospitaller are found on the north wall. On the south face of the wall are the arms of Grand Master Pierre d'Aubusson. He was responsible for rebuilding or strengthening the wall which was probably built by Fluvian (both overleaf).

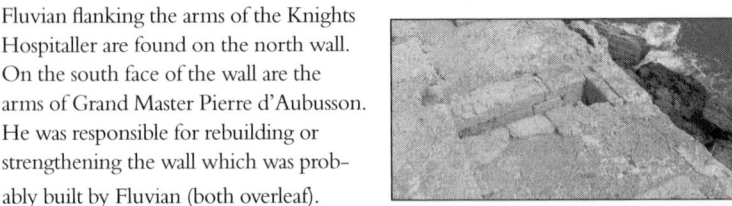

The Walls

Right: The arms of Grand Master Fluvian flanking the arms of the Knights Hospitaller.
Left: The arms of Grand Master Pierre d'Aubusson on the south face of the wall.

Windmill Mole and Tower[12]

The Tower of the Mills, or Windmill Tower, stands at the end of a spit of land which runs north from the north-east corner and which was, in the medieval period, lined with windmills. Alongside the Naillac Tower it controlled access into the commercial harbour and held the other end of the chain which closed off the harbour. The bulwark around the tower has suffered badly and much has been rebuilt (left).

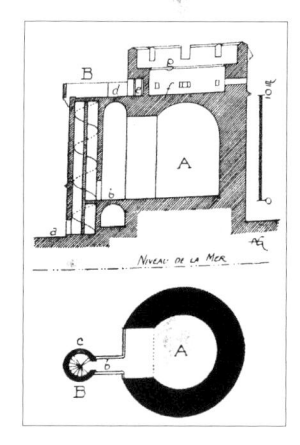

Like the early Tower of St Nicholas, the Tower of the Mills consists of a cylindrical tower with a curtain wall around the base and a separate stair tower. It was probably built between 1461 and 1475 – possibly about 1465 – as money for its construction came from King Louis XI of France.[13] In the Epernay painting the Tower of the Mills as it was in 1480 is clearly depicted, as are the large number of windmills on the mole (see the Colour Plates). Above, right is the plan and elevation of the Tower of the Mills from Gabriel.[14] The arms of the kingdom of France are on the south part of the tower (left), This is thought to mark the donation by Louis XI for the building of the tower.[15]

Although the Tower of the Mills was built around 1465, Grand Master d'Aubusson obviously had a hand in rebuilding or altering the tower as his arms, with those of the Knights Hospitaller, appear on the upper part of the tower (right).

The photograph to the left shows the Tower of the Mills from the south-west side. The artillery embrasures depicted here were later constructed by the Ottomans.

173

Rhodes Besieged

Scaffold Spit

Both the Epernay painting and the Caoursin illuminations show a spit of land curving round and running parallel to the Windmill Mole. The city scaffold stands at its tip and both show that it was used by the Turks to attack the city wall with gunpowder artillery. Today there is a large spit which runs parallel to the Windmill Mole, but at a considerable distance – in excess of 300m. Right is the view from the spit back towards the eastern side of the city. However, there is evidence that there may have been a spit closer to the eastern side of the city but that this has now largely disappeared. Indeed, this whole area has been badly affected by alterations, both in the construction of the existing *tenaille* after the 1480 siege, and more recently to make way for modern harbour facilities.

Windmill Mole to the Tower of Italy

The defences between the Windmill Mole, in the north-east corner of the city, and the Tower of Italy, in the south-east, is a very interesting section of the walls and often overlooked, or poorly treated, in earlier works. Today the road runs alongside the wall, but in the past it is clear that the sea came right up to the wall. The main section of the wall is still very much as it was before 1480 and has not been widened and thickened; it is still very much like the wall around the harbour. Where it angles to the south-west the wall has been widened and there are a series of artillery fortifications before the wall turns southward again to meet the Tower of Italy. The southern two-thirds of this section of wall are now protected by a complex *tenaille*. The *tenaille* has been pierced to make way for the road and the triangular lower section has been cut into two halves to accommodate a modern road to a new gate through the walls, the Acandia Gate. Gabriel's reconstruction shows the defences as they probably appeared in 1522 (right).[16]

The wall at the north-east of the city is still very much the medieval wall – high and thin with no thickening, and with its crenellations for the protection of men firing from the top of the wall. The *faussebraye* runs parallel to the wall and is pierced with simple circular gun loops (below).

The north-east corner of the walls – the modern road runs very close to the wall – appears to have been considerable damaged. From aerial views it seems that there was, originally, a circular tower here, now almost completely demolished, and that this was then fortified by a spur-shaped boulevard – very like that at the Tower of St John (right).

The Walls

The wall running south is tall and relatively thin. The northern section has the characteristic triangular crenellations but towards the south they are square. The *faussebraye* runs parallel down most of the wall although it has been destroyed by road building at its southern end. The southern part of this wall has been fortified by the addition of a *tenaille* running parallel to it (left). Below we see the southern tip of the *tenaille*, looking north along the outer face of the *tenaille* – the sea is just to the right. This 'spur' in the foreground, an extension of the *tenaille*, has embrasures from which medium or perhaps large artillery could fire. Below, left is one of the gun embrasures on the *tenaille* looking outwards.

The *tenaille* was built by Grand Master d'Aubusson before 1489 as his coat of arms, without the cardinal's hat, shows (below, right). Unlike many of the other *tenailles* this one must have been built up from the ground, rather than the result of excavation around it. Where the wall turns south-west it is protected by a polygonal tower with gun loops. The tower juts out from the wall and provides the ability to fire along it (below). A series of towers continues along where the wall turns south-west and the next section of wall, running south-east, has the *faussebraye* in front of it (below).

The south-east corner of the city wall has been altered by later work. The *tenaille* has been cut through for the road that now runs along the wall and a new gateway, called the Acandia Gate, has been made through the wall. The road to this gate has cut through the very large triangular part of the *tenaille* that protected the wall with the result that it now consists of two sections, north and south.

The image overleaf is of the northern section of the *tenaille*. The road in the foreground has been cut through the original *tenaille*. The Tower of Italy can be seen in the background.

Also overleaf is an image of the outer face of the southern section of the triangular *tenaille*. The gun embrasures are large and would have enabled great artillery to be mounted on the *tenaille*. The *tenaille* in front of the Acandia Gate is linked to the Tower of Italy by a single-storey 'firing gallery', allowing fire along the moat.

One of many gun embrasures.

Grand Master d'Aubusson's coat of arms (without cardinal's hat).

A section of wall with a faussebraye running south-east.

Polygonal tower with gun loops.

175

Rhodes Besieged

Above, left: The northern section of the tenaille.

Above, right: The outer face of the southern section of the tenaille, with large gun embrasures.

Left: A single-story 'firing gallery' linked to the Acandia Gate and the Tower of Italy.

Tower of Italy

The Tower of Italy was reconstructed by Grand Master Fabrizio del Carretto in 1515–17 (right). Originally the wall where the tower was built was pierced by a gate, but all traces have now disappeared except for the remains of the archway.[17] At some stage a semi-circular tower was built which connected with the *faussebraye*. Carretto strengthened this small tower and added a sloping parapet and embrasures.[18] Carretto then added a large semi-circular bastion around the existing tower and pierced it with large gunports to form a three-tiered artillery tower. At ground level, as the plan to the left shows, the gate originally pierced the wall and the gunports were angled to shoot along the moat.[19] At the next level the gunports are again positioned to provide fire along the moat (left).[20]

Ground level plan.

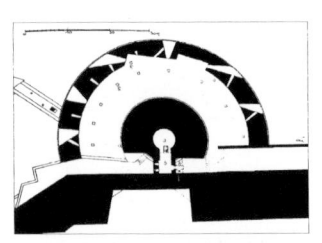

First level plan.

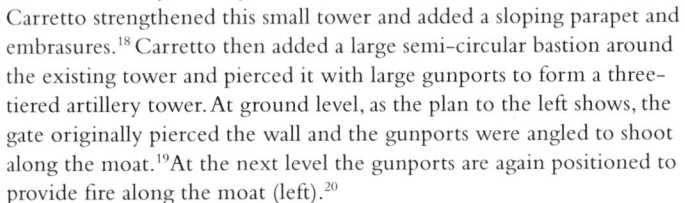

Below, left is the east side of the Tower of Italy. Here the three levels of gunports are clearly visible. The lower one provided fire across the moat while the upper levels enabled the defenders to fire across to the counterscarp and into the enemy's positions (below, centre).

The arms of Grand Master Carretto (1513–21) are portrayed in the outer bastion of the Tower of Italy (below, right).

The Walls

Walls from the Tower of Italy to St John's Gate[21]

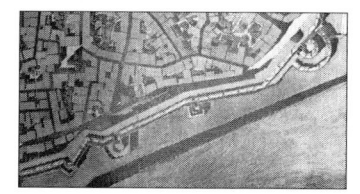

The wall running west from the Tower of Italy to St John's Gate is tall and, unlike in the moat to the east of the Tower of Italy and west of St John's Gate, there is no *tenaille* in front of it (left). The original wall was probably built by Grand Master Jean de Lastic between 1437 and 1454 as it bears his arms near the Tower of Italy (below).

The coat of arms of Grand Master Lastic are on the wall near the Tower of Italy (below). Here it is clear that the arms are those of Lastic, as a white band across a red shield, to distinguish them from those of Grand Master Fluvian whose colours are reversed. (In white stone the two are indistinguishable.)

After the 1480 siege the wall was substantially thickened to make a *terreplain* from which heavy artillery could be mounted as well as transported along the wall. In addition, a heavy sloping parapet was added to protect the gunners. It was pierced by widely splayed embrasures behind which guns could be mounted (right).

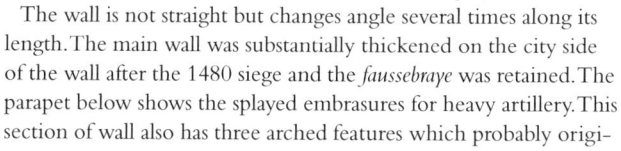

The wall is not straight but changes angle several times along its length. The main wall was substantially thickened on the city side of the wall after the 1480 siege and the *faussebraye* was retained. The parapet below shows the splayed embrasures for heavy artillery. This section of wall also has three arched features which probably originally held coats of arms – the balls there today are purely decorative as any stone ball fired at a wall would disintegrate on impact.

Originally there were three simple reinforcing towers along this stretch of wall, but these all had additional fortifications built around them. The first, nearest to the Tower of Italy, is a simple square tower. Originally a detached tower built on to the *faussebraye*, it was attached to the inner wall and augmented with an outer, embrasured wall. As Grand Master Pierre d'Aubusson's arms are found on the front of the tower these changes were made either shortly before or likely after the 1480 siege. The inner tower was originally only built to the *faussebraye* and was detached from the main wall.

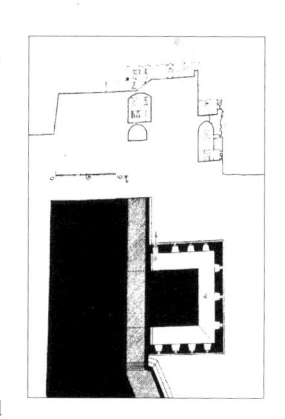

Later it was secured back to the wall and the outer work was built round it (above). The gunports and embrasures are at four levels in this tower – two in the outer wall firing along the moat, a third on top of the outer wall and a fourth from the top of the inner tower firing along and across the moat.[22]

The photograph to the left is of the front of the tower and shows the four levels of embrasures which enabled a greater concentration of fire. However, the front face of the tower seems very vulnerable to attack as it is not covered from the city walls

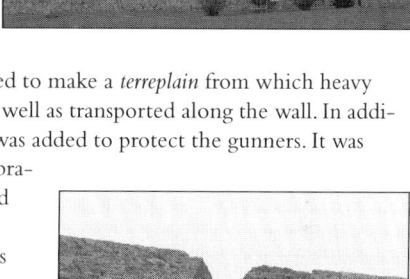

177

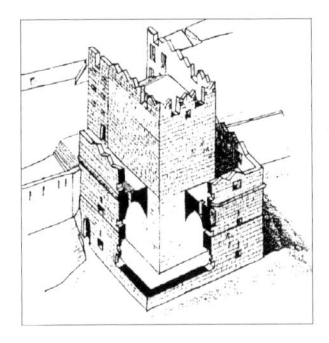

Rhodes Besieged

and cannot be easily defended. The arms are those of Grand Master Pierre d'Aubusson. Left is a reconstruction of the tower.[23]

The next section of wall is similar to the eastern section of wall, with its *faussebraye* and added parapet. The arms in the centre are again those of Grand Master Lastic, showing that he originally built this section of wall (below, right). To the west of the square tower is a small round tower with an added bulwark. Again, like the square tower, originally it was just a circular tower which was detached from the main wall. Later the tower was secured to the main wall and encased in a multangular bulwark. Below, left shows a reconstruction of the tower.[24] The photograph below, right is the wall to the west of the multangular tower. The small archway, bottom centre in the photograph, leads to a passage through the walls into the city. Between the multangular tower and St John's Gate the wall forms an angle which is protected by a tower.[25] It consists of an inner, faceted tower reinforced by a secondary bulwark built by Jacques de Milly while he was Grand Master, 1454–61 (below). The arms of Grand Master Milly are mounted on the inner tower (below).

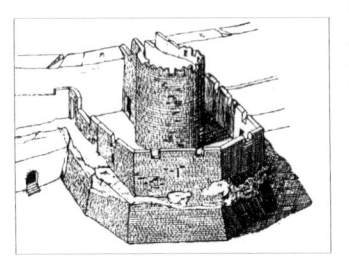

That the *faussebraye* was built around this inner tower indicates that the two were built at the same time – unlike the previous two towers which were reinforced by outer works by Grand Master d'Aubusson.

Small, keyhole-shaped gunports pierce the *faussebraye* around the small tower. These simple loops could only be used with handguns and contrast with the later, larger loops and embrasures elsewhere built at the end of the fifteenth century (below).

The wall to the east, continuing to St John's Gate, has been badly damaged – the *faussebraye*, bottom right of the below photograph, has been recently rebuilt.

Left: Inner, faceted tower built by Grand Master Jacques de Milly.

Right: The arms of Grand Master Milly, mouted on the inner tower.

Left: Small, keyhole-shaped gunports which pierce the Faussebraye.

Right: The wall to the east, continuing to St John's Gate.

St John's Gate

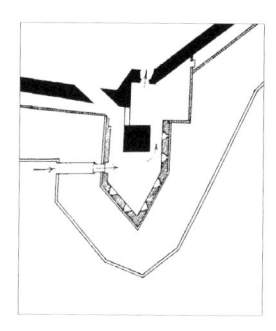

St John's Gate was one of the major gates of the city of Rhodes. The gate was built by Grand Master Milly, with a plaque also recording that the Greek mason Manolis Kountis worked on this section of the wall in 1457. Originally the gate to the city was protected by a simple tower separated from the main city wall. The tower bears the arms of Grand Master Fluvian – dating it to 1437–54 – with a relief of St John the Baptist. This tower was further protected by a spur-shaped bulwark probably built by Grand Master Zacosta between 1461 and 1467, meaning that it was built after the main gate.[26] The moat across this gate was quite narrow at the time.[27] After the siege of 1480 the earlier defences were strengthened by a large multangular bulwark built by Grand Master d'Aubusson, whose arms appear on it four times, sometime before 1489 as none of them incorporate the cardinal's hat which he was given in that year. It incorporates embrasures around its upper edge, but with none at a lower level – probably because the whole bulwark is a solid structure. Though the moat was widened to enable the bulwark to be built, it was still relatively narrow compared to other places along the wall (above, left).[28]

This elaborate gateway encapsulates the development of the defences of Rhodes from before the first siege. Though it was an important gateway, at first it was defended only by a simple tower. By 1467 this was then strengthened by a bulwark incorporating small gunports. The moat at this time was narrow and was crossed by a bridge on to this bulwark. After 1480 the moat was widened and the large bulwark formed by excavating around it. It was then encased in stone, forming an offensive fighting platform able to take large artillery (above, right).[29]

The east side of St John's Gate is photographed above. A series of tiered defences have been built to provide fire mainly along the moat. The arms of Grand Master d'Aubusson indicate that he added this outer defence.

The east side of the main bulwark outside St John's Gate (right). The absence of loops or embrasures below the parapet indicates that it is a solid structure. Fire along the moat to the east was provided by the firing gallery on the right side. The sloping parapet on top of the bulwark has splayed embrasures for mounting artillery and is very similar to the parapet on the main city wall.

The bridge across the moat to the outer bulwark (below). Above the gateway to the bulwark are the arms of Grand Master d'Aubusson.

The west side of the outer bulwark (left). The small building is a small firing gallery to provide fire along the moat to the west like that on the east of the bulwark.

Rhodes Besieged

Walls from St John's Gate to the Virgin's Tower[30]

The wall from St John's Gate to the Tower of the Virgin protects the southern part of the city and is, for much of its length, very straight (right). It has four interval towers and after the 1480 siege the moat was significantly widened. A long *tenaille*, to protect the city wall, was formed. The view below is from St John's Gate looking west towards the Virgin's Tower – at the top centre. The city wall, on the right, is protected by a *faussebraye* and the *tenaille* runs parallel to the wall. The interval wall towers are clearly visible.

The wall from St John's gate, westward, is very tall and has a *faussebraye*. It was built by Grand Master Lastic, whose arms are placed on the wall (below, right).

The first wall tower south from the Tower of St John. The tower was originally detached from the main wall but was later secured back – the arch to allow access along the *faussebraye* can just be seen.

The simple interval tower below, left has been strengthened by the addition of a strongly battered reinforcement to its base. Just when and by whom this was done is unclear. It may have been done before the 1480 siege to reinforce the tower, or it may have been done at the time that the moat was widened by Grand Master d'Aubusson, after the 1480 siege. The way that much of the bedrock has been exposed all along the stretch of wall from St John's Gate to the Virgin's Tower suggests that the moat might also have been deepened and this reinforcement added to shore up the tower. The wall to the west of the first tower is very tall and has the *faussebraye*. High up on the wall is a relief of an unknown saint surmounting the arms of the Order and those of Grand Master Pierre d'Aubusson. Just why the arms of d'Aubusson are here is unclear but may mark repairs to the walls or rebuilding and strengthening after the 1480 siege (below).

The second tower, west of St John's Gate, is quite similar to the first. Originally only attached to the *faussebraye*, it was, at a later date, secured back to the main wall. The rock base is evidence again that the moat must have been deepened. The arms on the tower are those of Grand Master Lastic (below).

The wall between the second tower and the third, west of St John's Gate, again shows evidence that the moat has been deepened. The wall behind the tower was built by Grand Master Lastic with his arms displayed.

The third tower is very similar the first two and also has a large reinforced base like the first. The arms of Grand Master Lastic are set

180

The Walls

into the wall and lower down is the remains of a gunport with a cross-shaped sighting slit (left).

The wall between towers three and four show the different building phases of the wall: the *faussebraye*; the lower part of the main city walls; and the rebuilding and raising the height of the wall at the top. In this case the three phases are marked by three coats of arms (below).

The arms of Grand Master Fabrizio del Carretto on the upper part of the wall show that he was responsible for heightening the walls and making the parapet (below, left). These arms may enable us to understand more clearly the construction of the walls in this part of the city. The probable explanation is that the walls and *faussebraye* were built by grand masters Fluvian and Lastic before the siege of 1480, with changes made by Grand Master Carretto between that siege and the one in 1522.

This included raising and widening the walls to provide a platform on which to mount artillery.

The fourth tower, called the Tower of Athanasios, is larger than the other three and extends further into the moat. It protects an entrance through the walls which, in its present state, extends from the Tower of the Virgin. The tower has a very similar base reinforcement as the first and third towers. It also has corbels at the roof level to support a fighting platform (below, right). The tower is adorned with a low relief carving of a saint, presumably St Athanasios (or Athanasius), with the arms of Grand Master Fluvian and the Knights Hospitaller (below, centre).

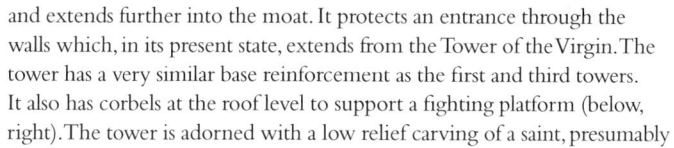

After the siege of 1480 Grand Master d'Aubusson was responsible for widening the moat. In doing so a long *tenaille* of rock was left standing, running parallel to the walls, which provided protection for them – thus the enemies' artillery was not able to attack the wall directly. The inner face of this *tenaille* was originally the outer face of the moat before 1480. The photograph below, left is the view from St John's Gate. The earth and rock was faced with stone, making a substantial obstacle to both artillery attack as well as scaling. No parapet exists for this *tenaille* and it is unclear whether this was as originally planned or it has been subsequently removed, although Jacques de Bourbon writes that the Hospitallers had soldiers who fought Turkish troops there until forced to retreat to the city.[31]

Rhodes Besieged

Tower of the Virgin

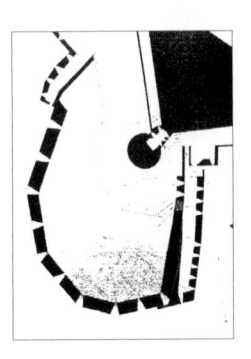

The Tower of the Virgin was originally a small circular defence tower built at the south-west corner of the city walls (right). Subsequently it was secured back to the wall and a large irregularly crescent-shaped bulwark was formed round it. The development can be seen very clearly on close inspection.[32] The original tower (left), which was not secured back to the main wall, was built in 1441 as stated by the inscription below the relief of the Virgin (from where the tower derives its name): EVITA EST ABINCARNATO D[OMI]NO ANNO M CCCC XLI (*this was built* – literally, *it began life* – *in the year 1441*) (below, right). The batter appears to have been added later.

The detached tower was then secured back to the main city wall in the time of Grand Master Orsini as shown by his arms built into the connecting wall between the tower and the city wall. The arms of Grand Master Orsini are mounted on the infill between the Tower of the Virgin and the main city wall.

After the siege of 1480 the moat was greatly widened around the Tower of the Virgin and a crescent-shaped *tenaille* of earth and rock was formed as an outer defence. This was faced with stone and given embrasures around its top edge. The bulwark surrounds the tower, providing both added defence as well as an artillery platform from which to fire into enemy positions. The bulwark appears to have been formed by leaving the rock and earth standing and then giving it a stone cladding (left). As the bulwark provided no means to protect the moat, additional defences were added to each side of it, providing low-level fire along the moat. To the east a three-storey defence was built against the bulwark, incorporating the entry into the city from across the moat via a bridge. Handgun and small artillery fire could be directed along both sides of the *tenaille* that protects the wall between the Tower of St John and the Virgin's Gate.

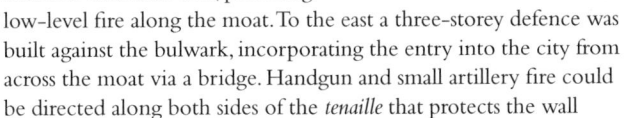

The photographs to the left and right are of the inside of the firing platform atop the bulwark, showing the loops at road level and the crenellations.

This 'firing gallery' incorporated the entry road into the gate. The photograph overleaf is of the outer gateway from the bridge over the moat and includes the arms of Grand Master Pierre d'Aubusson and an inscription which gives a date, 1486: AD FIDEI CATHOLICAE HOSTES ARCENDOS DIVVS F PETRUS DAUBUSSON RHODI DUM MAGNUS MAGISTER / DE TURCIS INCLITUS VICTOR RHODIAM URBEM MUNIENS ANTE MURALE EREXIT MCCCCLXXXVI (*When the Grand Master Blessed Brother Peter d'Aubusson for the Catholic Faith turned away the enemy, the celebrated victor, fortifying the city of Rhodes, built this tower before the walls, 1486*).

The Walls

The Tower of the Virgin and its bulwark defend a gateway into the city. This is now entered from the firing gallery on the east of the bulwark, turning right on to the *faussebraye*. The opening through the city wall is covered by a small tower. Originally this tower appears to have been detached from the main wall and was secured back later. Inside the tower the road turned to the left, through the wall (below, left). There is now an entrance into the city through the wall. There is some question as to whether there was an entrance into the city here at the time of the sieges or if it was made by the Turks after 1522.[33] Above the inner archway of this entrance are the arms of Grand Master Carretto who was probably responsible for the alterations to the walls (right).

The outer gateway.

A second firing gallery was added to the west side of the bulwark to provide fire along the moat. Unlike the firing gallery on the east side, this is only a single-storey building with gunports at low level and crenellations at roof level for small arms fire (below, right). The photograph below, centre shows the vaulted firing gallery with the gunports. These gunports were only suitable for handguns or small artillery pieces used as anti-personnel weapons.

The Gate of the Virgin from the west (below, left) – the tower is on the left, the bulwark in the centre, with the west firing gallery on the right of it. On the far right is the *tenaille* protecting the wall between the Virgin Gate and the Gate of Spain.

The Walls from Virgin's Tower to the Tower of Spain

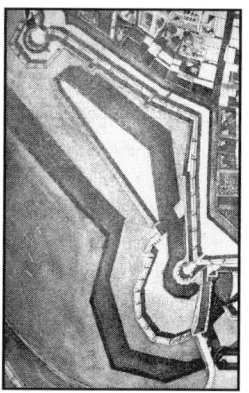

The city wall runs almost due north from the Virgin's Tower before turning, halfway along its length, north-west to join the Tower of Spain (left). It is strengthened by two small interval towers, both of which are still only attached to the *faussebraye*. The wall was built by Grand Master Lastic. They were heightened and thickened by Grand Master Carretto whose arms can be seen on the inside face. Almost the entire length is protected by a *tenaille* probably constructed by Grand Master d'Aubusson after the 1480 siege.[34]

Photographed overleaf is the stretch of wall from the Virgin's Gate to the Tower of Spain at the top centre. The large triangular *tenaille* can be seen on the left and the two interval towers along the wall. The wall runs due north and straight from the Virgin's Gate before turning to the north-west to the Tower of Spain. The first section is very tall and relatively featureless, with the *faussebraye* in front. The second section of the wall from the turn to the Tower of Spain is reinforced by two towers. They are very little changed and basically still as they were when

Rhodes Besieged

built some time before 1480. They are relatively low, not much taller than the *faussebraye*, and are only attached to the *faussebraye* – they have not been heightened and tied back to the main city wall as have all the other interval towers (right). The first of the two towers is a simple rectangular structure rising straight from the moat. Unfortunately the coat of arms set in the front is too damaged to be able to tell which Grand Master had it built. The gunport has a cross-shaped sight above it (below). The second tower is, like the first, a simple rectangular tower but it has been reinforced with a new base and a batter. The south face has a similar gunport with cross-shaped sight as the first tower. It also has a rectangular gunport with sight above. The photograph below shows the front of the tower and its height relative to the main wall. The north face has another of the circular gunports with a simple slit sight. The photograph below, right shows one of the circular gunports inside the tower. The stone hole into which the mounting of a swivel gun would have been placed is still in situ.

The wall from the Virgin's Gate to the Tower of Spain.

The wall continues to the Tower of Spain. The arms of Grand Master Lastic are set high up (below, left). The wall was evidently strengthened and/or widened by Grand Master Carretto. The wall was also given a new parapet, probably also the work of Grand Master Carretto. It slopes back sharply from the front of the wall. The photograph overleaf shows the top of the parapet to the south of the Tower of Spain, which is set with embrasures. Behind the embrasures, the *terreplein* had numerous specially built platforms for the guns – here evidently for the very largest pieces.

The wall from the Virgin's Gate to the Tower of Spain is protected from attack by a large triangular *tenaille* seen, in the photograph overleaf, from the Virgin's Gate. The arms of Grand Master Orsini are set high up on the rear face of the *tenaille*. However, it is unlikely that Orsini was responsible for the *tenaille* – as none of the 1480 artistic or written sources show one. It is more probable that this was originally the counterscarp of the moat before it was widened by Grand Master d'Aubusson after the 1480 siege. This then shows how wide the moat was before 1480 and also some clue as to the way the moat was formed. Originally quite narrow, it was faced in stone by Orsini. After the 1480 siege, d'Aubusson had the moat widened by digging to the west, leaving the original counterscarp intact as the rear wall of the *tenaille*.

The parapet of the *tenaille* incorporates both gunports for handguns as well as medium pieces of artillery. The gunports are both the usual simple slits or, as here, two angled slits meeting at the rear and offering a wider field of fire for the handgunner, whereas the gunports for larger guns are simple rectangular openings (overleaf).

The Walls

Above, left: Top of the parapet to the south of the Tower of Spain.

Above: The parapet of the tenaille, with gunports.

Above, right: Gunports for larger guns.

Left: The large triangular tenaille *seen from the Virgin's Gate.*

Tower of Spain

The Tower of Spain, like the other major gates and towers of Rhodes, was originally a small circular tower defence at a change in angle of the city walls to the west of the city (left). After the 1480 siege the tower was strengthened by a four-sided bulwark.[35] The drawing to the left is a cross section of the tower at ground level and elevation.[36]

Unlike the bulwarks at St John's Gate and the Tower of the Virgin, the bulwark around the original Tower of Spain was built rather than being formed by widening the moat and leaving a *tenaille*. There are two levels of gunports in the Tower of Spain bulwark: one at the level of the moat and the second around its upper edge. The lower gunports are relatively small and would only have been capable of mounting handguns or very small artillery pieces. Most have a separate sighting slit above the main opening. The front of the Tower of Spain bears the arms of Grand Master d'Aubusson, which incorporate the cardinal's hat and date of 1489 – the same year that he became a cardinal. The parapet on top of the bulwark has embrasures for medium-sized artillery. It is clear that they are not part of the original building of the bulwark, although when they were added is not certain (above). The photograph to the right is of the view looking down from the Tower of Spain on to the top of the bulwark, and clearly shows that the embrasures are not big enough for very large guns.

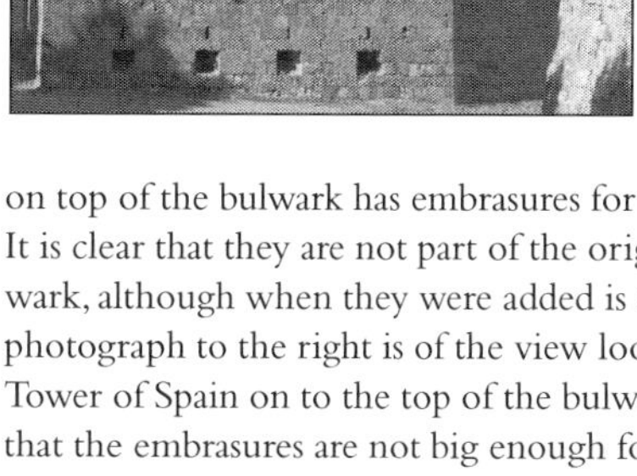

Rhodes Besieged

Wall from the Tower of Spain to St George's Bastion

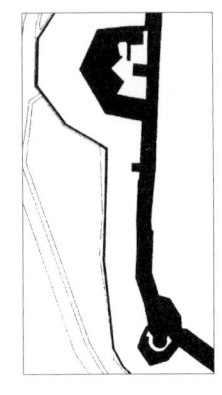

The wall from the Tower of Spain to St George's bastion is essentially a high wall, with the *faussebraye* in front (left). The moat is very wide but there is no *tenaille* as in other areas of the walls (below).

The main wall of the city has been raised in height and a large sloping parapet added with embrasures for large pieces of artillery. The wall has been greatly thickened and the wide *terreplein* along the top has paved artillery positions on which large guns could be positioned (below).

The wall between the Tower of Spain and St George's bastion has a single square tower along its length. Originally only extending out from the *faussebraye*, this tower was subsequently secured back to the main wall. It appears that the moat has been very significantly deepened between the Tower of Spain and St George's bastion, as can be seen in the photograph from below the interval tower (below, right).

Left: The wide terrplein, with paved artillery positions.

Left: The view looking along the top of the wall and into the faussebraye from the Tower of Spain.

St George's Bastion

Originally defending a gateway into the city, St George's defence was a detached square wall tower built by Grand Master Fluvian between 1421 and 1431 (left). This view below, right shows the upper part of the tower from the top of the city wall. The infilling between the tower and the wall is clearly visible. On the west wall of the tower is a relief of St George and the arms of the Knights Hospitaller, Grand Master Fluvian and Pope Martin V (1417–31) (overleaf). There is also a figure of St George and the dragon, from which the tower gets its name, with the arms of Grand Master Fluvian flanking the arms of the Knights Hospitaller and of Pope Martin V (overleaf).

At some time after the defence's initial construction the small detached tower was secured back to the main wall and a spur-shaped

The Walls

bulwark, very similar to that at the Virgin's Gate, was erected around it. There was probably a bridge over the moat and a gateway into the city which led around the front of the tower and through the wall.

The photograph below, right shows the original entrance into the city. In 1496 the relatively small tower and bulwark was completely enveloped within the largest bulwark of the city walls. The bastion of St George is a four-sided construction which projects out into a greatly widened moat.

The south face of the bulwark has two sets of gunports covering the moat (below, left). The lower gunports are relatively wide and could probably have mounted small- to medium-sized artillery. The upper gunports are smaller and were probably made for lighter artillery and handguns.

The chamber on the first floor of St George's bastion has the gunports down the left side, with vents for smoke in the ceiling and from the lower chamber in the floor.

The western faces of St George's bastion, facing the counterscarp, have no gunports below the parapet. The arms of Grand Master d'Aubusson are high up in the centre of one of these walls; they include both the cardinal's hat and the date, 1496 (below, left).

The north face of the bulwark has just two small gunports at the lower level. The arms of Grand Master Philippe Villiers de l'Isle Adam (1521–34) can be seen high on the wall, although just what he can have done in the short time of his rule before the siege of 1522 is difficult to determine. The arms of Grand Master de l'Isle Adam are mounted on the north face of St George's bastion (right). The photograph to the left is of the gun platform on top of St George's bastion. The crenellations were probably rebuilt following the 1522 siege by the Ottoman Turks.

The view right shows the interior of the bastion, and the drawing to the left is a reconstruction of St George's bastion.

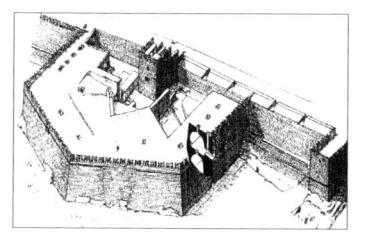

The west wall of the tower, with relief of St George and the arms of the Knights Hospitaller, Grand Master Fluvian and Pope Martin V.

The south face of the bulwark.

The western faces of St George's bastion.

A figure of St George and the dragon, with the arms of Grand Master Fluvian, the Knights Hospitaller and Pope Martin V.

The original entrance into the city of Rhodes.

187

Rhodes Besieged

Walls from St George's Tower to the Caponier and the Defences West of the Grand Masters' Palace

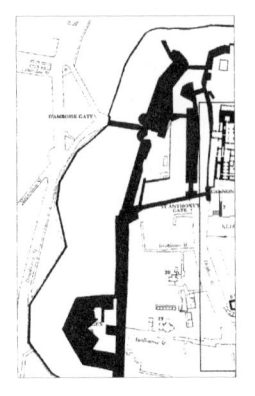

The drawing to the left shows the defences from St George's Tower to the *caponier*.[37]

North of St George's Gate the wall runs northwards to the north-west corner of the city. The first section of the wall was built by Grand Master Lastic and originally turned sharply east to the Grand Master's Palace. After the siege of 1480 Grand Master Pierre d'Aubusson extended the wall northwards, to the present north-west corner of the city. This area of the city suffered from a serious earthquake in 1513[38] and was subsequently partially rebuilt by Grand Master Carretto, who also added a *caponier* across the moat at the north-west corner of the walls.[39]

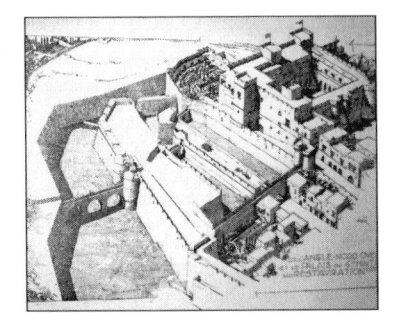

Grand Master d'Aubusson built a new bulwark, from the east due north to the present north-west corner of the city. He then re-modelled the defences around the Grand Master's Palace, joining back again to the original wall halfway along the north face. Grand Master Emery d'Amboise added an artillery defence, now called the Battery of the Olives, between 1502 and 1513 to cover the moat on the north side of d'Aubusson's bulwark. The serious earthquake in 1513 damaged the bulwark and it was rebuilt by Grand Master Carretto, who also added a *caponier* with gunports to defend the moat (above).[40]

The first section of the wall north of St George's Tower still has the *faussebraye* in front and was built by Grand Master Lastic. The *faussebraye* ends at the small projection, on the left of the picture above, which is the remains of an earlier tower and where the wall originally turned east to the Grand Master's Palace. The wall is again very high, with the *faussebraye* in front. It was built in the time of Grand Master Lastic, as shown by his arms set into the wall.

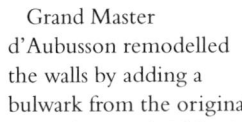

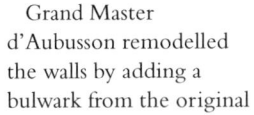

Grand Master d'Aubusson remodelled the walls by adding a bulwark from the original tower due north. This view above of the rear of the bulwark shows its immense thickness. The outer wall, with its crenellations, can be seen on the left and the top of the d'Amboise Gate, with its stepped crenellations and is at top centre.

A tunnel, presumably modern, now leads through the wall at the junction of where the bulwark meets the older tower. Grand Master d'Aubusson's bulwark is roughly the same height as the walls of Lastic to the south (left).

As originally built by d'Aubusson there was no gate in the bulwark he erected, but in 1512 Grand Master d'Amboise built a new gate into the city – now called the d'Amboise Gate. The d'Amboise Gate consists of an arched entrance between two drum towers. Above and behind it is the reconstructed Grand Master's Palace (right and overleaf).

Over the entrance is a relief of an angel with the arms of the Knights Hospitaller and of Grand Master d'Amboise. The

The Walls

The d'Amboise Gate.

inscription, DAMBOYSE / M D XII beneath, gives the date 1512 (below, right). The two towers flank the entrance passage which turns through a right angle (below, left).[41]

The bulwark north of the d'Amboise Gate was damaged in 1512 by the earthquake and was partly rebuilt by Grand Master Carretto. North of the d'Amboise Gate are the arms of Carretto with the inscription: F
FABR DE CARRETTO
MAGR COLLAPSAM A
FVNDAMENTIS RESTITVIT
(*Master Brother Fabrizio de Carretto rebuilt the collapsed wall from the foundations*). A second coat of arms, further north along the walls, has the same inscription but adds the date 1514 (below, right).

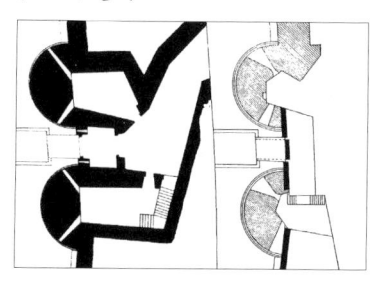

Grand Master Carretto was also responsible for building a single-storey *caponier* stretching across the bottom of the moat at the north-west corner of the city. On the south side it has three small gun-ports for handguns. On the north face is an entrance to the *caponier* and four gunports (below, left).

Internally the *caponier* is a barrel-vaulted chamber with splayed gunports on either side. The ports, though quite large on the inside, could only accommodate very small artillery pieces or handguns (below, right). The *caponier* was, like the repairs to the bulwark, also built in 1514 as shown by a coat of arms of Grand Master Carretto on the west end of the south wall.

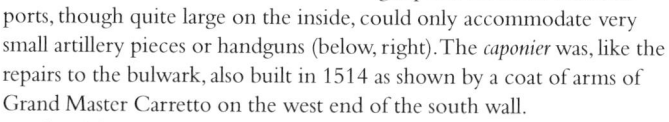

Behind the *caponier*, on the northern section of the walls, is a curious two-storey artillery tower now called the Battery of the Olives. It has gunports on two levels, angled through the walls, to provide small arms' fire across and around the moat. The end of the bulwark, which can be seen behind the battery, has the arms of Grand Master Carretto.

The Battery of the Olives was erected by Grand Master d'Amboise in 1511, as shown by the dated coat of arms on its south face. In the picture below the *caponier* is on the left, the bulwark built by Grand Master d'Aubusson on the right. Strangely, the bulwark here also includes the arms of Grand Master Carretto, indicating that the rebuilt bulwark was closely integrated with the battery.

The photograph overleaf is of the south side of the original city wall running east to the Cannon Gate. The Cannon Gate is situated in the corner where the pre-1480 wall turns north. The access is at first-storey level and seems to have served as a means to control access to the wall walk, and later the *terreplein*. It was built by Grand Master Lastic as shown by his arms above the entrance.

St Anthony's Gate is a small entrance through the older wall. Though originally it must have been protected by an outer work, which has

Rhodes Besieged

largely disappeared. The building of the bulwark by Grand Master d'Aubusson meant that the gate was within the defences and the outer work may then have been demolished. The statue of St Anthony sits above the gate with the arms of Grand Master Lastic (below, right).

This photograph below, left is of the pre-1480 wall to the east of St Anthony's Gate, built by Grand Master Lastic. Originally this was the outer face of the wall before the bulwark and other defences were built. Evidence of an outer work, to protect the gate, can be seen on the left. The Cannon Gate can also be seen on the extreme left, giving access to the top of the wall.

The south side of the original city wall running east to the Cannon Gate.

The drawing below, centre is a reconstruction of the north-west corner of the city as it might have appeared in 1522.[42]

The Cannon Gate.

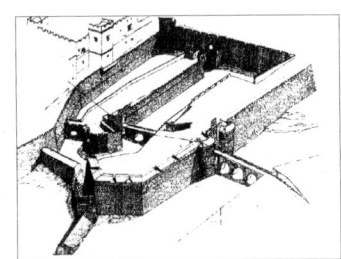

Walls from the Battery of the Olives to the Naillac Mole

To the left is a plan of the walls of the north-west corner of the city.[43] The defences of the city, from the Battery of the Olives in the north-west corner to the Naillac Tower Mole, are somewhat confusing and have been subject to some modern changes. The counterscarp around the Grand Master's Palace appears to have been greatly altered.

The view to the right shows the moat with counterscarp on the right looking west towards the reconstruction of the Grand Master's Palace.

St Peter's Tower, from the south, consists of a circular drum-tower around which an enclosing outer work has been constructed (left).

As originally built, St Peter's Tower was not secured to the main wall, but at some stage it was secured back to the wall and a polygonal outer work built around it. A barbican also ran down to the sea from the outer work.

The Walls

The arms on St Peter's Tower (left) – Pope Pius II (Aeneas Sylvius Piccolomini) (1458–64) on the left, the Knights Hospitaller in the middle and Grand Master Piero Raimondo Zacosta on the right. Zacosta did not become Grand Master until 1461 and Pius II died in 1464, so this tower can be dated to between 1461 and 1464.

The wall from St Peter's Tower runs east to the sea and consists of a tall wall with a *faussebraye* in front of it. The *faussebraye* is damaged and there is also a large area of damage to the main wall – possibly caused by an artillery shot.

This square tower (right) is dated by the coat of arms to Grand Master Jean Fernandez de Heredia (1376–96), indicating that this section of the city walls was among the first to be built by the Knights.

Left is a view of the wall east of the Tower of Heredia and showing the city wall, *faussebraye* and counterscarp. The bridge in the centre is a modern entrance into the city.

The photograph below, left shows the Tower of St Paul on the north-west corner of the city. It shows the figure of St Paul with the arms of the Knights Hospitaller, Pope Sixtus IV (1471–84) and Grand Master Pierre d'Aubusson, as on the Tower of St Paul. The inscription reads: DIVO PAULO VASI ELECTIONIS PETRUS DAUBUSSON RHODI MAGISTER DICAVIT (*Peter d'Aubusson, Master of Rhodes, consecrated this to Saint Paul at the time of his election*). This dedication implies that the tower was completed in 1476. There is a large bastion with gunports in front of the St Paul's Tower (below, right).

Notes

1. Obadiah of Bertinoro, in A. Neubauer, ed., 'Zwei breife obadjah's ous Bertinoro aus den Jahren 5248 und 5249 und ein anonymer Reisebrief aus den Jahr 1495', *Jahrbuch für die Geschichte der Juden und das Judenthums* 3 (1863), p. 40.
2. Gabriel.
3. Spiteri.
4. Fradin, Baron de Belabre, *Rhodes of the Knights* (Oxford: Clarendon Press, 1908).
5. Gabriel, II:62.
6. From Gabriel, II:81.

Rhodes Besieged

7   From Gabriel, II:89.
8   From Spiteri, p. 113.
9   From Gabriel, II:71.
10 From Gabriel, II:pl. xxiv.
11 Gabriel, II:73. The illustration is from his II:pl. xxiv.
12 From Gabriel, II:pl. xvi.
13 Gabriel, II:61.
14 From Gabriel, II:60.
15 Gabriel, II:60.
16 From Gabriel, II:pl. xiii.
17 Gabriel, II:55–6.
18 From Gabriel, II:pl. xiii.
19 From Gabriel, II:56.
20 From Gabriel, II:55.
21 From Gabriel, II:pl. xiii.
22 From Gabriel, II:54.
23 From Spiteri, p. 114.
24 From Spiteri, p. 114.
25 From Gabriel, pl. xiii.
26 From Spiteri, p. 115.
27 For an in-depth discussion of this gate, including what recent archaeological excavations have shown, see Anna-Maria Kasdagli and Katerina Manoussou-Della, 'The Defences of Rhodes and the Tower of St John', *Fort* 24 (1996), pp. 15–36.
28 From Spiteri, p. 115.
29 From Spiteri, p. 115.
30 From Gabriel, II:pl. vii.
31 Bourbon, p. 137.
32 From Gabriel, II:45.
33 Gabriel, II:47.
34 From Gabriel, II:pl. vii. Although the arms of d'Aubusson are not present, as he is the builder of the other *tenailles*, it is likely he built this one also.
35 From Gabriel, II:pl. vii.
36 From Gabriel, II:43.
37 From map inserted in Kollias, *Knights of Rhodes*.
38 Luttrell, 'Earthquakes in the Dodecanese', pp. 150–1.
39 From Gabriel, II:pl. ii.
40 From Gabriel, II:33.
41 Gabriel, II:32.
42 From Spiteri, p. 120.
43 From Gabriel, II:pl. ii.

Appendix 3: Grand Masters' Coats of Arms

Grand Masters of the Order of Knights Hospitallers

Juan Fernandez de Heredia 1376–96

Philibert de Naillac 1396–1421

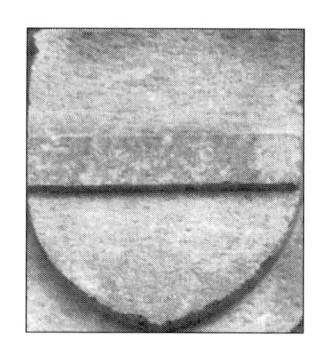

Antonio Fluvian 1421–37

Jean de Lastic 1437–54

Jacques de Milly 1454–56

Giovanni Battista Orsini 1467–76

Rhodes Besieged

Pierre d'Aubusson 1476–89

Pierre d'Aubusson 1489–1503

Emery d'Amboise 1503–12

Guy de Blanchefort 1512–1513

Fabrizio del Carretto 1513–21

Philippe Villiers de l'Isle Adam 1521–34

Bibliography

Original Unpublished Sources

Caoursin, Guillaume. *Obsidionis Rhodiae urbis description*. Paris, Bibliothèque Nationale, MS lat. 6067, 1480–1490.
Epernay painting of Siege of Rhodes, c.1480.
National Library of Malta, Valletta, Section 2, Libri Conciliorum.
National Library of Malta, Valletta, Section 5, Libri Bullarum.

Aubusson, Pierre d'. [Letter to emperor Frederick III]. In: *Scriptorum rerum germanicarum*, II. Berlin: 1602.
Amadi, Francesco. In: *Chroniques de Chypre d'Amadi et de Strambaldi*. Ed. R. de Mas Latrie. Paris, 1891–93.
Balbi di Correggio, Francisco. *The Siege of Malta, 1565*. Trans. Ernle Bradford. London: Folio Society, 1965; rpt. Woodbridge: The Boydell Press, 2005.
Barbaro, Nicolo. *Eidemerides de Constantinopoli anno 1453 obsessa atque expugnata*, in *Patrologia Graeca*, 158. Ed. J.P. Migne. Paris: Vrayet, 1866.
Basin, Thomas. *Histoire de Louis XI*. Ed. Charles Samaran. 2 vols. Paris: Société d'Édition 'Les Belles Lettres', 1963–72.
Baudin, P. *Le Siege de Rhodes: Chronique du XVIe siècle*. Constantinople, 1871.
Beg, Tursun. *The History of Mehmed the Conqueror*. Trans. Halil Inalcik and Rhoads Murphey. Minneapolis: Bibliotheca Islamica, 1978.
Belabre, Fradin, Baron de. *Rhodes of the Knights*. Oxford: Clarendon Press, 1908.
Blackmore, H.L. *The Armouries of the Tower of London. I: Ordnance*. London: Her Majesty's Stationery Office, 1976.
Bourbon, Jacques de. *The begynnynge and foundacyon of the holy hospytall, [and] of the ordre of the knyghtes hospytallers of saynt Johan baptyst of Jerusalem*. Trans. Robert Coplande. London, 1524.
Bourbon, Jacques de. *Relation de la grande et merveilleuse et trés cruelle expugnation de la noble cite de Rhodes*. Paris, 1527.
Bourbon, Jacques de. *Relation de la grande et merveilleuse et trés cruelle expugnation de la noble cite de Rhodes*. In: Abbé de Vertot. *The History of the Knights of Malta*. London, 1728, I: pp. 108–50.
Burchard, Johann. *At the Court of the Borgia, being an Account of the Reign of Pope Alexander VI written by his Master of Ceremonies, Johann Burchard*. Ed. and trans. Geoffrey Parker. London: The Folio Society, 1963.
Calendar of Patent Rolls, Henry VII. Vol. 1: 1485–94. London: Her Majesty's Stationery Office, 1914.
Cartulaire general de l'Ordre des Hospitaliers de St Jean de Jerusalem, 1100–1310. Ed. J. Delaville le Roulx, 4 vols. Paris: Ernest Leroux, 1894–1906.
Caoursin, Guillaume. *Obsidionis Rhodiae urbis descriptio*. Venice, 1480.
Caoursin, Guillaume. *Opera*. Venice, 1496.
Casola, Pietro. *Canon Pietro Casola's Pilgrimage in Jerusalem in the Year 1494*. Ed. M. Newett. Manchester: Manchester University Press, 1907.
Chalcocondylas, Laonicus. *Turkish History*, in *The Siege of Constantinople, 1453: Seven Contemporary Accounts*. Trans. J.R.M. Jones. Amsterdam: Adolf M. Hakkert Publisher, 1972.

Charrière, E. *Négociations de la France dans le Levant*. 4 vols. Paris, 1848–60; rpt. New York, 1965.
Curti, Giacomo. *Ad magnificum spectabilemque.* Venice: Erhaldus Radtolt de Augusta, c.1510.
Dolfin, Zorzi. 'Cronaca'. In: *The Siege of Constantinople, 1453: Seven Contemporary Accounts.* Trans. J.R.M. Jones. Amsterdam: Adolf M. Hakkert Publisher, 1972.
Ducas, Michael. 'Byzantine History'. In: *The Siege of Constantinople, 1453: Seven Contemporary Accounts.* Trans. J.R.M. Jones. Amsterdam: Adolf M. Hakkert Publisher, 1972.
Dupuis, Mary. In: Abbé de Vertot. *The History of the Knights of Malta.* London, 1728, I:598–616.
Ferrer, Francesc. *Romanç de l'armada del soldà contra Rodes.* In: L. Nicolau d'Olwer, 'Un témoinage catalan du siege de Rhodes en 1444', *Estudis universitaris catalans* 12 (1927), 376–87.
Firework Book, The: Gunpowder in Medieval Germany. Das Feuerwerkbuch c.1400. Ed. Gerhard W. Kramer. Trans. Klaus Leibnitz. In: *The Journal of the Arms and Armour Society* 17.1 (Mar 2001).
Fontanus, Jacobus. *De bello Rhodio libri tres.* Rome, 1525.
Housley, Norman, ed. and trans. *Documents on the Later Crusades, 1274–1580.* New York: St Martin's Press, 1996.
Imber, Colin, ed. *The Crusade of Varna, 1443–45.* Ashgate: Aldershot, 2006.
Justinianus, B. Paulus and Petrus Quirinus. *Erimatarum Carmaldulensium Libellus ad Leonum X Maximum.* In: G.B. Mittarelli and Anslemo Costadoni, ed. *Annales Carmaldulenses.* 9 vols. Venice, 1735–73.
Kaestlin, J.P., ed. *Catalogue of the Museum of Artillery in the Rotunda at Woolwich. Part I: Ordnance.* London: Her Majesty's Stationery Office, 1963.
Kritovoulos. *History of Mehmed the Conqueror.* Trans. Charles T. Riggs. Princeton: Princeton University Press, 1954.
L'Haridon, O. Penguilly. *Catalogue des collections composant le Musée d'Artillerie.* Paris: Charles de Mourgues Frères, 1862.
Mizzi, E., ed. *Le Guerre di Rodi: Relazioni di diversi autori sui due grandi assedi di Rodi, 1480–1522.* Turin, 1934.
Mohler, L., ed. 'Bessarions Instruktion für die Kreuzzugspredigt in Venedig (1463)', *Römische Quartalschrift* 35 (1927), 337–49.
Pius II. *The Commentaries of Pius II.* Trans. F.A. Gragg. Northampton: Smith College, Department of History, 1937, 1940, 1947, 1951, 1957.
Roberts, Nicholas Wentworth Porter. *A History of the Knights of Malta or the Order of St. John of Jerusalem.* 2nd ed. London: Longmans, Green and Co., 1883, App. 8 to ref.
Röhricht, R. and H. Meisner, ed. *Deutsche Pilgerreisen nach dem Heiligen Lande.* Berlin: Weidmann, 1880.
Rossi, Ettore, ed. *Assedio e conquistadi Rodi nel 1522 secondo le relazioni edite e inedite dei Turchi.* Rome, 1927.
Rossi, Ettore, ed. 'Nuove ricerche sulle fonti turche relative all' assedio di Rodi nel 1522', *Rivista di studi orientali*, 15 (1934), 97–102.
Sanudo, Marino. *I diarii di Marino Sanuto (MCCCCXCVI–MDXXXIII) dall 'autografo Marciano ital. cl. VII codd. CDXIX–CDLXXVII.* Ed. Rinaldo Fulin et al. 59 vols. Venice: 1879–1903 to ref.
Sphrantzes, George. *The Fall of the Byzantine Empire: A Chronicle of George Sphrantzes, 1401–1477.* Trans. M. Philippides. Amherst: University of Massachusetts Press, 1980.
Tedaldi, Giacomo. 'Letter to Alain de Coëtivy, the Cardinal of Avignon'. In: *The Siege of Constantinople, 1453: Seven Contemporary Accounts.* Trans. J.R.M. Jones. Amsterdam: Adolf M. Hakkert Publisher, 1972.
Tercier, M., ed. 'Mémoire sur la prise de la ville et de l'ile de Rhodes en 1522 par Soliman II', *Memoirs de l'Académie des inscriptions et belles-lettres*, 26 (1759).
Voisin, Philippe de. *Voyage à Jérusalem de Philippe de Voisin.* Ed. Tamisey de Laroque. Paris: Société historique de Gascogne, 1883.
Winter, J. Maria van. *Sources concerning the Hospitallers of St John in the Netherlands.* Leiden: Brill, 1998.

Secondary Sources

Ágoston, Gábor. *Guns for the Sultan: Military Power and the Weapons Industry in the Ottoman Empire.* Cambridge: Cambridge University Press, 2005.
Arnold, Thomas. *The Renaissance at War.* London: Cassell, 2001.
Atiya, Aziz Suryal. *The Crusade of Nicopolis.* London: Methuen and Co. Ltd, 1934.
Babinger, Franz. *Mehmed the Conqueror and His Time.* Trans. Ralph Manheim. Ed. William C. Hickman. Princeton: Princeton University Press, 1978.

Bibliography

Bacheca, Michelangelo. *Il prodigio mariano nell'assedio di Rodi del 1480 in due documenti pontifici inediti.* Assisi: Porziuncola, 1954.

Bain, R.N. 'The Siege of Belgrade by Muhammed II, July 1–23, 1456', *English Historical Review* 7 (1892), 235–52.

Balard, Michel. 'The Urban Landscape of Rhodes as Perceived by Fourteenth- and Fifteenth-Century Travellers', *Mediterranean Historical Review* 10 (1995), 24–34.

Baldwin, Marshall W. 'The Decline and Fall of Jerusalem, 1174–1189'. In: *A History of the Crusades. Vol. I: The First Hundred Years.* Ed. M.W. Baldwin. Madison: University of Wisconsin Press, 1969.

Baray, Bernard, ed. *De Rhodes à Malte: Le grand maître Philippe de Villiers de L'Isle-Adam (1460-1534) et l'ordre de Malte.* Paris: Musée d'Art et d'Histoire Louis-Senlecq, 2004.

Barber, Malcolm. *The New Knighthood: A History of the Order of the Temple.* Cambridge: Cambridge University Press, 1994.

Barber, Malcolm. *The Trial of the Templars.* Cambridge: Cambridge University Press, 1978.

Barker, John W. *Manuel II Palaeologus (1391-1425): A Study in Late Byzantine Statesmanship.* New Brunswick: Rutgers University Press, 1969.

Bartusis, Mark C. *The Late Byzantine Army: Arms and Society, 1204–1453.* Philadelphia: University of Pennsylvania Press, 1992.

Biebel, Franklin M. 'The 'Angelot' of Jean Barbet', *The Art Bulletin* 32 (1950), 336–44.

Blackmore, H.L. *The Armouries of the Tower of London. I: Ordnance.* London: Her Majesty's Stationery Office, 1976.

Bradford, Ernle. *The Great Siege: Malta, 1565.* London: The Reprint Society, 1961.

Bradford, Ernle. *The Shield and the Sword: The Knights of St. John.* London: Penguin, 2002.

Brockman, Eric. *The Two Sieges of Rhodes: The Knights of St. John at War, 1480–1522.* New York: Barnes and Noble Press, 1969.

Bronstein, Judith. *The Hospitallers and the Holy Land: Financing the Latin East, 1187–1274.* Woodbridge: Boydell and Brewer, 2005.

Brummett, Palmira. *Ottoman Seapower and Levantine Diplomacy in the Age of Discovery.* Albany: State University of New York Press, 1994.

Brummett, Palmira. 'The Overrated Adversary: Rhodes and Ottoman Naval Power', *Historical Journal* 36 (1993), 517–43.

Caron, Marie-Thérèse. '17 février 1454: le Banquet du Voeu du Faisan, fête de cour et stratégies de pouvoir', *Revue du nord* 78 (1996), 269–88.

Caron, Marie-Thérèse and Denis Clauzel, ed. *Le Banquet du Faisan.* Collection 'Histoire.' Arras: Artois Presses Université, 1997.

Cianchi, Marco. *Leonardo's Machines.* Trans. Lisa Goldenberg Stoppato. Florence: Becocci editore, 1984.

Crowley, Roger. *Constantinople: The Last Great Siege, 1453.* London: Faber and Faber, 2005.

Crowley, Roger. *Empires of the Sea: The Siege of Malta, the Battle of Lepanto, and the Contest for the Center of the World.* New York: Random House, 2008.

Delaville le Roulx, J. *Les Hospitaliers à Rhodes jusqu'à la mort de Philibert de Naillac, 1310–1421.* Paris: E. Leroux, 1913.

Delaville le Roulx, J. *Les Hospitaliers en Terre Sainte et Chypre, (1100–1310).* Paris: Ernest Leroux, 1904.

Demurger, Alan. 'Templiers et Hospitaliers dans les combats de Terre Sainte'. In: *Le combattant au moyen âge.* 2nd ed. Paris: Publications de la Sorbonne, 1995, pp. 77–92.

DeVries, Kelly. 'Conquering the Conqueror at Belgrade (1456) and Rhodes (1480): Irregular Soldiers for an Uncommon Defense'. In *A Guerra, Revista de História das Ideias* 30 (2009), 219–32.

DeVries, Kelly. 'The Effectiveness of Fifteenth-Century Shipboard Artillery'. *The Mariner's Mirror* 84 (1998), 389–99.

DeVries, Kelly. 'Facing the New Military Technology: Non-*Trace Italienne* Anti-Gunpowder Weaponry Defenses, 1350–1550'. In: *Heirs of Archimedes: Science and the Art of War through the Age of Enlightenment.* Ed. Brett Steele and Tamara Dorland. Cambridge: The MIT Press, 2005, pp. 37–71.

DeVries, Kelly. 'Gunpowder Weaponry at the Siege of Constantinople, 1453'. In: *War, Army and Society in the Eastern Mediterranean, 7th–16th Centuries.* Ed. Yaacov Lev. Leiden: E.J. Brill, 1996, pp. 343–62.

DeVries, Kelly. 'The Impact of Gunpowder Weaponry on Siege Warfare in the Hundred Years War'. In: *The Medieval City Under Siege.* Ed. Ivy A. Corfis and Michael Wolfe. Woodbridge: The Boydell Press, 1995, pp. 227–44.

DeVries, Kelly. 'The Lack of a Western European Military Response to the Ottoman Invasions of Eastern Europe from Nicopolis (1396) to Mohács (1526)', *Journal of Military History* 63 (1999), 539–59.

DeVries, Kelly. '"The Walls Come Tumbling Down": The Myth of Fortification Vulnerability to Early Gunpowder Weapons'. In: *The Hundred Years War*. Ed. L.J. Andrew Villalon and Donald Kagay. Leiden: Brill, 2005, pp. 429–46.

Egg, Erich. *Der Tiroler Geschutzguss 1400–1600*. Innsbruk: Universitatsverlaf Wagner, 1961, pp. 39–48.

Eltis, David. *The Military Revolution in Sixteenth-Century Europe*. London: I.B. Tauris Publishers, 1995.

Engel, Pál. 'János Hunyadi: The Decisive Years of his Career, 1440–1444'. In: *War and Society in Eastern Central Europe. Vol. III: From Hunyadi to Rákóczi: War and Society in Late Medieval and Early Modern Hungary*. Ed. J.M. Bak and B.K. Király. New York: Brooklyn College Press, 1982, pp. 103–23.

Essenwein, August von. *Quellen zur Geschichte der Feuerwaffen*. 2 vols. 1877; rpt. Graz: Akademische Druck - u. Verlagsanstalt, 1969.

Fisher, Sidney. *The Foreign Relations of Turkey, 1481–1512*. Urbana: University of Illinois Press, 1948.

Forey, Alan. 'The Militarisation of the Hospital of St. John'. *Studia monastica* 26 (1984), 75–89.

Forey, Alan. *The Military Orders: From the Twelfth to the Early Fourteenth Centuries*. Toronto: University of Toronto Press, 1992.

Freely, John. *Jem Sultan: The Adventures of a Captive Turkish Prince in Renaissance Europe*. London: Harper Collins, 2004.

Gabriel, Albert. *La cité de Rhodes*. 2 vols. Paris: E. de Boccard, 1921–23.

Guilmartin, John Francis, Jr. 'Ballistics in the Black Powder Era'. In: *British Naval Armaments*. Ed. Robert Douglas Smith. London: Trustees of the Royal Armouries, 1989., pp. 73–98.

Guilmartin, John Francis, Jr. *Gunpowder and Galleys: Changing Technology and Mediterranean Warfare at Sea in the Sixteenth Century*. Cambridge: Cambridge University Press, 1974.

Hale, John R. 'The Early Development of the Bastion: An Italian Chronology'. In: *Europe in the Late Middle Ages*. Ed. J.R. Hale, J.R.L. Highfield and B. Smalley. Evanston: Northwestern University Press, 1965, pp. 466–94.

Hale, John R. *Renaissance Fortification: Art or Engineering?* London: Thames and Hudson Press, 1977.

Halecki, Oscar. *The Crusade of Varna*. New York: Polish Institute of Arts and Sciences in America, 1943.

Hall, Bert S. *Weapons and Warfare in Renaissance Europe: Gunpowder, Technology, and Tactics*. Baltimore: The John Hopkins University Press, 1997.

Hedenborg, Johannes. *Geschichte der Insel Rhodes, von der Urzeit bis auf die heutigen Tage nebst einer historischen Übersicht der Völker, Griechen, Römer, Araber, Franken und Türken, welche die Insel beherrscht haben, mit einer Sammlung vieler Inscriptionem so wie vieler Abbildungen von Monumenten besonders aus dem Mittelalter*. Vol. 2.3, Rhodes, Historical and Archaeological Institute of Rhodes Library, Manuscript·

Held, Joseph. *Hunyadi: Legend and Reality*. Boulder: East European Monographs, 1985.

Hess, Andrew C. 'The Evolution of the Ottoman Seaborne Empire in the Age of the Oceanic Discoveries, 1453–1525'. *American Historical Review* 75 (1970), 1892–1919.

Hess, Andrew C. 'The Ottoman Conquest of Egypt (1517) and the Beginning of the Sixteenth-Century World War'. *International Journal of Middle Eastern Studies* 4 (1973), 55–76.

Hichner, Nicole. 'Louis XII and the Porcupine: Transformatuions of a Royal Emblem'. *Renaissance Studies* 15 (2001), 17–36.

Hughes, Quentin and Athanassios Migos. 'Rhodes: The Turkish Sieges'. *Fort* 21 (1993), 2–17.

Imber, Colin. *The Ottoman Empire, 1300–1650*. Houndmills: Palgrave Macmillan, 2002.

Inalcik, Halil. *An Economic and Social History of the Ottoman Empire. Vol. I: 1300–1600*. Ed. Halil Inalcik and Donald Quataert. Cambridge: Cambridge University Press, 1994.

Inalcik, Halil. 'Mehmed the Conqueror (1432–1481) and His Time'. *Speculum* 35 (1960), 408–27.

Inalcik, Halil. *The Ottoman Empire: The Classical Age, 1300–1600*. Trans. Norman Itzkowitz and Colin Imber. New York: Praeger Publishers, 1973.

Inalcik, Halil. 'The Ottoman Turks and the Crusades, 1451–1522'. In: *A History of the Crusades. Vol. VI: The Impact of the Crusades on Europe*. Ed. Norman P. Zacour and Harry W. Hazard. Madison: University of Wisconsin Press, 1989, pp. 311–53.

Kaestlin, J.P. *Catalogue of the Museum of Artillery in the Rotunda at Woolwich. Part 1: Ordnance*. 2nd ed. London: Her Majesty's Stationery Office, 1970.

Karcheski, Walter J., Jr. and Thom Richardson. *The Medieval Armour from Rhodes*. Leeds: Royal Armouries and Higgins Armory Museum, 2000.

Bibliography

Kasdagli, Anna-Maria and Katerina Manoussou-Della. 'The Defences of Rhodes and the Tower of St. John'. *Fort* 24 (1996), 15–36.

Keen, Maurice H. 'The Changing Scene: Guns, Gunpowder, and Permanent Armies'. In: *Medieval Warfare: A History*. Ed. Maurice Keen. Oxford: Oxford University Press, 1999), pp. 273–91.

Kennard, A.N. *Gunfounding and Gunfounders: A Dictionary of Cannon Founders from Earliest Times to 1850*. London: Arms and Armour Press, 1986.

Kollias, Elias. *The Knights of Rhodes: The Palace and the City*. Athens: Ekdotike Athenon S.A., 1991.

Kollias, Elias. *The Medieval City of Rhodes and the Palace of the Grand Master*. 3rd ed. Athens: Archaeological Receipts Fund, 2005.

Kritovoulos [sic]. *History of Mehmed the Conqueror*. Trans. Charles T. Riggs. Princeton: Princeton University Press, 1954.

Kunt, Metin and Christine Woodhead, eds. *Süleyman the Magnificent and His Age: The Ottoman Empire in the Early Modern World*. London: Longman, 1995.

Lafortune-Martel, Agathe. *Fête noble en Bourgogne au XVe siècle. Le banquet du Faisan (1454): Aspects politiques, sociaux et culturels*. Montreal: Bellarim, 1984.

Lane, Frederic C. 'Naval Actions and Fleet Organization, 1499–1502'. In: *Renaissance Venice*. Ed. John R. Hale. Totowa: Rowan and Littlefield, 1973, pp. 146–73.

Lefroy, J.H. 'An Account of the Great Cannon of Muhammad II. Recently Presented to the British Government by the Sultan, With Notices of Other Great Oriental Cannon'. *Minutes of Proceedings of the Royal Artillery Institution* (1870); rpt. Cambridge: Ken Trotman, 2005.

Leluc, Sylvie. 'L'artillerie des chevaliers Hospitaliers de Saint-Jean de Jérusalem de Rhodes à Malte / The Artillery of the Knights of the Hospitaller Order of St John of Jerusalem from Rhodes to Malta'. In: *Entre glaive et la croix: Chefs-d'œuvre de l'armurerie de Malta / Between the Battlesword and the Cross: Masterpieces from the Armoury of Malta*. Paris: Musée de l'Armée and Heritage Malta, 2008, pp. 80–99.

Lopez-Martin, Javier. *Historical and Technological Evolution of Artillery from its Earliest Widespread Use until the Predominance of Mass-Production Techniques*. PhD dissertation. London Metropolitan University, 2007.

Luttrell, Anthony. 'The Earliest Hospitallers'. In: *Montjoie: Studies in Crusade History in Honour of Hans Eberhard Meyer*. Eds Benjamin Z. Kedar, Jonathan Riley-Smith and Rudolf Hiestand. Aldershot: Ashgate, 1997, pp. 37–54.

Luttrell, Anthony. 'Earthquakes in the Dodecanese, 1303–1513'. In: *Natural Disasters in the Ottoman Empire*. Ed. E. Zachariadou (Rethymnon: Crete University Press, 1999).

Luttrell, Anthony. 'The Hospitallers at Rhodes, 1306–1421'. In: *A History of the Crusades. Vol. III: The Fourteenth and Fifteenth Centuries*. Ed. Harry W. Hazard. Madison: University of Wisconsin Press, 1975, pp. 278–313.

Luttrell, Anthony. 'The Hospitallers at Rhodes, 1421–1523'. In: *A History of the Crusades. Vol. III: The Fourteenth and Fifteenth Centuries*. Ed. Harry W. Hazard. Madison: University of Wisconsin Press, 1975, pp. 314–60.

Luttrell, Anthony. *Hospitallers of Rhodes and Their Mediterranean World*. Aldershot: Ashgate, 1992.

Luttrell, Anthony. 'The Hospitallers of Rhodes Confront the Turks: 1306–1421'. In: *Christians, Jews and Other Worlds: Patterns of Conflict and Accommodation*. Ed. P.F. Gallagher. Lanham: University of America Press, 1988.

Luttrell, Anthony. *The Town of Rhodes, 1306–1356*. Rhodes: City of Rhodes Office of the Medieval Town, 2003

Mallett, Michael. *The Borgias: The Rise and Fall of a Renaissance Dynasty*. London: Granada, 1981.

Manoussou-Della, Katerina. *Medieval Town of Rhodes: Restoration Works (1985–2000)*. Rhodes: Ministry of Culture, 2001.

Medieval Gunpowder Research Group, Report number 2, August 2003: *The Ho Experiments* on www.middelaldercentret.dk/pdf/gunpowder2.pdf.

Migos, Athanassios. 'Rhodes: the Knights' Background'. *Fort* 18 (1990), 5–28.

Morgan, David. *Medieval Persia, 1040–1797*. London: Longman, 1988.

Nicholson, Helen. *The Knights Hospitaller*. Woodbridge: The Boydell Press, 2001.

Nicholson, Helen. *Templars, Hospitallers and Teutonic Knights: Images of the Military Orders, 1128–1291*. Leicester: Leicester University Press, 1995.

Nicolle, David. *Acre 1291: Bloody Sunset of the Crusader States*. London: Osprey, 2005.

Nicolle, David. *Constantinople 1453: The End of Byzantium*. London: Osprey Publishing, 2000.

Nicolle, David. *Knights of Jerusalem: The Crusading Order of Hospitallers, 1100–1565*. Oxford: Osprey, 2008.

Nicolle, David. *Nicopolis, 1396: The Last Crusade*. London: Osprey, 1999.

O'Neil, B.J. St. J. 'Rhodes and the Origin of the Bastion'. *Antiquaries Journal* 34 (1954), 44–54.

Parker, Geoffrey. *The Military Revolution: Military Innovation and the Rise of the West, 1500–1800*. Cambridge: Cambridge University Press, 1988.

Paviot, Jacques and M. Chauney-Bouillot, eds. 'Nicopolis, 1396–1996: Actes du Colloque international'. *Annales de Bourgogne* 68 (1996).

Pepper, Simon. 'Fortress and Fleet: The Defence of Venice's Mainland Greek Colonies in the Late Fifteenth Century'. In: *War, Culture and Society in Renaissance Venice: Essays in Honour of John Hale*. Eds D.S. Chambers, C.H. Clough and M.E. Mallett. London: 1993, pp. 29–55.

Pepper, Simon and Nicholas Adams. *Firearms and Fortifications: Military Architecture and Siege Warfare in Sixteenth-Century Siena*. Chicago: University of Chicago Press, 1986.

Petrovic, Djurdica. 'Fire-arms in the Balkans on the Eve of and after the Ottoman Conquests of the Fourteenth and Fifteenth Centuries'. In *War, Technology and Society in the Middle East*. Eds V.J. Parry and M.E. Yapp. London: Oxford University Press, 1975, pp. 164–94.

Phillips, Jonathan. *The Fourth Crusade and the Sack of Constantinople*. New York: Viking, 2004.

Picenardi, Guido Sommi. *Itinéraire d'un chevalier de Saint Jean de Jérusalem dans l'île de Rhodes*. Lille: Société de Saint Augustin, Desclée, de Brouwer et cie, 1900.

Puype, Jan Piet. 'The Basilisk *Stuerghewalt* of 1511 in Hertogenbosch, the Netherlands'. In: *ICOMAM 50: Papers on Arms and Military History, 1957–2007*. Ed. Robert D. Smith. Leeds: Basiliscoe Press, 2007, pp. 360–87.

Queller, Donald E. and Thomas F. Madden. *The Fourth Crusade: The Conquest of Constantinople, 1201–1204*. 2nd ed. Philadelphia: University of Pennsylvania Press, 1997.

Ridella, Renato. 'Two 16th century Papal Esmerils in the Cleveland Museum of Art, Ohio, and Some Notes on Bronze Pieces of Ordnance with a Polygonal Section'. *Journal of the Ordnance Society* 19, 2007, 5–38.

Riley-Smith, Jonathan. *Hospitallers: The History of the Order of St. John*. London: The Hambledon Press, 1999.

Rogers, Clifford J. 'The Age of the Hundred Years War'. In: *Medieval Warfare: A History*. Ed. Maurice Keen. Oxford: Oxford University Press, 1999, pp. 136–60.

Rogers, Clifford J. 'The Military Revolutions of the Hundred Years War'. *Journal of Military History* 57 (1993), 241–78.

Rossi, Ettore. 'Memorie dei cavalieri di Rodi a Costantinopoli'. *Annuario della Scula archeologica di Atene e delle missioni italiane in Oriente* 8–9, 1920, 331–40.

Rossignol, Gilles. *Pierre d'Aubusson: 'le boucleir de la chétienté' Les Hospitaliers à Rhodes*. Besançon: Editions la Manufacture, 1991.

Runciman, Steven. *The Fall of Constantinople, 1453*. Cambridge: Cambridge University Press, 1965.

Russell, Jocelyne G. 'The Humanists Converge: The Congress of Mantua (1459)'. In: *Diplomats at Work: Three Renaissance Studies*. Stroud: Sutton, 1992.

Setton, Kenneth. *The Papacy and the Levant (1204–1571). I: The Thirteenth and Fourteenth Centuries*. Philadelphia: The American Philosophical Society, 1976.

Setton, Kenneth. *The Papacy and the Levant (1204–1571). II: The Fifteenth Century*. Philadelphia: The American Philosophical Society, 1978.

Setton, Kenneth. *The Papacy and the Levant (1204–1571). III: The Sixteenth Century to the Reign of Julius III*. Philadelphia: The American Philosophical Society, 1984.

Setton, Kenneth. *The Papacy and the Levant (1204–1571). IV: The Sixteenth Century from Julius III to Pius V*. Philadelphia: The American Philosophical Society, 1984.

Seward, Desmond. *The Monks of War: The Military Religious Orders*. London: Eyre Methuen, 1972.

Sire, H.J.A. *The Knights of Malta*. New Haven: Yale University Press, 1994.

Smith, Robert Douglas. 'The Technology of Wrought-Iron Artillery'. *Royal Armouries Yearbook* 5 (2000), 68–79.

Smith, Robert Douglas and Kelly DeVries. *The Artillery of the Dukes of Burgundy, 1363–1477*. Woodbridge: The Boydell Press, 2005.

Smith, Robert Douglas and Ruth Rhynas Brown. *Mons Meg and Her Sisters*. London: Trustees of the Royal Armouries, 1989.

Sommé, Monique. 'L'armée Bourguignonne au siège de Calais de 1436'. In: *Guerre et société en France, en Angleterre et en Bourgogne XIVe-XVe siècle*. Ed. Philippe Contamine et al. Lille: Centre d'histoire de la région du Nord et de l'Europe du Nord-Ouest, 1991, pp. 197–219.

Sommi Picenardi, Guido. *Itinéraire d'un chevalier de Saint Jean de Jérusalem dans l'île de Rhodes*. Lille: Société de Saint Augustin, Desclée, de Brouwer et cie, 1900.

Bibliography

Spiteri, Stephen C. *Fortresses of the Knights*. Malta: Book Distributors Ltd, 2001.

Stefanidou, Alexandra. 'The Cannon of the Medieval City of Rhodes, based on the Manuscript and Illustrations of Johannes Hedenborg (1854)'. In: *Greek Research in Australia: Proceedings of the Sixth Biennial International Conference of Greek Studies, Flinders University June 2005*. Ed. E. Close, M. Tsianikas and G. Couvalis. Adelaide: Flinders University Department of Languages – Modern Greek, 2005, pp. 293–304.

Szakály, F. 'Phases of Turco-Hungarian Warfare before the Battle of Mohács'. *Acta orientalia academia scientia Hungarensis* 33, 1979, 65–111.

Tubersac, M. de. 'Les bouches à feu de Rhodes du musée d'artillerie de Paris'. *Journal des arms spéciales* 5e ser., 3.3, May–June 1862, 415–24.

Turnbull, Stephen. *The Walls of Constantinople, AD 324–1453*. London: Osprey, 2004.

Valentini, R. 'L'Egeo dopo la caduta di Costantinopoli nelle relazioni dei Gran Maestri di Rodi'. *Bullettino dell'Istituto storico italiano per il medio evo e Archivio Muratoriano* 51 (1936), pp. 137–68.

Vatin, Nicolas. 'La conquête de Rhodes'. In: *Soliman le Magnifique et son temps: Actes du Colloque de Paris Galeries Nationales du Grand Palais, 7–10 mars 1990/Süleyman the Magnificent and His Time: Acts of the Parisian Conference, Galeries Nationales du Grand Palais, 7–10 March 1990*. Ed. Gilles Veinstein. Paris: La Documentaiton Française, 1992, pp. 435–54.

Vatin, Nicolas. 'The Hospitallers at Rhodes and Ottoman Turks, 1480–1522'. In: *Crusading in the Fifteenth Century: Message and Impact*. Ed. Norman Housley. Basingstoke: Palgrave Macmillan, 2004, pp. 148–62, 231–35.

Vatin, Nicolas. *L'order de Saint-Jean-de-Jérusalem, l'empire Ottoman et la Méditerrannée orientale entre les deux sièges de Rhodes, 1480–1522*. Paris: Peeters, 1994.

Vatin, Nicolas. 'Le siège de Mytilène (1501)'. *Turica* 21–23, 1992, 437–59.

Vatin, Nicolas. *Sultan Djem: Un prince Ottoman dans l'Europe du XVe siècle d'après deux sources contemporaines: Vâki'ât-i Sultân Cem / Oeuvres de Guillaume Caoursin*. Ankara: Société Turque d'Histoire, 1994.

Vatin, Nicolas. 'Les tremblements de terre à Rhodes en 1481 et leur historien, Guillaume Caoursin'. In: *Natural Disasters in the Ottoman Empire*. Ed. E. Zachariadou. Rethymnon: Crete University Press, 1999, pp. 153–84.

Vaughan, Richard. *Philip the Good: The Apogee of Burgundy*. London: Longmans, 1970.

Index

Acre 13, 14, 15, 16, 21, 86
Adrian V, Pope 13
Adrian VI, Pope 98
Adrianople 9, 28
Ahmed Pasha 106, 116, 127, 129
Aleppo 83
Alexander VI, Pope 67, 79, 80, 82, 84
Alexandria 86, 99
Amaral, Andrea d', Chancellor 113, 123, 129, 130
Amboise, Emery de, Grand Master 78, 85, 86, 104, 127, 143, 145–8, 156, 188, 189, 194
Andronicus III Palaeologus, Emperor 21
Ankara 22, 23
Antioch 14, 15
Armenia 15, 16, 22, 23
Arsuf, battle of 15
Ar-Zahir Sayf ad-Din Jaqmaq, Mamluk Sultan 23
Ascalon, Siege of 15
Atlit 13
Aubusson, Pierre d', Grand Master 32, 33, 34, 44–9, 51–3, 55–9, 63–8, 70, 75–81, 84–7, 97, 104, 115, 125, 126, 135, 137, 138, 142, 170, 172–3, 175, 177–91, 194
Auvergne 20, 33, 66, 101, 107, 110, 111
Ayas Pasha, Beylerbey of Rumeli 97, 106

Bait Nūbā 15
Bali Pasha, Agha of the Janissaries 97, 111
Balian of Ibelin 9
Baphaeus, Battle of 21
barque 95
basilisk 101–5, 114, 128, 148, 155
Bastion (Tower) of St George 77, 78, 85, 88, 113, 127, 186–8
batons de feu 49
Battery of the Olives 85, 127, 188, 189, 190–1
Bāyezīd I, Ottoman Turkish Sultan 21, 22, 23, 64, 67, 68, 82, 83

Bāyezīd II, Ottoman Turkish Sultan 65, 81, 83, 84–6, 126
Beauvais, Siege of 126
Beirut 13
Belgrade, Siege of (1456) 30, 31, 79, 83, 97, 126
Belgrade, Siege of (1521) 23, 130, 131
Belvoir 15
Bessarion, Cardinal 29
Bethlehem 14
Blanchefort, Gui de, Grand Master 86, 194
Bodrum 64
Bombard 11, 20, 26, 45, 47–53, 55, 57–9, 64, 100–4, 109, 111, 1234, 128, 159, 160, 164
Bonaldi, Jehan Anthonio 99
boulevard 47, 76, 87, 103, 105–7, 109, 110–16, 123, 128, 129, 174
Bourbon, Jacques de 95, 96, 98, 99, 100, 102–4, 106–19, 127, 128, 130, 181
Bourganeuf 66
Bourges, Pierre (Pedro) de 47
brigantine 63, 95
Bulgaria 22
bulwark 76–8, 87, 171, 173, 178, 182, 183, 185, 186–90
Burgundy 22
Bursa 22

Cairo 83, 86, 102
Callixtus III, Pope 30, 31
cannon 8, 11, 27, 28, 44, 46, 50–3, 56, 69–74, 87, 88, 95, 96, 97, 100, 101–5, 108, 114, 123, 125–8, 131, 133–166
cannon Perrier 101–4
Caoursin, Guillaume 18, 19, 34, 43–8, 53–8, 64, 65, 67, 68, 75, 87, 174
Capistrano, John of (Giovanni da), Franciscan Friar 30, 31, 83
caponier 85, 87, 127, 188–9

203

Cardonna, John de 33
Carretto, Fabrizio del, Grand Master 25, 85, 86, 87, 88, 105, 127, 151, 152, 176, 181, 183
Castile 64
Cem 64–8, 79, 81, 82, 84, 126
Chaldiran, Battle of 83
Charles V, Holy Roman Emperor 131
Charles VIII, France, King 67, 84
Chios 31, 43, 97
Clement V, Pope 17
Collachium 18, 19, 20, .24
Constantinople 9, 16, 21, 22, 26, 27, 29, 30, 31, 43, 44, 45, 64, 67, 79, 96, 97, 99, 124
corning 71
Cos 31, 64, 68, 124
coulovrine 100, 114
counterscarp 76–8, 85, 96, 106–7, 109, 110, 127, 176m 184, 187, 190–1
courtau 49, 55
Crete (Candia) 31, 98, 108, 109, 124
Curti, Giacomo 45, 46
Cyprus 14, 16, 19, 20, 31, 32

d'Amboise Gate 188–9
Damascus 15, 83
Damietta 15, 86
Deventer, Siege of 30, 126
double cannon 100–3, 109
Dupuis, Mary 43, 45, 46, 51–5, 57, 59, 63

Edessa 14
Egypt 15, 16, 33, 34, 79, 82, 83, 86, 88, 97, 113, 126, 165, 166
England 20, 22
Epernay painting 55–7, 75, 87, 173, 174
Eugenius IV, Pope 23

Faussebraye 25, 27, 58, 109, 115, 174–8, 180, 183, 184, 186, 188, 191
Feast of the Pheasant 29
Ferdinand I, King of Naples 63
Fernandez de Heredia, Juan, Grand Master 24, 191, 193
Ferrer, Francesc 23
Fluvian de Riviere, Antonio, Grand Master 24, 172–3, 177, 179, 181, 186–7, 193
Fontanus, Jacob 95, 99, 103, 105, 119
France 20, 22, 55, 66, 79, 97, 104, 137, 153, 173
Frederick II, Holy Roman Emperor 15
Frederick III, Holy Roman Emperor 53, 59
fustes 53, 54

galleass 95
galleon 86, 95
galley 16, 17, 30, 44, 46, 52, 53, 54, 64, 84, 85, 86, 95
Genoa 15
Gerard, the Blessed, Grand Master 14
Germany (Holy Roman Empire) 22, 26, 101, 104, 160
Ghāzi 'Osmān, Ottoman Turkish Sultan 21
Giustinian, Cardinal 88
Golubac, battle of 23
Gozo 131
Grand Master's Palace 18, 19, 47, 55, 78, 80, 84, 105, 08, 152, 188, 190
Gregory X, Pope 13

hacquebut 106, 110
Haifa 13
Harbour Tower 56–7
Hattin, battle of 15
Henry II, King of Cyprus 16
Henry VII of England, King 73
Honorius IV, Pope 13
Hungary 22, 26, 65, 181

Innocent V, Pope 13
Innocent VIII, Pope 66, 67, 79

Jaffa 15
Janissaries 26, 29, 64, 83, 97, 106, 107, 111, 112, 119, 127, 130
János Hunyadi, King of Hungary 23, 30
Jerusalem 9, 13, 14, 15, 83, 138
Jewish Quarter 55–9, 75, 114, ,124–6
John XXI, Pope 13

Karamani Mehmet Pasha, Grand Vizier 64
Kemel Reis, Ottoman Turkish Sultan 82, 84
Knights Templar 13, 80
knollenpulver 71
Koskino Gate 106, 115
Kosovo 9, 22, 23
Kountis, Manolis, mason 179

l'isle Adam, Philippe Villiers, Grand Master 56, 86, 88, 97, 98, 99, 104, 105, 107, 111, 114, 115, 117, 118, 123, 127, 129, 130, 155, 156, 187, 194
la Mote, Pierre de, gunner 73
Lambadis, Georgios 151, 152
Lambadis, Manolis 151, 152
Langues (tongues) 20
Lastic, Jean de, Grand Master 24, 30, 31, 126, 177, 178, 180, 181, 183, 184, 188, 189, 190, 193
Leo X, Pope 88
Lindos 17
Louis IX, King of France (Saint Louis) 15

Index

Louis XI, King of France 33, 129, 140, 149, 173
Lufti Pasha, Grand Vizier 108

Malta 9, 10, 131
Mamluks 13, 14, 16, 20, 23, 32, 65, 82, 83, 86
Mandraki (Military) Harbour 49, 108
Marj Dâbik, Battle of 83
Marmaris 45, 97
Martin IV, Pope 13
Martin V, Pope 24, 186, 187
Master George of Constantinople, gunner 43–5, 47–9, 73
Mecca 83
Medina 83
Mego, Nicolaos 99
Mehmed I, Ottoman Turkish Sultan 23
Mehmed II, Ottoman Turkish Sultan 10, 26, 29, 30, 31, 34, 43, 47, 54, 64, 66, 82, 83, 123, 124, 126, 129, 159
Mesīh Pascha, Ottoman general 45, 53, 55, 57, 123, 124, 125
Milly, Jacques de, Grand Master 24, 31, 126, 178, 179, 193
moat 25, 27, 32, 44, 46, 47, 55, 56, 58, 59, 64, 75, 76–8, 85, 87, 103, 107, 109, 110, 113–16, 125, 127, 129. 175, 176, 177, 179–90
mortar 47, 48, 49, 55, 57, 58, 101, 102, 103, 138
Mount Kunovica, Battle on 23
Murād I, Ottoman Turkish Sultan 21, 23
Mustafa Pasha 96, 106, 107, 112, 113, 116, 129
Mytilene 79, 80, 84

Napoleon Bonaparte 131, 134, 136, 138, 139, 144, 145, 147, 148, 149, 153, 154
Naxos, Jacomo Crispo 99
Neuss, Siege of 126
Nicaea 21
Nicholas III, Pope 13
Nicholas IV, Pope 13, 16
Nicholas V, Pope 31
Nicomedia 21
Nicopolis 9, 22, 79
Nordlingen, Johannis Berger de, gunner 33, 45

Orkhān I, Ottoman Turkish Sultan 21
Orsini, Giovanni Battista, Grand Master 24, 31, 32, 33, 77, 170, 182, 184, 193
Otranto 81, 82
Our Lady of Victory (Notre-Dame de la Victoire) Church 56, 75, 115

Pagnac, Maurice de, Grand Master 17
Paschal II, Pope 14
passevolan 100, 101, 103

Paul II, Pope 32
Pelekanon, Battle of 21
Philadelphia, Siege of 21
Philibert de Naillac, Grand Master 22, 24, 170, 193
Philip II Augustus, King of France 13
Philip the Good, Duke of Burgundy 25, 29, 30, 51, 171
Phisco 44–5
Piccolomini, Aeneas Silvius, Cardinal (Pope Pius II) 30, 191
Pir Mehmed Pasha, Grand Vizier 106
Portugal 64
Provence 16, 20, 85, 100, 105, 107, 109, 110, 111

Raymond du Puy 15
Rhodius, Manoli Calodi 33, 34
Richard I, King of England 13
Richard III of England, King 73
Roberts, Nicholas 96, 116, 117, 119, 128
Rūm 22

Safavî, Ismaîl, Shah of Persia 83
Saint-Gilles (St Gilles) 33, 117, 143
saker 100–1, 103, 109
Saladin 9, 13, 15
Salonika 22, 23
Santa Maria del Borgo Church 19
Santa Maria del Castello Church 19
Sanudo Torsello, Marino 21, 95
Selim I, Ottoman Turkish Sultan 83, 86, 88, 97, 102, 112, 126
serpentine 49, 52, 58
Sidon 13
Sixtus IV, Pope 32, 33, 34, 191
Smyrna 21, 23, 32
Spain 20
Spring of the Cresson, battle of 15

St Anthony's Gate 23, 189, 190
St Athanasios Church 76, 181
St John Church 18, 19, 80, 85, 108
St John's Gate 76, 77, 106, 177–81, 185
St Nicholas Tower (Fort) 20, 23, 25, 32, 47, 48, 49, 51–5, 64, 78, 86, 101, 108, 113, 124–8, 147, 151, 171–3
St Paul's Gate 24
St Sabas, Monastery 15, 16
St Anthony Church 19, 47, 49, 50, 51, 53, 64, 78, 108, 171
Suleyman I (the Magnificent), Ottoman Turkish Sultan 10, 81, 83, 84, 88, 95, 96–8, 101, 106, 108–12, 114, 116–119, 123, 127–31
Syria 16, 22, 33, 34, 83, 95

205

Tadini di Martinengo, Gabriel, Hospitaller engineer 109,–14, 117, 128–30
Tamerlane 22, 23, 27
Tartus 13
tenaille 75–8, 85, 87, 103, 106, 107, 109, 111, 112, 115, 116, 123, 127, 128, 129, 174–7, 180–6
Teutonic Knights 13, 14, 22, 33
Third crusade 13, 15
Tower of Athanasios 181
Tower of Auvergne 101, 107, 110, 115
Tower of Italy 55, 56, 57, 76, 85, 87, 106, 125, 127, 174–7
Tower of Naillac 24, 25, 108, 151, 172–3, 190, 193
Tower of Spain 25, 77, 106, 111, 114–6, 128, 129, 152, 183–6
Tower of the Virgin 25, 76, 110, 180–3, 185
Transylvania 22, 23
traverse 109, 110–12, 114–17, 129

Urban (Orban), gunner 27, 44

Valette, Jean de, Grand Master 131

Vandalus, Seringus 99
Varna, Battle of
Venice 15, 31, 32, 82, 86, 88, 99
Vidal, Michel 99
Villaret, Foulques de, Grand Master 16, 17
Villeneuve, Hélion de, Grand Master 17, 18, 19, 20
Vladislav, King of Poland and Hungary 23

Wall of Auvergne 111, 112
Wall of England 100, 107–12, 115
Wall of Italy 109, 115, 128, 129
Wall of Provence 109–11
Wall of Spain 100, 108–12, 115, 129
Wallachia 22
Windmill Mole 24, 55, 56, 57, 173, 174
Windmill Tower (Tower of the Mills) 24, 25, 108, 172, 173

Zacosta, Piero Raimondo, Grand Master 24, 25, 31, 171, 179, 191
Zonchio, Battle of 82